Conversations with
Lorraine Hansberry

Literary Conversations Series
Monika Gehlawat
General Editor

Conversations with Lorraine Hansberry

Edited by Mollie Godfrey

University Press of Mississippi / Jackson

Publication of this work was made possible in part by
a generous grant from James Madison University.

The University Press of Mississippi is the scholarly publishing agency of
the Mississippi Institutions of Higher Learning: Alcorn State University,
Delta State University, Jackson State University, Mississippi State University,
Mississippi University for Women, Mississippi Valley State University,
University of Mississippi, and University of Southern Mississippi.

www.upress.state.ms.us

The University Press of Mississippi is a member
of the Association of University Presses.

First printing 2021
∞

Library of Congress Cataloging-in-Publication Data available

LCCN 2020044651
ISBN 9781496829634 (hardback)
ISBN 9781496829641 (trade paperback)
ISBN 9781496829658 (epub single)
ISBN 9781496829665 (epub institutional)
ISBN 9781496829672 (pdf single)
ISBN 9781496829689 (pdf institutional)

British Library Cataloging-in-Publication Data available

Works by Lorraine Hansberry

Plays and Screenplays

A Raisin in the Sun: A Drama in Three Acts. Acting edition. New York: Random House, 1959.

The Sign in Sidney Brustein's Window. New York: Random House, 1965.

To Be Young, Gifted and Black: Lorraine Hansberry in Her Own Words. Adapted by Robert Nemiroff. Englewood Cliffs, NJ: Prentice Hall, 1969.

The Drinking Gourd in the Voices of Man Literature Series. Ed. by Vincent L. Medeiros and Diana B. Boettcher. MA: Addison-Wesley Publishing Company, 1969.

Les Blancs in *Les Blancs: The Collected Last Plays of Lorraine Hansberry.* Ed. Robert Nemiroff. New York: Random House, 1972.

What Use Are Flowers? in *Les Blancs: The Collected Last Plays of Lorraine Hansberry.* Ed. Robert Nemiroff. New York: Random House, 1972.

Raisin. Musical adaptation by Robert Nemiroff and Charlotte Zaltsberg. New York: Samuel French, 1978.

Toussaint: Excerpt from Act I of a Work in Progress (1961) in *Nine Plays by Black Women.* Ed. Margaret Buford Wilkerson. New York: New American Library, 1986.

A Raisin in the Sun: The Unfilmed Original Screenplay. Ed. Robert Nemiroff. New York: Plume Book, 1992.

Nonfiction

The Movement: Documentary of a Struggle for Equality. New York: Simon & Schuster, 1964.

Films and Audio Recordings

A Raisin in the Sun. Directed by Daniel Petrie. Columbia Pictures, 1961.

Lorraine Hansberry: A Raisin in the Sun. Full cast recording with Ruby Dee, Ossie Davis, Steve Mitchell, Diana Sands, Claudia McNeil, Zakes Mokae, Harold Scott, Sam Schacht, and Leonard Jackson. New York: Caedmon Records, 1969.

To Be Young, Gifted and Black. Directed by Michael Shultz. PBS, 1972.

Lorraine Hansberry: To Be Young, Gifted and Black. Full cast recording with James Earl Jones, Camille Yarborough, John Towey, Barbara Baxley, Garn Stephens, Claudia McNeil, and Tina Sattin. New York: Caedmon Records, 1972.

Lorraine Hansberry Speaks Out: Art and the Black Revolution. A collection of seven interviews and speeches recorded between 1959 and 1964. New York: Caedmon Records, 1972.

A Raisin in the Sun. Directed by Bill Duke. American Playhouse (PBS), 1989.

A Raisin in the Sun. Directed by Kenny Leon. Sony Pictures, 2008.

Collected Works

A Raisin in the Sun and The Sign in Sidney Brustein's Window. Ed Robert Nemiroff. New York: New American Library, 1966.

Les Blancs: The Collected Last Plays. Includes *Les Blancs, The Drinking Gourd*, and *What Use Are Flowers?* Ed. Robert Nemiroff. New York: Random House, 1972.

The Lorraine Hansberry Audio Collection. Includes the 1969 recording of *A Raisin in the Sun*, the 1972 recording of *To Be Young, Gifted and Black*, and the 1972 collection, *Lorraine Hansberry Speaks Out.* New York: HarperCollins, 2009.

Contents

Introduction

It is hard to think of another writer whose career was as brief as Lorraine Hansberry's, yet whose artistic and political impact was as transformative. Spanning from the debut of *A Raisin in the Sun* on Broadway in 1959 to her early death from cancer in January of 1965, Hansberry's short stint in the public eye changed the landscape of American theater. With *A Raisin in the Sun*, she became both the first African American woman to have a play produced on Broadway and the first to win the prestigious New York Drama Critics' Circle Award. In 1961, the film version of *Raisin* starring Sidney Poitier won the Gary Cooper Award for Human Values at the Cannes Film Festival and was nominated for best screenplay of the year by the Writers Guild of America. *Raisin*'s plot resonated deeply with the aims of the civil rights movement—in the play, a working-class Black family struggles to decide how to spend the insurance money left by their father's death. The family finally bands together and decides to move into an all-white neighborhood over the neighborhood association's efforts to bribe them into staying away. Quickly becoming one of the defining works of art of the period, *Raisin* also ushered in a new era of Black representation on the stage and screen, displacing the cartoonish stereotypes that were the remnants of blackface minstrelsy in favor of complex three-dimensional portrayals of Black characters and Black life. Hansberry's public discourse in the aftermath of *Raisin*'s success also disrupted mainstream critical tendencies to diminish the work of Black artists, which helped to pave the way for future work by Black playwrights such as Amiri Baraka, Ntozake Shange, August Wilson, Lynn Nottage, and Suzan-Lori Parks.

Within a few years of her play's Broadway debut, Hansberry had become not only one of the best-known Black writers in the United States, but also one of the nation's most outspoken public intellectuals. Before *Raisin* premiered, Hansberry had been working for several years as a writer and editor for Paul Robeson's left-wing anticolonial Black newspaper, *Freedom*. In 1952, she traveled to Uruguay to speak at the Intercontinental Peace Conference on Robeson's behalf and was put under surveillance by the FBI upon her return. After *Raisin*, Hansberry suddenly had a much wider audience. Her letters to the editor, essays, and interviews were published in a wide range of publications; she appeared as a guest on popular radio and television programs; and she gave speeches at venues such as the American Academy of Psychotherapists and the United Negro College Fund. Even as illness began to overtake her, she threw her full weight behind the civil rights movement, taking part in the historic 1963 meeting between civil rights activists and Bobby Kennedy and writing the text for *The Movement: Documentary of a Struggle for Survival* (1964) to raise money for the Student Nonviolent Coordinating Committee (SNCC).

Hansberry was committed to her art and to the idea that art should speak for itself; however, her editorials, speeches, and interviews also reveal her deep awareness of the biases that white audiences brought to their expectations of Black art. Her first post-*Raisin* editorial responded to critics' efforts to align her play with the stereotypes of the dialect tradition. Hansberry explained:

> "Dialect" is the traditional product and device of careless or indifferent artists who are preoccupied with stereotypes rather than true characterization . . . [But] the characters in *A Raisin in the Sun* do not speak "dialect." The dialogue has . . . the idiom, typical vocabulary, and rhythm of Chicago's South Side where I grew up. It was not something for which I had to turn to racist imagination. ("*Raisin* Author"; see also Hentoff)

In a subsequent piece for the *Village Voice*, she unpacked the racist undertones of the critical failure to recognize the connection between her character Walter Younger and the white "everyman" figure of Willy Loman in Arthur Miller's 1949 play, *Death of a Salesman*. As she put it, "Despite the simple line of descent between Walter Lee Younger and the last great hero in American drama to also accept the values of his culture . . . in the minds of many, Walter remains . . . an exotic" ("Author's Reflection"). With her earliest editorials, Hansberry was already showcasing the fearless candor she would bring to racial justice issues—both in the arts and beyond.

Hansberry's political commitments had their roots in her childhood experience as the daughter of Carl Hansberry, a successful Black businessman who worked closely with the National Association for the Advancement of Colored People (NAACP), the Urban League, and civil rights activists and artists throughout his career. In 1937, her father moved the family to an all-white neighborhood in Chicago to deliberately challenge the constitutionality of racial restriction clauses. In response, a white mob gathered and threw a brick through their window, narrowly missing eight-year-old Lorraine. The Hansberry case moved through the court system, with the Supreme Court of Illinois upholding the legality of restrictive covenants and forcing the Hansberrys out of their home. The case then went all the way to the United States Supreme Court in *Hansberry v. Lee*, 311 U.S. 32 (1940), which reversed the lower court's decision without providing a more general ruling on the constitutionality of such covenants. Not long after a failed bid for Congress in 1940, Hansberry's father bought a house in Mexico and prepared to move the family out of the United States. As Hansberry herself put it in her interview with Lillian Ross, "Although he had tried to do everything in his power to make it otherwise, he felt he still didn't have his freedom." He died in Mexico in 1946 before his family could join him. According to Hansberry, "American racism helped kill him" (Ross).

In Hansberry's early interviews, interviewers often focused on this story as the inspiration behind *Raisin*, while describing Beneatha—the younger sister who wants to use her father's insurance money to pay for her medical degree—as a stand-in for Hansberry. Hansberry, however, was always quick to complicate such claims. Although she frequently admitted that Beneatha was something like herself "eight years ago," she also compared herself to George Murchison, Beneatha's American suitor, and described Joseph Asagai, Beneatha's Nigerian suitor, as her "favorite character" and the play's most "sophisticated figure" (Wallace, Terkel, and Fischer). Hansberry was also quick to point out the sharp difference between her relatively affluent middle-class background and the working-class background of her characters. Rather than focus on her own "atypical" experience, she consciously chose to portray a family whose experience she considered "more relevant" to "our political history and our political future" (Terkel). While some critics have argued that Hansberry "never fully resolved the duality of her life and works—upper-middle-class affluence and Black heritage and revolution," Hansberry's interviews suggest that she openly acknowledged and embraced these tensions (Poston, Wallace, Hentoff, Fischer, Marx, "Author's Reflection," "Images and Essences").[1] Prefiguring contemporary understandings of intersectionality, Hansberry would insist on the racial, regional, cultural, economic, and gender specificity of the experiences depicted in her play (Terkel, Fischer). At the same time, she often articulated a Pan-African sensibility—a sense that black people of all classes and nationalities were united by their oppression under global white supremacy and should look to one another for paths toward achieving their liberation (Isaacs, Fischer, Marx, Fisher).

Hansberry's sense of the complexity within and connections across Black communities reveals itself in her interviews in many ways. In "An Author's Reflection," Hansberry would describe it as a dramatic fault of her play that "neither Walter Lee nor Mama Younger loom large enough to monumentally command the play." And yet, as she shared this observation with interviewers, she would go on to observe that this "weakness" in her play might, in fact, be a strength: "When you start breaking rules you may be doing it for a good reason" (Terkel). She flatly rejected certain interviewers' efforts to see individual characters as representative of the race, pointing instead to the ways in which her characters enabled her to draw out different sentiments within the Black community (Wallace). It was this, indeed, that drew her to the dramatic form. As she put it, "I'm particularly attracted to a medium where . . . [you can] treat character in the most absolute relief—one against the other—so that everything, sympathy and conflict is played so sharply you know—even a little more than a novel" (Perry).

Just as Hansberry refused her reviewers' and interviewers' efforts to see her characters as monolithic representations of "the race," she also resisted their efforts to whitewash race entirely out of the play. Hansberry clearly stated that she saw her characters as fundamentally different from the stereotypical representations of Black people that dominated the stage (Hammel, Poston, Terkel, Hentoff). In one particularly contentious dialogue with Otto Preminger—the director of *Carmen Jones* (1954) and *Porgy and Bess* (1959)—Hansberry described those films as "bad art" because the stereotypes therein demonstrate that "the artist hasn't tried hard enough to understand his characters."[2] Many audiences understood that Hansberry's characters were different from such exoticized and stereotypical representations; nevertheless, they often deeply misunderstood the significance of that difference. In interview after interview, Hansberry was asked to comment on the common but deeply racist refrain that hers was "not a Negro play at all, but a play about people" (Hamilton; see also Terkel, Wallace, Hentoff). Over and over again, and with truly remarkable patience, Hansberry pointed out that this was, in fact, "a misstatement"—that her play was both "a play about people" and "a play about Negroes" (Hamilton), and to "get to the universal you must pay very great attention to the specific" (Terkel). Against the racist fictions of her time, Hansberry insisted not only on the obvious humanity of Black people, but also on the historical construction of all human experience. As she put it, "Virtually all of us are what our circumstances allow us to be" (Perry).

Hansberry also repeatedly refused reviewers' and interviewers' efforts to oppose protest to art (Terkel, Hentoff, Hamilton, Wallace), or their efforts to single her work out as exceptional (Wallace, Terkel, Hentoff, Susskind, Fischer). To those who complimented her for rising above protest, she would respond: "My play is actively a protest play, actively so. There is no contradiction between protest and art and good art. You know, that's an artificial argument" (Wallace). She would also insist—though occasionally to nonlistening ears (Wallace, Susskind, Hentoff)—on the obstacles that stood in the way of Black playwrights seeing their work staged and appreciated in its fullness and complexity. As her interviews turned more and more toward the political issues of the day, she expressed this support for other Black writers' and activists' works by appreciating the value of any and "all ideologies which point toward the total liberation of the African peoples all over the world" (Wallace). When pushed as to whether she considered herself an integrationist or a revolutionary, she simply replied, "The latter may be necessary to make the first possible" (Association of Artists for Freedom).

Taken together, the concerns that emerge most forcefully in these interviews are Hansberry's investment in global Black liberation, her commitment to her craft, and her sense that these two things go hand in hand. Although she was extraordinarily open toward different approaches to overcoming oppression, she was also quite forceful in arguing her own point of view. In fact, she preferred realism over other dramatic forms for precisely this reason, because it demanded "the imposition" of a "specific intellectual point of view" (Terkel, Ross; see also Perry and Susskind). As she put it: "In realism I think the artist who is creating the realistic work imposes on it not only what is, but what is possible . . . because this is part of reality, too—so that you get a much larger potential of what man can do" (Perry). Just as she refused the binary oppositions of art and protest, or the intellectual and the masses, Hansberry refused any opposition between treating the points of view of others with empathy and forcefully articulating her own.

Hansberry's historically informed sensitivity toward different points of view also helps to explain the diversity of material in her larger creative opus. Though she died too young to discuss her work in progress in much detail, she often made brief references to these projects (see Poston, Hentoff, and especially Perry).[3] Indeed, although *Raisin* was praised for breaking barriers and shattering critical expectations of Black theater, Hansberry's later works defied expectations in an even wider range of ways and—for the two that she tried to see produced in her lifetime—arguably failed to succeed as a direct result. *The Sign in Sidney Brustein's Window*—a play about white

Greenwich Village intellectuals—ran on Broadway for 101 performances but received mixed reviews, and it only stayed open as long as it did because her friends and colleagues raised enough money to keep the play afloat. It closed the night of her death. Her television play, *The Drinking Gourd*, commissioned by NBC to celebrate the Civil War Centennial, was deemed too controversial for NBC's audience and was never filmed (Hentoff). Her other plays moved beyond the national context—one, *Toussaint*, was about the 1791–1804 Haitian revolution; another, *Les Blancs*, was a mythologized reimagining of the 1952–1960 Mau Mau rebellion in Kenya. Finally, in *What Use Are Flowers?*, Hansberry traded the realism of her successful debut for philosophical fantasy, exploring how a man living in self-imposed isolation from civilization would choose to raise children orphaned by a nuclear holocaust. Taking part, in turns, in the emerging genres of white-life literature and literary Pan-Africanism, neoslave narratives, and Afrofuturism, Hansberry's later plays reach far beyond the domestic realism of her best-known work, and complicate the image of the author that *Raisin*, on its own, projects.

Hansberry's interviews similarly attest to the range of conversations within which and audiences to whom Hansberry spoke with ease. Her interviews cover everything from classic European literature and aesthetics to the forms and functions of Black folk traditions, from European philosophical concepts to revolutionary histories of the African Diaspora. They also take place in a wide range of spaces, including Black intellectual spaces supported by the Association of Artists for Freedom and *Phylon;* mainstream, middlebrow spaces such as the *New Yorker* and *New York Times*; and niche theater spaces such as the *Mitch Miller Show, Open End*, and *Playwright at Work.* In her fictional dialogue, "Images and Essences: 1961 Dialogue with an Uncolored Egghead," Hansberry would poke fun at the dynamic of some of these spaces, but while her impatience is visible in a few interviews (Wallace, Association),[4] she typically responded to white presumptions of superiority with magnificent yet quite diplomatic sophistication. In fact, although she has been credited with some spectacular takedowns—such as James Baldwin's claim that she walked out of the meeting with Bobby Kennedy—her interviews complicate that image. To the *Village Voice*, she explained, "I did not . . . as was reported in some quarters, walk out. When I got up to leave, the meeting had gone on for about three hours, and everyone got up, said goodbye, and left" (Fisher).[5] Similarly, although she has been quoted responding with biting sarcasm to Studs Terkel asking whether her play is about Negroes or people—"Well, I hadn't noticed the contradiction because I'd always been under the impression that Negroes *are* people"—the line does not appear in the original interview; it appears to have been added posthumously, likely based on private conversations.[6] In 1964, Hansberry would "thank God" for Baldwin's willingness to use "shock" to get people "to talk to each other," while admitting that she had always "hesitated" to do the same (Association).

Perhaps because of Hansberry's diplomacy in speaking to such a wide range of audiences, her underlying radicalism was often missed by members of the mainstream white establishment, and by many of her Black contemporaries. Early interviews often described Hansberry as a housewife (Fields), asked questions about how her husband was handling her success (Miller) and how she felt about housework (Ross), or even mischaracterized her as supporting her interviewers' own problematic assumptions about the play. In one of the most egregious cases, Nan Robertson, writing for the *New York Times*, incorrectly quoted Hansberry as saying that her play "wasn't a 'Negro play'" but a play about "people who happened to be Negroes," a misquote that would haunt Hansberry for the rest of her career (see Wallace).[7] In some interviews, Hansberry's extended discussions of her Nigerian character, whom both Hansberry and the FBI considered *Raisin*'s most radical, seem to have been cut before the interviews aired (Fischer, Marx; see also Terkel and Isaacs).[8] Hansberry's combative interview with Mike Wallace, in which she refused to cooperate with his caricatures of Black Nationalism, never aired at all.

Such omissions in the framing of Hansberry's work, along with the play's many misguided reviews, no doubt contributed to Amiri Baraka's dismissal of *A Raisin in the Sun* as a representative of the Black middle class's enthrallment with integration, or Harold Cruse's dismissal of the play as the "culmination of the efforts of the Harlem leftwing literary and cultural in-group to achieve integration of the Negro in the arts."[9] In reality, Hansberry had little patience for those who characterized either her characters or her work in exceptional or assimilationist terms, and in the case of the Nan Robertson interview, she even wrote a letter to the editor demanding— though not receiving—a retraction.[10] Hansberry would insist that the play was not about integrating with whites, but about asserting Black dignity (Susskind, Marx, Poston) and that it was not about achieving the trappings of the American Dream, but about exploring the corrosiveness of that dream's materialism (Hammel, Marx, "An Author's Reflection").

Although Hansberry's radicalism extended to her feminism, this aspect of her work was only lightly touched on by her interviewers, with most simply noting her stature as the first Black female playwright to have a play on Broadway (Hammel, Fields, Gaver, Miller, Fischer).[11] But Hansberry was an astute reader of Simone de Beauvoir, and her early embrace of what we would now call intersectional feminism was grounded in her sense that people's identities were constructed by material conditions.[12] In response to Terkel's question about the "strength" of the Black woman in "Negro families," Hansberry quickly moved the discussion away from essentialist stereotypes and toward systemic social constructions. As she put it, Black women were "twice militant" because they were "twice oppressed"; it was this experience, she argued further, that gave Black women strength—not only within the domestic space of the family, but also within the public sphere as ideal leaders in the struggle for their own and for Black liberation (Terkel; see also Perry, Hentoff, Marx).

Absent from the record of Hansberry's life and career that her interviews provide, however, is any discussion of her sexuality. Hansberry's separation and subsequent divorce from Robert Nemiroff remained a secret during her life. It wasn't until 1970 that Barbara Grier, editor of the lesbian journal *The Ladder*, revealed Hansberry to have been the author of two 1957 letters to the journal.[13] Several of Hansberry's earliest, still unpublished plays—"The Apples of Autumn," "Flowers for the General," and "Andromeda the Thief"—featured lesbian characters, and two of her later plays—*The Sign in Sidney Brustein's Window* and *Les Blancs*—featured gay male characters. But while Hansberry's opus suggests that she was working toward deeper explorations and expressions of gay and lesbian issues, she clearly felt the need to keep this part of her life hidden from the public eye while she was alive, which was a full decade before the Black lesbian feminist Combahee River Collective formed in 1973–74.[14] As critic Lisbeth Lipari argues, "considering her peers—she was one year older than Toni Morrison, four years older than Audre Lorde, two years younger than Maya Angelou, and one year younger than Adrienne Rich—one can only imagine the contribution Hansberry might have made had she lived longer."[15]

Since Hansberry's death, her loved ones, friends, colleagues, and acolytes have gone to extraordinary lengths to preserve and extend her legacy. Robert Nemiroff, her ex-husband and literary executor, created the play *To Be Young, Gifted and Black* out of her published and unpublished work, edited and published most of her completed plays, adapted *Raisin* into an award-winning musical, and helped to establish the Lorraine Hansberry Papers and the Lorraine Hansberry Literary Trust. Essays by Hansberry's close friends James Baldwin and Ossie Davis have interwoven biography with critical appreciation.[16] Others, such as those by Harold Cruse and Adrienne Rich, have used her life and work to flesh out their own differing political commitments.[17] Still others—by Amiri Baraka, Lloyd Brown, and bell hooks—have presented themselves as necessary critical reevaluations.[18] The conversation featured at the end of this volume—between Lerone Bennet Jr. and Margaret Burroughs—has been included to capture the spirit of some of these various efforts. Representing Hansberry variously as a friend, a foil, and a foremother, these attempts to continue speaking with and through Hansberry remind us that she can no longer speak back. It is my hope that these interviews will open a small window into the eloquence, intensity, and insight with which she once did.

In selecting the interviews for his book, I have prioritized her most substantive interviews, as well as those that are hardest to find in print. Where indicated, radio and television interviews have been transcribed directly from the original audio, and I have tried to preserve as much of the nonverbal components of these interviews as possible in order to convey a sense of the dynamic, sometimes warm and full of laughter, occasionally stiff and full of frustration. Three interviews—those with Mike Wallace, Eleanor Fischer, and Patricia Marx—were either fully or partially unaired in Hansberry's lifetime, and I have included editorial prefaces and footnotes for clarification purposes. When using previously published printed transcripts of radio interviews such as "The Black Revolution and the White Backlash," I have used the printed version of the transcript but added editorial footnotes to indicate significant differences from the original audio. Minor errors in print interviews, such as spelling mistakes or typographical inconsistences, have been corrected silently.

In compiling this volume, I have been assisted enormously by two colleagues at James Madison University (JMU). My student Mary Catherine Landy transcribed many of the interviews in this book, edited the volume for consistency, and kept a record of the permissions status of each item. Howard S. Carrier, JMU Libraries' Copyright Librarian, investigated the copyright status of each interview and provided invaluable consultation on especially difficult cases. Simply put, I could not have completed this volume without their contributions. I am also indebted to the support of JMU's Department of English, College of Arts and Letters, and Cross-Disciplinary Studies, as well as the support of a JMU Provost's Faculty Development Support Award, which enabled me to take multiple trips to New York to transcribe interviews and made it possible to include a fuller representation of Hansberry's interviews than I could have otherwise hoped.

In several cases it was difficult to find either the original audio or the copyright holder of a particular interview, and I am deeply indebted to the help provided during my research by Jane Klain from the Paley Center for Media, Randall MacLowry from the Film Posse, Rebecca Fraimow and Ryn Marchese from WGBH, Josie Walters-Johnston from the Library of Congress, Traci Marks and Shola Lynch from the Schomburg Center for Research in Black Culture, Sara Rzeszutek from St. Francis College, Keith Gilyard from Penn State University, Andy Lanset from the WNYC Archive Collections, Allison Schein Holmes from the WFMT & Studs Terkel Radio Archive, Jennifer Bertani from WNET, Diana Bachman of the Bentley Historical Library, and the Library-Archives Reference Staff of the Wisconsin Historical Society. I am also deeply indebted to the many copyright holders who have granted their permission to reprint Hansberry's interviews in this volume, with special thanks to Esther Cooper Jackson, Stephen Kahn, Margaret Miller, and, of course, the Lorraine Hansberry Literary Trust and their literary agent, Matt Belford. Finally, I would like to thank my colleagues David Babcock, Allison Fagan, Heidi Pennington, Mary Thompson, and Sian White for reading an early draft of this manuscript, and my partner Jim Bywater for supporting me, as always, throughout.

MG

Notes

1. Anne Cheney, *Lorraine Hansberry* (Boston: Twayne, 1984), ii.

2. Lorraine Hansberry, quoted in Jack Pitman, "Deplores *Porgy*: Racial Stereotype Air Debate a Feathers-Stirrer—Preminger in Rebuttal," *Variety*, May 27, 1959, 16. Aside from this brief summary of the debate, no known recording or transcript exists of Hansberry's original conversation with Preminger, which aired on Irv Kupcinet's TV show *At Random*, WBBM-TV, May 26, 1959. According to Pitman, Preminger's claim that Hansberry's dismissal of his films as stereotypical rendered her a "minority of one" set the show's switchboard ablaze "with a twenty-to-one ratio of callers objecting to [Preminger's] utterance" (Pitman, 16).

3. See also Lorraine Hansberry, "Village Intellect Revealed," *New York Times*, October 31, 1964, X1, X3.

4. See also Pitman, "Lorraine Hansberry Deplores *Porgy*," 16.

5. See James Baldwin, "Lorraine Hansberry at the Summit," *Freedomways: A Quarterly Review of the Freedom Movement* 19, no. 4 (1979): 269–72.

6. Robert Nemiroff, *To Be Young, Gifted and Black: Lorraine Hansberry in Her Own Words* (New York: Vintage Books, 1995), 113.

7. Nan Robertson, "Dramatist Against Odds," *New York Times*, March 8, 1959, X3, discussed at length in Robert Nemiroff's "Cautionary Note on Resources" in "A Lorraine Hansberry Bibliography," with Ernest Kaiser, *Freedomways* 19, no. 4 (1979): 285–304.

8. Cheryl Higadisha, *Black Internationalist Feminism: Women Writers of the Black Left, 1945–1995* (Urbana: University of Illinois Press, 2011), 62–63.

9. Amiri Baraka, "A Wiser Play than Some of Us Knew," *Los Angeles Times*, March 22, 1987; Harold Cruse, *The Crisis of the Negro Intellectual* (1967; New York: New York Review Books, 2005), 278–79.

10. See Hansberry's letter exchange with the *New York Times* in the Lorraine Hansberry Papers at the Schomburg Center for Research in Black Culture at the New York Public Library.

11. See also Penny Fox, "Success Makes Work Easier for Prize-Winning Author," *Newsday*, February 16, 1960, 29.

12. See Lorraine Hansberry, "Simone De Beauvoir and the Second Sex: An American Commentary, an Unfinished Essay-in-Progress," in *Words of Fire: An Anthology of African-American Feminist Thought*, ed. Beverly Guy-Sheftal (New York: New Press, 1995), 128–42.

13. Barbara Grier, "Lesbiana," *The Ladder* 14, no. 5–6 (February–March 1970): 19.

14. Richard Goldstein, "Go the Way Your Blood Beats: An Interview with James Baldwin," *The Village Voice*, June 26, 1984, 13–14, 16.

15. Lisbeth Lipari, "The Rhetoric of Intersectionality: Lorraine Hansberry's 1957 Letters to the *Ladder*," in *Queering Public Address: Sexualities in American Historical Discourse* (Columbia, SC: University of South Carolina Press, 2007), 221–22.

16. James Baldwin, "Sweet Lorraine," *Esquire*, November 1969, 139–40; Ossie Davis, "The Significance of Lorraine Hansberry," *Freedomways: A Quarterly Review of the Freedom Movement* 5, no. 3 (1965): 396–402.

17. Cruse, *The Crisis of the Negro Intellectual*; Adrienne Rich, "The Problem with Lorraine Hansberry," *Freedomways: A Quarterly Review of the Freedom Movement* 19, no. 7 (1979): 247–55.

18. Baraka, "A Wiser Play than Some of Us Knew"; Lloyd W. Brown, "Lorraine Hansberry as Ironist: A Reappraisal of *A Raisin in the Sun*," *Journal of Black Studies*, 4, no. 3 (1974): 237–47; bell hooks, "*Raisin* in a New Light," *Christianity and Crisis* 49, no. 1 (February 1989): 21–23.

Chronology

1930   Lorraine Vivian Hansberry is born on May 19 in Chicago, Illinois.

1937–38   Hansberry's family buys a home in an all-white neighborhood. Hostile neighbors throw a brick through the window, which narrowly misses Lorraine. The Hansberry family is evicted by Illinois courts and Hansberry's father, Carl Augustus Hansberry Sr. appeals the case in federal courts with the help of NAACP lawyers.

1940   Carl makes an unsuccessful bid for Congress. On November 12, the United States Supreme Court rules in favor of Carl in the case of *Hansberry v. Lee.*

1946   Carl dies of a cerebral hemorrhage in Mexico while making plans to move his family there to escape US racism.

1948   Hansberry attends the University of Wisconsin. Joins the Communist Party and becomes Chairperson of the Young Progressives of America.

1949–50   After studying art at the University of Guadalajara in Mexico and at Roosevelt University, leaves the University of Wisconsin and moves to New York. Writes for Young Progressives of America magazine and begins working as an editorial assistant at Paul Robeson's *Freedom* newspaper. Her poem "Flag from a Kitchenette Window" is published in *Masses & Mainstream*, a Marxist magazine.

1951–52   Becomes associate editor of *Freedom.* Travels to Montevideo, Uruguay to speak on behalf of Paul Robeson at the Intercontinental Peace Conference. Upon her return, her passport is revoked, and the FBI begins to surveil her, which lasts for the rest of her life. Meets Robert Nemiroff in July at a racial discrimination protest at New York University.

1953   Marries Robert Nemiroff in Chicago on June 20. Moves into an apartment at 337 Bleecker Street in Greenwich Village. Resigns from full-time work at *Freedom* to devote more time to her writing.

1956   In August, Nemiroff's song "Cindy, Oh Cindy" becomes a hit. Hansberry is free to write full time and begins work on *A Raisin in the Sun.*

1957   Secretly separates from Nemiroff. Reads the first draft of *A Raisin in the Sun* to Phil Rose, who options the play and secures Sidney Poitier to star and Lloyd Richards to direct. Her anonymous letters to the editor appear in *The Ladder*, a lesbian journal.

1959   Tryouts of *A Raisin in the Sun* are held in New Haven, Philadelphia, and Chicago. The play is well-enough received to secure a Broadway opening at the Ethel Barrymore Theater on March 11. Hansberry gives the keynote speech, "The Negro Writer and His Roots" at the American Society of African Culture (AMSAC) in March. Wins the New York Drama Critics' Circle Award in April. The play is published by Random House and the movie rights are sold to Columbia Pictures.

1960   Completes *Raisin* screenplay for Columbia Pictures. Commissioned in 1959 by NBC to write *The Drinking Gourd*, Hansberry completes work on the script, but it is deemed too controversial and canceled before production begins. Works on *Toussaint*, *The Sign in Jenny Reed's Window* (later *The Sign in Sidney Brustein's Window*), and *Les Blancs*. Ossie Davis replaces Sidney Poitier in *A Raisin in the Sun*, and in October, the play moves to the Belasco Theater.

1961   Moves to Croton-on-Hudson in the Hudson Valley of New York. A film version of *A Raisin in the Sun*, starring Sidney Poitier and Claudia McNeil and directed by Daniel Petrie, is released. The film wins the Gary Cooper Award for Human Values at the Cannes Film Festival and is nominated for best screenplay of the year by the Writers Guild of America.

1962   Completes *What Use Are Flowers?* Actively supports the Student Nonviolent Coordinating Committee (SNCC). In October, delivers "My Government Is Wrong" speech at a rally opposing the House Un-American Activities Committee (HUAC).

1963   Becomes ill with cancer in April. On May 24, attends a meeting with Attorney General Robert Kennedy along with other Black leaders, artists, and activists. Delivers the "We are One People!" speech to a civil rights rally in Croton-on-Hudson on June 16. Undergoes two unsuccessful operations.

1964   Secretly divorces Nemiroff. Delivers "To Be Young, Gifted and Black" speech, also known as "The Nation Needs Your Gifts," to the winners of a United Negro College Fund writing contest. Publishes *The Movement: Documentary of a Struggle for Equality*, the proceeds of which go to SNCC. On October 15, *The Sign in Sidney*

Brustein's Window opens on Broadway. After mixed reviews, friends and supporters work to keep the play open for 101 performances.

1965   Hansberry dies of cancer on January 12 at the age of thirty-four. *The Sign in Sidney Brustein's Window* closes that day. A memorial service is held three days later in Harlem. Over six hundred people attend. *The Sign in Sidney Brustein's Window* is published that year by Random House.

1969   *To Be Young, Gifted and Black*, adapted by Nemiroff, opens at the Cherry Lane Theater off Broadway on January 2. Nina Simone first performs song of the same name inspired by Hansberry. *To Be Young, Gifted and Black: Lorraine Hansberry in Her Own Words* is adapted by Nemiroff, with illustrations by Hansberry and an introduction by James Baldwin, and is published by Prentice-Hall.

1970   *Les Blancs*, completed by Nemiroff, opens at the Longacre Theater on Broadway on November 15. Former editor Barbara Grier publicly identifies Hansberry as the author of two anonymous letters to *The Ladder*.

1972   PBS remakes *To Be Young, Gifted and Black* as a television film starring Ruby Dee, Al Freeman Jr., and Claudia McNeil. *Les Blancs: The Collected Last Plays of Lorraine Hansberry*, edited by Nemiroff, is published by Random House.

1973   The musical *Raisin*, produced by Nemiroff, opens at the 46th Street Theater on Broadway on October 18. It wins the Tony Award for best Broadway musical.

1979   A special retrospective issue of *Freedomways* is published, called *Lorraine Hansberry: Art of Thunder, Vision of Light*, edited by Jean Carey Bond.

1989   PBS remakes *A Raisin in the Sun* as a television film starring Danny Glover and Esther Rolle and directed by Bill Duke.

2004   A revival of *A Raisin in the Sun* opens at the Royale Theater on Broadway, starring Sean "P. Diddy" Combs and Phylicia Rashad; a television film version of this production airs on ABC in 2008.

2010   Bruce Norris's *Clybourne Park*—a spin-off of *A Raisin in the Sun* set both during and fifty years after the events of her play—premieres in New York. The play wins a Pulitzer Prize in 2011 and a Tony Award in 2012.

2017–18   A full-length documentary, *Lorraine Hansberry: Sighted Eyes/Feeling Heart*, directed by Tracey Heather Strain, premieres at the Toronto Film Festival on September 7 and airs on PBS the following January.

**Conversations with
Lorraine Hansberry**

Raisin Author Tells Meaning of Her Play

Lorraine Hansberry / 1958

From *New York Age*, December 20, 1958, p. 27. Reprinted by permission of the Lorraine Hansberry Literary Trust.

(The author of *Raisin in the Sun*, a drama which will star Sidney Poitier on Broadway early next year, explains what she is trying to accomplish in this exclusive article for the [New York] *Age*).

A Negro playwright faces certain socially built-in expectations about his work. I, for instance, have already read several press accounts purportedly telling what *A Raisin in the Sun* is about. These include a Chicago item to the effect that it is about "block-busting" (Negroes moving into a restricted neighborhood); elsewhere that it is about the aspirations of a Negro family for "middle-class status"—whatever we may suppose that to precisely mean—and so on. I have also heard about the Negro society columnist who has apparently advised her readers that some of that dialect in *Raisin in the Sun* must go.

The first two reports are not particularly true or false, but the mistaken remark "dialect" is inadvertently pertinent to the entire question of contemporary Negro drama. The fact is that I am quite in agreement with the lady who penned the complaint. If there were dialect in *Raisin*—it would most certainly need to go. "Dialect" is the traditional product and device of careless or indifferent artists who are preoccupied with stereotypes rather than true characterization. It tends itself to sloppy and superficial characterization and is therefore not only offensive—but bad art. This, it seems to me, is too seldom said. In my view, all writers inclined to this approach of "type" writing should hasten to canning factories where presumably it is desirable that one pea look quite like another.

3

Typical Dialogue

The characters in *A Raisin in the Sun* do not speak "dialect." The dialogue has, to the best of my creative ability, the idiom, typical vocabulary, and rhythm of Chicago's South Side where I grew up. It was not something for which I had to turn to racist imagination; it is speech which has surrounded my life and senses since birth.

However, I have not the least intention of falling victim to either of two desires for misrepresentation of the Negro character. Neither that which demands the hip-swinging, finger-snapping race of prostitutes and pimps which people the imagination of white writers of musical comedy "Negro" shows, or what I personally consider the misguided and almost traumatic desire of certain elements of the Negro middle class to see that particular horror replaced with well-heeled, suave, Oxfordian types. While both exist within the framework of our life, neither, it seems to me, is profoundly representative of the kind of true typicality which more often than not has been at the core of fine drama.

Obsessed with Ideas

Rather, I am virtually obsessed with the observation that we are a people who are 90 percent working folk desperately beset with all the problems and joys that living implies. And—all the contradictions: pettiness and greatness, disgusting capitulations and heroic struggles, cowardice and incredible courageousness. The truth is that we did produce Stepin Fetchit and "Motherless Child"—but also—Paul Robeson and "Go Down Moses"!

I like to think my play begins to say some of those things.

A Playwright, a Promise: Lorraine Hansberry Reveals a Major Talent in the Forthcoming *A Raisin in the Sun*

Faye Hammel / 1959

From *Cue*, February 28, 1959, pp. 20, 43.

When the curtain goes up on *A Raisin in the Sun* on March 11 at the Ethel Barrymore Theater, New York will be witnessing two important firsts—the first bid for Broadway success by film actor Sidney Poitier and the first play by a writer of unusual promise. Her name is Lorraine Hansberry.

Lorraine is twenty-eight. She is a Negro. She is the first woman of her race to have a play produced on Broadway. She is being heralded, by out-of-town critics and audiences, as a major talent. Some compare her to Sean O'Casey and Arthur Miller. But there is no one to compare her to except herself.

Lorraine is a young woman who believes in dreams—the dreams of all men for dignity, for a place in the sun—be they Black or white. But she has gone far beyond writing a "problem play," and this is what makes her work larger than the specific identity of its characters, a Negro family aiming for middle-class status. "What I wanted to do," said Lorraine, "was to avoid the stereotypes of so many plays about Negroes—stereotypes that come from telling only half the truth about a man. I felt that if I could take a group of Negroes and successfully *involve* them in life, I could get the audience to accept them as people with whom they share common ground. Then I could introduce any question at all—not just Negro-white conflict. We have plenty of problems besides that one," she said.

The question Lorraine chooses to pose in *A Raisin in the Sun* is *how* men achieve their dreams—and how they, and the dreams themselves, are changed in that very process. The hero of her play (Sidney Poitier) is forced to make a decision: whether he will "buy" the wherewithal for his family's very pressing dreams by stooping, or whether he will take a stand for freedom, for dignity. His decision is one which, like most choices in life, assures no happy ending. But it moves him, and symbolically, every man faced with a moral dilemma, onto a new—and higher—level of struggle.

Like Langston Hughes in the poem from which she drew her title, "What happens to a dream deferred / Does it dry up like a raisin in the sun / Does it fester like a sore and then run / . . . or does it explode?" Lorraine offers no easy answers. What she has done is simply to pose a basic question: how shall men, oppressed and tortured almost to cowardice, behave like human beings? On these solid roots she has fashioned a play that is at once uproariously funny and intensely moving, that sings and soars and tears the heart all at the same time. It is rich in the double-edged, bittersweet humor of the Negro people, ironic, rollicking—and hard hitting. Her characters are so vividly realized that the audience, Black and white, is irresistibly drawn into their struggles.

A Raisin in the Sun is Lorraine Hansberry's first play, and its production on Broadway, that hard-headed street of balance sheets and expense accounts, is in the nature of a small coup. Lorraine had been writing plays for only about five years, since her marriage to Bob Nemiroff, a young songwriter and music publisher (he is coauthor of "Cindy, Oh Cindy"). The daughter of a comfortably middle-class Chicago family, Lorraine attended the University of Wisconsin and Roosevelt College in Chicago and came to New York in 1950, with aspirations to be a painter. Her first encounter with theater was at the age of fourteen when she went to see a performance of *Dark of the Moon* and was struck by its marvelous theatricality. Since then she has been a tireless playgoer. "I keep on looking for the magic," she says.

Lorraine's first attempts at creating her own brand of theater magic were "really exercises to teach myself how to write. I did the things you might expect—a fantasy, a dramatization of a nineteenth-century novel, a play about girls living in New York. I tore them up as soon as my husband read them and agreed they were meant for the wastebasket."

One night, however, in the fall of '57, Lorraine happened to read a scene from what was to become *A Raisin in the Sun* to some friends who had come over for dinner, among them, Phil Rose, a music publisher. "We stayed up very late, reading and arguing about the play," Lorraine recalls, "and suddenly I realized that it had taken on a life of its own." The next morning, Phil woke her with a phone call and told the astonished Lorraine that he wanted to produce her play. In a few days a legal contract was drawn up, and the long, hard pull to get backing began—not at all helped by the fact that Lorraine was a beginner, that Rose had never produced a play, and that they had chosen as their director another unknown, a young Negro from Detroit named Lloyd Richards (no Negro had directed a Broadway show since Jesse Shipp did *Abyssinia* in 1907). Dave Cogan, a tax accountant, became coproducer. It took over a year to get enough money—most of it in small amounts from many people—to put the show into rehearsal. After that first run-through, the tide turned. The show drew high critical and popular praise in New Haven and Philadelphia, and a New York theater at last became available.

Sidney Poitier just sort of naturally came by his role. He and Lorraine are old friends who have spent many a long hour arguing about the theater. Sidney is tremendously excited about the play. "I feel it's the most important work of my career," he said in Philadelphia a few weeks ago. "More than that, I believe it's the first step by the Negro to real participation in American theater." The other members of the splendid cast—among them, Ruby Dee, Claudia McNeil, and Diana Sands—are equally enthusiastic. Diana commented, "This isn't just a play. It's history!"

Whether Lorraine Hansberry makes history with this particular play, time—and the critics—will tell. For her, it is only the beginning of a career which is also a dedication. An intense, vibrant young woman, Lorraine cares deeply about the theater—and deplores the fact that theater in America has become, for the most part, a study in subjectivity, an exploration of man's inner nature unrelated to the larger world from which he takes his shape. "All art is social," says Lorraine; "the problem is not whether you write 'social dramas,' but what you say about society—and whether you say it with artistic integrity. If you say nothing at all, that too, is making a comment about society.

"Here in America," Lorraine continued, "we have been suffering from an imposed intellectual impoverishment in the last decade. We were told there were areas of life we were not to examine, problems we dare not investigate. So, we chose the easy way out; all our problems became subjective. If we couldn't look at the world, we'd look only at ourselves."

What Lorraine hopes to do in her plays is to "reexamine our sources of strength as a people." As a Negro, she feels she shares the vantage point which oppression provides. "Look at the great Irish writers—Shaw, O'Casey, Joyce—all members of the outgroup. When you're at the bottom, you can't help but see things more clearly."

Most importantly, Lorraine feels that good theater can *affect* American life—by reflecting and thereby encouraging its best elements. Says this young playwright in America: "American life, with all its problems, still has within it areas of vitality and persistence and search and dignity that are going to be the source of our survival."

Lorraine Hansberry's determination to involve her characters in the main currents of contemporary life, to have them struggle—and triumph—in its swirling waters, is what gives her work its vitality, its stature. Perhaps her play—if it does nothing else—will break through some arid ground and show the way to new writing in our theater—writing that is seeking a retreat in neither obscurantism or sensationalism, that is not afraid to tackle the big questions.

Housewife's Play Is a Hit

Sidney Fields / 1959

From *New York Daily Mirror*, March 16, 1959.

Before last Wednesday, whenever anyone asked Lorraine Hansberry her occupation, she was afraid to say, "writer." That sounded too artsy-craftsy. She always answered, "housewife."

And the usual reaction was, "Why don't you do something useful!" Lorraine said.

But since last Wednesday, Lorraine replies, "Writer!"

It was last Wednesday that her play, *A Raisin in the Sun*, opened. It's an enormous hit, as much for the play as for the brilliant performances by Sidney Poitier, Claudia McNeil, and Ruby Dee.

Lorraine is only twenty-eight, slight, small, pretty, with a soft voice and a skyful of life and ideas for opera librettos and new plays. We met in the cluttered Greenwich Village flat where she lives with her husband, Robert Nemiroff, a music publisher.

"He's really a literary critic and a good one," Lorraine said. "That's what he went through NYU for. But since we were married six years ago, he wanted me to write and he'd pay the bills."

They haunt movies, plays, ski trails, and now that she's tasting success, Lorraine will satisfy an old and deep frustration: She wants her own ping-pong table. Must be good at it.

"More form than content." she confessed. "At the start I look devastating. At the finish everybody beats me badly."

■ ■ ■

For the first few years of her marriage, she worked at a variety of jobs. Four days in a department store, quitting because she couldn't stand the ringing bells that told the girls what to do and when. In the office of a theatrical producer. Six months putting tags on fur coats. And over a period of years in the restaurant her in-laws owned, as a waitress, hostess, cashier.

"Not too much cashiering," Lorraine said, "because I can't count very well."

But during all this she was writing. Fact is she's been writing since she was fourteen, though she always was reluctant to show any of it to anyone.

"My father was a real estate man in Chicago, and in my milieu, you just didn't admit you wrote a poem, you hid it," Lorraine said. Once she almost died of mortification when her high school teacher came upon something she wrote and proudly read it to the class.

■ ■ ■

Of the bearing on Chicago's South Side she and her sister and two brothers got from their parents, Lorraine said, "We were properly housed, clothed, fed, and schooled. There were no money problems. When my father died, my brothers took over and ran the business.

"I was not a particularly bright student. I had some popularity, and a premature desire, probably irritating, to be accepted in my circle on my terms. My dormitory years, which numbered only two at the University of Wisconsin, were spent in heated discussions on everything from politics to the nature of art, and I was typically impatient at people who couldn't see the truth—as I saw it. I must have been a horror."

When, at nineteen, she assessed American higher education, found it deficient, packed, and left the campus, her mother's reaction was, "Do what you think you must." (Lorraine dedicated *A Raisin in the Sun* to her mother.)

She lounged around Chicago for six months, studying German at Roosevelt College, though she didn't know why, and finally got her mother's permission to come to New York.

Here, she tried short stories and TV plays, collected a volume of notes for a novel, but never had anything published. In 1954 she began writing plays, struggling to learn the difficult arts of sincerity, dialogue, and structure.

"I didn't have to change dialogue much, but constantly revised the structure," she said. "Boy, if plays didn't have to make sense, I'd be a genius."

■ ■ ■

She wrote four plays before *A Raisin in the Sun*. Practice. In college she was more painter than art student and always knew there's always a lot of sketching before the painting even begins.

In *A Raisin in the Sun* she says with magnificent simplicity that all men have dignity but often distort it with greedy dreams and strange hungers at the expense of their happiness, if not their sanity. She says it with great humor, deep compassion, and love.

"All the love I can," Lorraine said, "which I do not apologize admitting I feel for the human race."

We Have So Much to Say

Ted Poston / 1959

From *New York Post*, March 22, 1959, p. M2. Reprinted by permission of the *New York Post*.

Success rests very lightly on the slender shoulders of Lorraine Hansberry, the tousle-headed gamin whose *A Raisin in the Sun* has made her Broadway's latest Cinderella Girl.

And the comely but strong-minded lass, who looks even younger than her twenty-eight years, is determined to keep it that way.

There'll be no rags-to-riches moving, for instance, from the third-floor walkup apartment in Greenwich Village where she lives with her husband, Robert Nemiroff, and her happily neurotic collie, Spice.

She seemed horrified at the idea the other day as she sat half curled in a living room chair, her black-sweatered arms clasped around slim legs clad in rumpled brown corduroy trousers.

"I'm a writer," she said rather indignantly (an opinion endorsed by every first-string drama critic in town), "and this is a workshop. We're not celebrities or anything like that."

She added with a pixyish smile, "But I am going to try to get the landlord to paint that hall. We're not bohemians. They can't carry us that far."

In the Offing

And there'll probably be few changes in her work habits, which she termed "sloppy," but which somehow managed in one concentrated year to produce Broadway's latest dramatic hit.

"Basically," she said, "I'm an extremely undisciplined person. I sleep every day until 11:00 or 12:00. Then I'll get up and have coffee with anyone who drops in.

"I'll go out and sit in the park when I should be working, or sit right here and stare at the floor. I'll get on a movie-going kick that lasts for weeks and really do nothing at all."

Now Broadway and Hollywood, the latter of which has turned its early nibblings into an all-out race to grab *Raisin* for the screen, are likely to force some delay on two other Hansberry projects.

One is the book for a modern opera based on Toussaint L'Ouverture, the slave who liberated Haiti from the France of Napoleon. "It won't deal much with the revolution, but with the man himself. The shadings of that man's character are fascinating."

The other is an adaptation of *The Marrow of Tradition* by the early Negro novelist Charles Chesnutt, dealing with the postreconstruction re-enslavement of the new freedmen in Carolina. The book deals mainly with two families, one of white aristocrats and the other of middle-class long-free Negroes, but:

"In my treatment, I'm dropping the Negro family. I want to study the white wife who doubts her sanity because her honest values are in conflict with her surroundings, with her effort to relate herself to the blind fight to reinstitute slavery.

"If I finish it, it won't be Chesnutt at all, but me. But I hope to feature him somehow with my dramatization, and make people wonder who the hell was this Negro doing all this writing, before the turn of the century."

But if Hollywood succeeds in buying Miss Hansberry's current drama about an impoverished Negro family trying to drag itself out of Chicago's South Side slums through a $10,000 insurance policy left by the father, then Toussaint and Chesnutt will have to wait a while.

"If there's a motion picture sale, I'll do the script. I'm adamant on that. Nobody's going to turn this thing into a minstrel show as far as I'm concerned. And if this blocks a sale, then it just won't he sold."

A phone call from her husband on a new unlisted number—which rings just as constantly as the old one—interrupted her, but she persuaded him to hang up.

"That husband of mine," she said affectionately, gesturing vaguely around the cluttered living room, where scores of telegrams bearing such signatures as David Susskind, Kermit Bloomgarden, Tennessee Williams, Langston Hughes, and Julie Styne cover two whole walls with a third taken up with local critics' raves.

"For a born New Yorker," she went on, "he's the, biggest yokel I know. He finds every item ever published about the play and gets excited anew about every one."

The pixyish smile came back as she added, "But he's a swell guy, though. And if it hadn't been for him, this play would never have hit the boards."

She recalled the night she had read through the almost-completed script of *Raisin* and decided it was "the worst effort I'd ever made at anything."

So, she threw the whole thing at the ceiling and, as the sheets fluttered all over the living room, went to get a broom to sweep them all into the fireplace.

"Bob didn't rebuke me at all, except with a look," she recalls. "He just got down on the floor and picked up every sheet of it. He put it back in order and kept the whole thing out of my sight for several days. And then one night when I was moping around, he got it out and put it in front of me. I went to work and finished it."

The day she finished *Raisin*, she called Bert Long, her husband's songwriting associate and partner, and invited him to dinner to listen to it. Long brought a mutual friend, Philip Rose, a music publisher.

"I started out reading it in this chair and ended up sprawled down on the floor. We started discussing it and found ourselves arguing about the characters as people. It lasted almost all night.

"Phil called me up at eight the next morning and said he wanted an option on it. I jokingly told him I'd keep the five hundred dollars and not give it back to him, but later that day we went to the lawyer's office and signed the papers."

Rose and David J. Cogan, an accountant, eventually became the producers of the play, but not until Lorraine had read it about eighty times to small groups of six or seven people—some one hundred of whom put up small sums for a "piece" of the production—were they on their way.

"Sidney Poitier came to one of the early readings," she remembers, "and he liked it very much. He committed himself early to the lead, but we still weren't sure we could get him."

Another early listener was Lloyd Richards, young Negro actor-director whose eventual direction of *Raisin* drew almost as much praise as the writer's contribution. Lorraine Hansberry feels very strongly about him.

"If Lloyd Richards doesn't get any worthwhile work out of this in the future," she says, "then America is a lot sicker than I thought."

Although she had never finished any of the four plays she started before, nor had ever had any of her literary efforts published or produced, the budding dramatist was not overly surprised at the acclaim that greeted her first effort. Nor did she suffer first-night jitters on Broadway.

"I'd had my real case of butterflies back during rehearsals," she recalls, "the first time we invited an audience to the New Amsterdam roof.

"And I'd gathered confidence through the New Haven, Philadelphia, and Chicago tryouts, although it was pretty tough in Chicago with practically everyone who had known me from infancy sitting out front.

"So, I couldn't really believe that the people of New York would be much different."

But she was surprised to find that many people wondered how she, with her own upper-middle-class upbringing in Chicago, had been able in *Raisin* to depict so realistically the aspirations and frustrations of the low-income Younger family on the South Side.

"These people," she says of her characters, "are here for everyone to see, every day. But we've all been so blinded by stereotypes both on the stage and off that we just don't recognize them. Many people are so accustomed to accepting and laughing at the stereotypes that they miss the remarkable sophistication of Negroes; they don't understand the ability of Negroes to turn things around and laugh at their own antagonists."

To her, Lena Younger, the mother (brilliantly portrayed by Claudia McNeil) "can be seen any day in Harlem or the South Side and is instantly recognized by any Negro who encounters her."

The Old and the New

And there is much of her own brother, now a highly successful Chicago realtor, in Lena Younger's son, Walter Lee (Poitier).

"My brother had the opportunity and accomplished the things Walter Lee vainly hoped to do," she says, "but the drive which impelled them both is the same."

And Lena's flip, collegiate daughter, Beneatha (Diana Sands), "is just me at that age, during my two years at the University of Wisconsin. And maybe a lot of me now."

"The thing I tried to show," she said, "was the many gradations in even one Negro family, the clash of the old and the new, but most of all the unbelievable courage of the Negro people. Where they get it, I don't know, but they have it, and it needed showing."

She paused. "Maybe someday, someone else in America other than us will appreciate the innate dignity and persistence of the Negro people. And if there is any 'message' in my play, it is simply this: the ghettoization of any people, Black or white, is lousy and sickening, and I tried to say it the best way I could."

Lorraine Hansberry came here in 1950 after quitting the University of Wisconsin and studying briefly at Roosevelt College, Chicago's Art Institute, and in Guadalajara, Mexico.

She studied briefly at the New School for Social Research, gave it up "along with the family's support," and got a series of jobs as department store clerk, tag girl in a fur shop, and aide to a theatrical producer.

She met Nemiroff about six years ago through friends. They were married in June 1953. The next year, at his insistence, she pushed aside a projected novel and several short stories and set out to be a serious dramatist, between brief working stints as waitress, hostess, and cashier in his family's Village restaurant.

Her main form of relaxation is still "to have friends in and run my mouth interminably." But both she and her husband are inveterate movie- and show-goers, and she prides herself on her ping-pong game, "which dazzles everybody and defeats no one." They both ski.

She had never met Langston Hughes, from the lines of whose poem "Harlem" she took the title of her play, until earlier this month, when she addressed the American Society of African Culture's Conference of Negro Writers. She was impressed by the fact that so many of the participating writers were so young.

"I'd always dismissed my own youth and had been amused by people who met me expecting that this Miss Hansberry was a little old lady of sixty or so. But I decided at the conference that there was a reason why so many of the current Negro writers are young."

She paused and summed it up. "Maybe because we have so much to say, we start earlier," she said. "I only hope I can keep on saying it."

Ex-UW Co-ed Becomes "The Toast of New York"

Jack Gaver / 1959

From *Wisconsin State Journal*, March 29, 1959, section 4. Reprinted by permission of the *Wisconsin State Journal*.

NEW YORK—Offhand, the matter of becoming a successful playwright seems simple in the case of Lorraine Hansberry. Bullseye first time out.

But, of course, it isn't simple, never was, and never will be.

"I had spent a lot of time and considerable money trying to be an artist," said the comely twenty-eight-year-old author of *A Raisin in the Sun*, Broadway's latest dramatic hit.

"I Didn't Have It"

"I came to New York from my home in Chicago in 1950, after a couple of years in college (at the University of Wisconsin), with art in mind. Finally, I had to admit to myself that I just didn't have it as a painter.

"I had been trying to write various things for years, and I decided that I would concentrate on writing. But not just any sort of writing. Six years ago or so, with nothing to prove my point, I just told myself that I was a playwright and began working at it."

Miss Hansberry's method may be unique.

"I didn't set out to write anything in finished form," she explained. "I didn't have a complete play idea in my head. I wrote experimentally, only to give myself experience. I would think of a dramatic situation that would interest me, write as much dialog as necessary to work out that situation, and go on to another such exercise."

Only Husband Saw Scripts

This went on year after year, with fragments of scripts piling up unseen by anyone except the writer's husband, Robert Nemiroff, member of a music publishing firm, whom she married in 1953. But a couple of years ago, her "exercising" led to the characters and basic situation of *A Raisin in the Sun*.

This one she didn't put aside; she wound up with a complete play.

"Four hours of play, to be exact," Miss Hansberry said. "And not quite the one now on view at the Barrymore theater, although the first act, through all the rewrites that followed, has remained essentially the same."

The historic facts must intrude here, although they have nothing to do with the fact that *A Raisin in the Sun* is a brilliant first play that would loom large in any season. Miss Hansberry is a Negro, the first woman of her race to have a play presented on Broadway. Her play is about Negroes living in a slum section of Chicago and hoping for a better life.

Read Play to Friends

"The play originally was much more of a social problem drama than it is now," the author went on. "There was heavy stress on Negroes moving into a white community.

"After I had finished the first draft, we had some dinner guests one night and I read the script to them. One of the guests was the actor, Sidney Poitier, who is our leading man.

"There was considerable criticism of the script after my four hours of reading. Mainly, the objection was that I had two plays. I'm stubborn and I argued, but I thought it over for a few days, then went back to work."

It "Worked Out"

"I wound up with a much shorter play that concentrated on the characters and their intimate problems and dreams. All persons have problems and dreams. No one was more surprised than I was when a music business associate of my husband's, Philip Rose, told me he wanted to produce the play.

"It took about a year to raise the money to produce it and to get the right cast, and we had to open our tryout tour without assurance of a Broadway house, but things worked out all right."

And Miss Hansberry is the toast of the town.

Talk of the Town: Playwright

Lillian Ross / 1959

First published in the *New Yorker*, May 9, 1959, pp. 33–35. Reprinted by permission of the Estate of the author. All rights reserved.

We had a talk recently with Lorraine Hansberry, the twentyeight-year-old author of the hit play *A Raisin in the Sun*. Miss Hansberry is a relaxed, soft-voiced young lady with an intelligent and pretty face, a particularly vertical hairdo, and large brown eyes, so dark and so deep that you get lost in them. At her request, we met her in a midtown restaurant so that she could get away from her telephone. "The telephone has become a little strange thing with a life of its own," she told us, calmly enough. "It's just incredible! I had the number changed and gave it to, roughly, twelve people. Then I get a call from a stranger saying, 'This is So-and-So, of the BBC!' It's the flush of success. Thomas Wolfe wrote a detailed description of it in *You Can't Go Home Again*. I must say he told the truth. I enjoy it, actually, so much. I'm thrilled, and all of us associated with the play are thrilled. Meanwhile, it does keep you awfully *busy*. What sort of happens is you just hear from *everybody*!"

Miss Hansberry gave a soft, pleased laugh. "I'm going to have some scrambled eggs, medium, because, as far as I know, I haven't had my breakfast yet," she went on. "I live in the Village, and the way it's been, people sort of drop in on me and my husband. My husband is Robert Nemiroff, and he, too, is a writer. Yesterday, I got back to writing, and I wrote all day long. For the first time in weeks. It was wonderful. We have a ramshackle Village walkup apartment, *quite* ramshackle, with living room, bedroom, kitchen, bath, and a little back workroom, and I just stayed in that little old room all day and wrote. I may even get time now to do some of my housework. I don't want to have anyone else to do my housework. I've always done it myself. I believe you *should* do it yourself. I feel very strongly about that."

The medium scrambled eggs arrived, and Miss Hansberry sampled them vaguely and went on to tell us something of what life has been like since her play opened a few weeks ago. "I now get twenty to thirty pieces of mail a day," she said. "Invitations to teas, invitations to lunches, invitations to dinners, invitations to write books, to adapt mystery stories for the movies, to adapt novels for Broadway musicals. I feel I have to answer them, because I owe the people who wrote them the courtesy of explaining that this is not my type of thing.

"Then, there are so many organizations that want you to come to their meetings. You don't feel silly or bothered, because, my God, they're all doing such important work, and you're just delighted to go. But you're awfully busy, because there are an awful lot of organizations.

"The other morning, I came downstairs to walk my dog—he's sort of a collie, and he'll be six in September—and there, downstairs, were the two most charming people, a middle-aged couple who wanted me to have dinner with the New Rochelle Urban League before it went to see the play. I just couldn't say no. Meanwhile, I'd been getting telegrams from Roosevelt University, in Chicago, which is a very wonderful institution back home, asking me to come and speak. I kept sending telegrams back saying I couldn't come, and then they got me on the phone, and they had me. Once I'm on the phone, I just can't say no. I sometimes find myself doing things for three or four organizations in one day. The other morning, I started the day by taping a television program. Then I went to the National Association of Negro Business and Professional Women's Clubs Founders' Day Tea, at the Waldorf, where they were giving out Sojourner Truth Awards—awards named for Sojourner Truth, who was a very colorful orator who went up and down New England and the South speaking against slavery. Then I went home and went to the Square with my dog.

"When I got back home, I fed the dog and put on a cocktail dress, and my husband and I had dinner in a new Village steakhouse. Then we went to a reception for a young Negro actor named Harold Scott, who had just made a record album of readings from the works of James Weldon Johnson. A very beautiful album. Then we went home and had banana cream pie and milk and watched television—a program with me on it, as a matter of fact. It was terrifying to see. I had no idea I used my face so much when I talked, and I decided that that was the end of my going on television. The next day was quiet. I had only one visitor—a young Negro writer who wanted to drop off a manuscript for me to read. We had a drink and a quick conversation, and he was off. I actually got to cook dinner—a pretty good one, with fried pork chops, broccoli *au gratin*, salad, and banana cream pie. I'm mad for banana cream pie. Fortunately, there's a place in the neighborhood that makes marvelous ones."

Miss Hansberry told us that she had written her play between her twenty-sixth and twenty-seventh birthdays, and that it had taken her eight months. "I'd been writing an awful lot of plays—about three, I guess—and this happened to be one of them," she told us. "We all know now that people like the play, including the critics. Most of what was written about the play was reasonable and fine, but I don't agree that this play, as some people have assumed, has turned out the way it has because just about everybody associated with it was a Negro. I'm pleased to say that we went to great pains to get the best director and the best actors for this particular play. And I like to think I wrote the play out of a specific intellectual point of view. I'm aware of the existence of Anouilh, Beckett, Durrenmatt, and Brecht, but I believe, with O'Casey, that real drama has to do with audience involvement and achieving the emotional transformation of people on the stage. I believe that ideas *can* be transmitted emotionally."

"Agreed," we said, and asked Miss Hansberry for some autobiography.

"I was born May 19, 1930, in Chicago," she told us. "I have two brothers and one sister. I'm the baby of the family. My sister Mamie is thirty-five and has a three-year-old daughter, Nantille, who is divine and a character. She was named for my mother, whose name is Nannie, and her other grandmother, Tillie. My older brother, Carl Jr., is forty, and my other brother, Perry Sr., is thirty-eight and has an eighteen-year-old daughter, who is starting college and is very beautiful. Carl, Perry, and Mamie run my father's real-estate business, Hansberry Enterprises, in Chicago. My father, who is dead now, was born in Gloster, Mississippi, which you can't find on the map, it's so small. My mother comes from Columbia, Tennessee, which *is* on the map, but just about. My father left the South as a young man, and then he went back there and got himself an education. He was a wonderful and very special kind of man. He died in 1945 [sic], at the age of fifty-one, of a cerebral hemorrhage, supposedly, but American racism helped kill him. He died in Mexico, where he was making preparations to move all of us out of the United States. My brother Carl had just come back from Europe, where he fought with Patton's army. My father wanted to leave this country because, although he had tried to do everything in his power to make it otherwise, he felt he still didn't have his freedom. He was a very successful and very wealthy businessman. He had been a US Marshal. He had founded one of the first Negro banks in Chicago. He had fought a very famous civil-rights case on restricted covenants, which he fought all the way up to the Supreme Court and which he won after the expenditure of a great deal of money and emotional strength. The case is studied today in the law schools. Anyway,

Daddy felt that this country was hopeless in its treatment of Negroes. So, he became a refugee from America. He bought a house in Polanco, a suburb of Mexico City, and we were planning to move there when he died. I was fourteen at the time. I'm afraid I have to agree with Daddy's assessment of this country. But I don't agree with the leaving part. I don't feel defensive. Daddy really belonged to a different age, a different period. He didn't feel free. One of the reasons I feel so free is that I feel I belong to a world majority, and a very assertive one. I'm not really writing about my own family in the play. We were more typical of the bourgeois Negro exemplified by the Murchison family that is referred to in the play. I'm too close to my own family to be able to write about them.

"I mostly went to Jim Crow schools, on the South Side of Chicago, which meant half-day schools, and to this day I can't count. My parents were some peculiar kind of democrats. They could afford to send us to private schools, but they didn't believe in it. I went to three grade schools—Felsenthal, Betsy Ross, and A. O. Sexton, the last of them in a white neighborhood, where Daddy bought a house when I was eight. My mother is a remarkable woman, with great courage. She sat in that house for eight months with us while Daddy spent most of his time in Washington fighting his case in what was, to put it mildly, a very hostile neighborhood.

"I was on the porch one day with my sister, swinging my legs, when a mob gathered. We went inside, and while we were in our living room, a brick came crashing through the window with such force it embedded itself in the opposite wall. I was the one the brick almost hit. I went to Englewood High School and then to the University of Wisconsin for two years. Then I just got tired of going to school and quit, and came to New York, in the summer of 1950. The theater came into my life like *k-pow!*" Miss Hansberry knocked a fist into the palm of her other hand. "In Chicago, on my early dates, I was taken to see shows like *The Tempest*, *Othello*, and *Dark of the Moon*, which absolutely flipped me, with all that witch-doctor stuff, which I still adore. In college, I saw plays by Strindberg and Ibsen for the first time, and they were important to me. I was intrigued by the theater. Mine was the same old story—sort of hanging around little acting groups and developing the feeling that the theater embraces everything I like all at one time. I've always assumed that I had something to tell people. Now I think of myself as a playwright."

Interview with Lorraine Hansberry, Peter Glenville, Dore Schary, José Quintero, Lloyd Richards, and Arthur Laurents

David Susskind / 1959

Broadcast on *Open End*, WNTA-TV, April 26, 1959. Printed by permission of the David Susskind Estate on behalf of *Open End*, © Pamandisam, LLC.[1]

David Susskind: Good evening, and welcome to Open End. My name is David Susskind . . . Tonight, our subject is the theater this year, a summing up. And we have six talented and excellent guests to discuss it. I will present them in a moment, but I would like to suggest to you that a craft, the theater specifically, that has these kinds of people is a prideful and exciting craft.

And now I'd like to introduce our guests. Our first is Miss Lorraine Hansberry. Miss Hansberry is the author of the highly acclaimed *A Raisin in the Sun*, which has just recently won the Critics' Circle Award for the best American play of the season. *A Raisin in the Sun*, incidentally, is Miss Hansberry's first play to be produced on Broadway.

Our next guest is a familiar and a much-admired guest on this program. Mr. Peter Glenville. He began his theatrical career as an actor, while a student at Oxford and later appeared in many starring roles in London. Mr. Glenville is most known in our country as a director for many fine productions. He recently directed the Columbia feature *Me and the Colonel*. He has directed *Separate Tables*, he has directed *The Innocence*, and most recently *Rachimo*, which opened earlier this year on Broadway.

Our next guest Mr. Dore Schary has the enviable distinction of having two plays on Broadway at the same time, now. He is the author and coproducer of the prize-winning *Sunrise at Campobello*, and he is the director and again coproducer of *A Majority of One*. An easterner by birth, Mr. Schary spent many years in Hollywood where he was vice president in charge of production at Metro-Goldwyn-Mayer.

Our next guest, Mr. José Quintero, is director, cofounder, and coproducer of *The Circle in the Square*, and he has staged all but two of the seventeen productions in the nine-year history of the theater, where *Our Town* is presently playing. Mr. Quintero also brought to Broadway Eugene O'Neill's *Long Day's Journey into Night*, which won the Pulitzer Prize and the Drama Critics' Circle Award prize for the 1956–57 season.

Our next guest, Mr. Lloyd Richards, is the director of *A Raisin in the Sun*. And although it is his first venture on Broadway, Mr. Richards has been active in the theater for a number of years as an actor, director, and teacher, and he has had his own theater group in Detroit.

Our last guest is Mr. Arthur Laurents, who is the author of *Home of the Brave, The Birdcage, A Time of the Cuckoo,* and *A Clearing in the Woods.* His *West Side Story* is now in its brilliant second year on Broadway and will soon be joined by the incoming production *Gypsy,* which opens in New York on May 14.

■ ■ ■

Susskind: Well, I want to thank you all for being here, and I'm also going to tell you that I'm personally very stimulated at the prospect of your all being guests simultaneously, because you all represent adventures on Broadway that I respect and like enormously, and you're not going to be in placid agreement with each other all through the evening, are you? [*laughter*]

Peter Glenville: Well, that remains to be seen.

Lorraine Hansberry: Yes, it does.

Susskind: I had to choose a subject tonight, and so I thought since the theater season customarily begins in September and winds up the first of May, to all intents and purposes, this theater season is just about over. And so, I thought we might discuss a summing up of this year. Has it been a good theater year? Peter, has it?

Glenville: I don't know, David, I've been too occupied in the affairs that have occupied me in the season to really be able to judge. I think reading the critics, I would think not, perhaps, one of the most scintillating or stimulating. I think if one reads the critics regularly right through the season, I would get the impression that there were many good things in it, but it hasn't been one of the most exciting for years.

Susskind: Well, of the things you did see personally, which will be nameless for the moment, how would you apprise the total of those?

Glenville: Um, I would apprise them as good, average, mixed, mixed fair. And I think that I would assess most seasons that way. A lot of it is in the luck, for certain very good shows and very good productions that I haven't seen, that from everything I hear are very good, and I've missed those, so that makes one less good judge. I haven't seen all the shows, but I think every season, one likes some things, and one likes others less, and sometimes one is not necessarily right in one's own preferences.

Susskind: You know, the more you talk to Peter the more you understand [*laughter*] why the English ruled for centuries.

Hansberry: Mmm-hmm. For the moment. [*laughs*]

Susskind: José, what about the year? You've seen a good deal of theater.

José Quintero: Well, I really don't have much more to add than what Peter said. I don't think that this has been the most exciting season that I have seen since I have been in New York. I think there've been some things that I've enjoyed enormously. But as a whole I don't think that we have as many exciting things this year as we've had . . .

Glenville: May I add, perhaps, that talking about a season is difficult to discuss anyway, because we don't want to get down to the shows we liked and we didn't, because we don't wish to either overpraise or criticize our colleagues.

Arthur Laurents: Oh, I do.

Susskind: Now wait a minute, that collective "we" that you used—you mean you.

Glenville: May I suggest that possibly an all-over average, good season is sometimes possibly less stimulating than a season in which one remembers one or two highlights of such brilliance, originality, and excitement that the two or three really exciting things in a season make a season in some ways preferable to a just good, general, high average. For instance, your show, Arthur, that was a season before last, is to me a musical that gives a real kick in the pants to musical comedy by showing an entirely new sort of musical with excitement and brilliant choreography and drama, *West Side Story*. That to me makes a season exciting just to see a couple of those. I think that your show this season, *A Raisin in the Sun*, lifts a whole season up. I don't think you can judge a season necessarily by how many out of a hundred were really good, I think, where there's some really stimulating, exciting, original evenings. And I think two or three do that.

Dore Schary: I think there were. I think there were. I think it was a very good season.

Susskind: What specifically, Dore . . .

Schary: I think that a season that gives you *A Touch of the Poet,* and *J.B.,* and *A Raisin in the Sun, Sweet Bird of Youth,* along with perhaps minor successes like *Disenchanted* and *Rachimo* and many others—I think is a very, very good season. I don't see anything wrong with this season at all. I think it was provocative, I think it had a wonderful divergence of material, diversity of material, and I enjoyed myself in the theater very, very often this year. I disagreed with some people on some of the plays I saw, but I thought it was a very stimulating season with the exception of the musical field. The musical field was not a very good field, but we're hoping to overcome that with Arthur's new show, *Gypsy.*

Susskind: Lorraine, what did you see this season that particularly excited you?

Hansberry: Hmm, I saw *J.B.*

Susskind: Did that excite you?

Hansberry: In terms of the production, I thought it was very exciting, very much so. The imagination that went in to go ahead to making this particular statement is very beautiful and excellent theater in my opinion. I also saw *Sweet Bird* in rehearsal in Philadelphia; I haven't seen it here, and discussing the season I would just treat it differently. I would be more inclined to wonder, not so much in terms of what was "successful" in quotes, but if there are any implications of trends in American drama—or American musical comedy, for that degree—and to what extent those shows that we did see reflected them.

Susskind: Well, did you see any new thrust in American drama this year? I saw Tennessee Williams repeating his theme a bit in *Sweet Bird of Youth.* I saw shows that represented good theater, but no particular new dimension in the theater.

Laurents: I think there's a beginning of a new trend. I think the season was good for two reasons: One is I think it's very rare when you have a really good new playwright such as Miss Hansberry. Too often I think plays are produced as a great deal of what Lorraine called "success" in quotes, and it's really kind of slick writing. But I think it's—this season alone, you know, we always want so much quantity. And here is a genuine playwright. And the other good thing about it, and this is my personal taste, it seems to me to be a trend away from naturalistic theater. No matter what you might have thought of *J.B.* or *Sweet Bird,* and I haven't seen *Rachimo*—I'm going tonight, but I'm sure it's there too—it's making the theater something that I would like to see, which is more lyrical and more theatrical in its whole statement, and I think there is a trend toward that, which I am very happy about.

Glenville: Yes, I think that the period of plays in box sets with purely naturalistic dialogue and never projecting outside the limitations of naturalistic acting is on the way out, and I think that can give rise to very interesting productions.

Schary: Do you really believe that, Peter? That what you call the natural theater is on the way out?

Glenville: Well, it'll never go, but I think that it's now shared pretty equally with productions that are not naturalist. For instance, *Sweet Bird of Youth*. Nobody's particularly pointed this out as it's a very exciting theatrical evening, and the production is brilliant, and the acting is fine, but it is not in any sense, naturalistic acting. I mean, I was fascinated to see people say in a scene for duologues—and there were many duologues in the play, very exciting ones—the actors walking, literally, up and down the footlights, talking to the audience with the person to whom they're speaking being behind, say, sitting on a bed. [*laughter*] And all sorts of conventions of acting which are terribly bold. They need to be terribly well done to succeed, and I think they are well done in that particular instance, but I can imagine people copying that method and not succeeding at all. I think also when we're talking about new trends, they're not necessarily good because they're new. I'd rather see old-fashioned theater superbly done, naturally, than a new trend rather inadequately done, because, in the end, it's the performance, the art of the actor and the art of the writer being at its best. Whether it's in an old style or a new. I think that we—on one of your former programs, David—we discussed—Ken Tynan was here, who was giving us, I think, some very brilliant criticisms during the season—and he was maintaining that he didn't feel that a playwright, unless there was some sociological comment in the play, was an important playwright. I don't know whether you'd agree with that.

Hansberry: Well, I think that has to be put in a certain kind of context. First of all, I hope we are using the same terms—naturalism to me is not realism. It's something else, apart and different . . .

Glenville: No, of course. I think we all know what naturalism is; in a box set, it's difficult to define, but I think we all know what we mean by it. I think most people . . .

Hansberry: Yes, I hope so, because I don't think, for instance, that realism has the particular limitations that naturalism does. Right. There's no reason why the realistic exploration of a subject can't just explode our imagination, and hopefully, usually it does in the best of the realistic writers. I have a subdivision which I call romantic realism, which I hope is what my play reflects. In terms of this trend, and what Mr. Tynan said—I believe I saw that show—the reason I say it has to be said in the context is because I'm inclined to the view that a lot of people have—it isn't just me—that virtually all art makes some sort of sociological statement. It can't help it. If you make a statement, then obviously you also have a point of view. If you make a film and you say that the villain is executed at the end of it, then you are posing that your audience must share the view that this is justice.

Glenville: But the social comment can be either implicit and incidental or explicit and at the core.

Hansberry: Well, but that always gets to, and I think that is usually lost is: what is art? I don't think that to say that something having sociological implications takes it out of the realm of art.

Glenville: Oh, no! Of course.

Hansberry: Exactly. I'm aware that you're European, and in America we've made a rather peculiar delineation between something that's supposed to be a social play and something that's supposed to be the art play, and I don't really think that this great enormous difference exists. So to that degree, I think that if the artist is trying to say something of substance, that he is going to have to have some measure of commentary. It can just be objective dissection. I'm not so anxious that he try and tell us what to do about it. But I think that a certain degree of conscious treatment of any question is relevant and pertinent, and rather than detracting from art, it probably heightens it.

Glenville: I think that is true, and I think everything that we say and do has with it the implications of our upbringing, our point of view, our ideas, but that isn't necessarily the core of what we want to express. You enter a play just about two human beings and their love or their hate for one another, and the sociological comment, which is bound to go with any statement of any writer, is either explicit and is the point of the play or is purely incidental. You can have, say, a good Agatha Christie thriller, if you like that, and it can be very well done and at the end, the man is condemned to death, and the point is that he was found guilty, and he did the murder, and he's condemned to death. Now, I very much doubt if there's any sort of comment about capital punishment in that.

Hansberry: Exactly! But of course, that's my point. You see, it presupposes that we think that there is some justification of capital punishment.

Glenville: You can always find it, but whether the author wishes to write about it is the point.

Hansberry: No, no, but you're saying that his lack of consciousness that some of us sitting out in the audience might not think that this is the thing to do with either a murderer, or any other kind of criminal, the fact that we are not able to answer back doesn't remove the fact of the question. In other words, it has to do with the artist assuming that if he is writing about what is accepted and he simply reflects that, then this is not controversial. This is not social writing. But of course, it is because . . .

Laurents: Yeah, but there's a picture called *Rififi*, a French picture, which I liked until the point it got very moral, when it was about robbing a jewelry store or something, and I really wanted them to get away with the money.

Hansberry: Didn't we all?

Laurents: Yes, well, that's the whole point! And then they have to be sorry and get knocked off, because they've done a bad thing.

Susskind: It's really blasphemous for a French movie to get moral.

Laurents: It was made by an American.

Susskind: Oh, was it? That's right, Jules Dassin. Could we climb up on your mountain, or would you come down, because I wanted to ask you about, perhaps—the Cinderella play this season is certainly *A Raisin in the Sun*, because with very little fanfare and almost no expectations on the part of, not alone the public, but the professionals. *Raisin in the Sun* has just taken the theatrical season by storm. It's sold out. It's a raging commercial hit. It's won the Drama Critics' Prize. It's acknowledged to be one of the really important plays of the season, and you two are fellow conspirators in its birth. What was that experience like? I mean, it was unprecedented, and I'd wonder if you'd describe it a bit, Lloyd.

Lloyd Richards: The experience?

Susskind: Well, I mean, just getting the play on, for example.

Richards: Well, it was a fabulous experience for me, and that's why I haven't seen much of this year's product—

Hansberry: [*laughs*] We worked.

Richards: —because we spent so long on that. And from that point of view, from my personal point of view, it's been a very successful season. I found many, many interesting, exciting things in doing the play. One of the most exciting, and I think this accounts for a great deal of the audience acceptance of it, was, I think it gave something that I've seen very few plays do recently, and that is it gave the audience a chance almost to participate and to participate experientially. It was a point of view from which I felt the material would be most or best received, and the greatest joy in doing it was just to see that happen, to see people drawn into the point of—I know, an audience experiences empathically; they have an empathic reaction, or they observe, and they enjoy something. But the thing that happened within this play was that they got a chance to actually live and experience it, and I felt that many people in the audience, or most of our audiences, experience actually what is going on. This is a thing that I haven't seen happen in plays very much, to the point that people just get involved in it, and they feel with them, and they hope with them, and they pray with them, and they enjoy with them, and they laugh with them and really become a part of it. And that's the most exciting aspect of the play for me, and I think one of the reasons why it has been received to the extent that it has.

Susskind: The thing that fascinates me about *A Raisin in the Sun*, beyond its obvious wonderful qualities as a play, are the unprecedented aspects of it in every direction. It's your first play, Lorraine. Now you select Lloyd Richards, who has never directed a Broadway play, and it has an all-Negro cast, and you had great trouble raising the money. I mean, it had to have been a labor of incredible effort. The raising of the money, for example . . .

Glenville: Was it difficult to get up?

Susskind: Oh, extremely.

Glenville: It was, was it?

[unintelligible conversation]

Hansberry: I think other people seem to know more about how difficult it was. . . . *[laughter]* I keep reading about how extraordinarily difficult it was to get *Raisin* on the boards. I guess I was so removed from that. I was doing revision through the whole period. I really didn't know that our number of investors was an uncommon number. Someone told me this recently, we have a hundred and some-odd people—by the way who've been paid off—and this, apparently is not ordinary—that you do it with far smaller numbers. But in another way, of course, I, above all, know how difficult and how unique it is that our particular material did get to Broadway. I don't like so much to speak of it in terms of the specific property—as they say in the industry—*Raisin in the Sun*—but in terms of materials and art which is withheld from the public for various reasons that the commercial theater thinks is or is not good material, that won't sell, or won't get an audience.

Glenville: I can't believe that *Raisin in the Sun* would not have been put on under any circumstances. I don't say that it mightn't have been delayed a season or there mightn't have been problems, as there are with many plays. But I think that a play such as *A Raisin in the Sun* would've been put on in

the end. It might not have been a great success, I think that's a more interesting point—it is a real genuine, universal success.

Richards: Well, I think . . .

Glenville: That is more special, but I can't believe that a good play isn't
put on in the end.

Richards: No, but it will be put on . . .

Quintero: Sometimes it is important to get a play done at a certain time,
not so much in terms of the—well, that enters into it, too, in the society
and the world in which you live—but in terms of your own development
and your own growth and your own accumulation of knowledge of the particular feeling which you're working, and I think that it's marvelous that it
should have happened this season.

Laurents: I think it's important for the play and for the playwright who
can sit and wait so long, and every playwright, no matter how good, needs
encouragement. If this play hadn't been done now and hadn't been a success, I'm sure your confidence would have been less.

Hansberry: May I say something about this question of time, and when
something appears on the scene, you know, because I have very strong feelings about it. I go to the theater now, and I don't watch the play. I watch the
audiences. And . . .

Laurents: What a commentary on the plays.

Hansberry: [*laughs*] It's very long. [*laughter*] But, this is true, and I've had
occasion, honestly, and before many people to say that I have cried, sometimes. Not just because of the play, but watching these American audiences,
which by-and-large are traditional theater-going audiences: the American,
New York middle class which goes to the theater. And their response, which
Lloyd spoke of, is something other . . . that I didn't know how to anticipate.
And the question of time that you speak of I think is pertinent and important. Frankly, I think we did a good play. I think we did it well, and it's a
respectable script, and it is honest and so forth—and I like to think that it's
art. But aside from that, in terms of the question of time, it seems to me
that's a whole climate, the whole atmosphere in our country that perhaps
might be the backwash of something that we went through for eighty years
when we were so afraid of so many things, and we turned toward so many
things that were negative, and we turn toward an overexamination of our
inner selves, which is valid. I have nothing against psychological drama. I
have nothing against anything that has to do with the inner man or anything
of the kind. I'm not posing one cliché against another. But I'm trying to say

that I think there exists in American life at this moment some sort of hunger for even the most rudimentary kind of affirmation, and that part of the response to this play undoubtedly has to do with the fact that people are feeling very warm toward anything that says man has a lot of dignity, he's very complicated, he's very mixed up, and he's even cruel. But he has a little nobility, and I really feel, sitting watching the audience, is this response. And Lloyd, it's very true, I think we have the most vocal audiences in New York. You hear the women at the end of the play saying, "Don't forget to take the plant." You hear this murmur.

Quintero: That really is very funny that you should say that, because when down at the Circle we were choosing, trying to choose another play to do, and we couldn't find a new play, which I think is something we should do more often, but it was very difficult to find one, because the play that we had before was not very successful. We had to get it out in a hurry and bring in something right away. And I said best do *Our Town*. And I said, "Why?" Everybody said, well, it's been done in the movies, and you see it in television all the time, and nobody's going to come—there's no audience for it, because they'll stay home and watch the movies. And why do you want to do it? Aside from, everybody agreed it was a marvelous play and almost an American classic. And I said, well, I don't know, before we leave, I'd like to have somebody stand in the middle of that stage and scream out—you know despite all of the dreariness and all of the monotony that we have in everyday life—that there is something worth all of that. Something, absolutely—probably small—but absolutely precious and marvelous. And the response of the audience to the play—it's like that.

Glenville: It's interesting that at the same time of the success of *Our Town* and *Raisin in the Sun* you have, at the same time, the great success—and indeed I would couple your play in that feeling—you get the *Sweet Bird of Youth*, which is—with all its theatrical splendor—the exact opposite, because it is not an affirmation of the ordinary warmth and humanity and fundamental simplicity and, in a way, goodness of people at all. It's quite the reverse.

■　■　■

Susskind: I wanted to ask you this question. You know, three of you are represented here tonight with plays that I think are really affirmative. That say that life is good and decent and worthwhile. And I welcome them. The three plays are *A Raisin in the Sun* and *Our Town* and *The Majority of One*. I wonder if we haven't had our fill—I personally have had my fill—of aberration, of degeneracy, of drug addiction, alcoholism, marital infidelity, impotency. How do we . . .

Glenville: If you cut out marital infidelity, already I mean . . .

Hansberry: That's royally popular.

Susskind: But you know what I mean. The downbeat, gloomy . . . Tennessee Williams, poet that he is, passionate though he be, is invariably dealing with a level of humanity that's mired in sickness and hopelessness . . .

Schary: Well, except he's reflecting, and so many playwrights have been reflecting in recent years, the state of the world. I think that we're in a very unhappy and sick period of time. I think many playwrights search for some answers to the problems that are constantly besetting us—where we have fears. We have worries. You look at the daily papers, and they certainly reflect some of the horrible problems that all of us are facing and future generations are facing. And inevitably, then, they begin to search for subject material that we may consider—and there certainly are aberrations—but they look for something beyond that. They're trying to point out that this is a reflection of sickness somewhere within us all.

Glenville: Do you think that's true, Dore? Do you think that he is reflecting that? I think that I would have thought that he's a very subjective writer, because you're talking now about a writer like Arthur Miller, for instance, who makes an objective comment on his surroundings.

Schary: Yes, but I don't think that any playwright can remain totally objective. I think that all of us who create, we are all subject to theses influences around us, and we may not be objective about what we're doing at that particular time, but we are certainly affected by the world around us. We are depressed, we are alarmed, we are confused, we want to strike out, and all of these emotions finally articulate themselves in what we finally put down to paper. Miss Hansberry does it one way, we do it another way, Leonard Spigelgass does it another way—*A Majority of One*—and all of us search for ways of making a statement. But all those statements, there is some reflection . . .

Laurents: . . . the pertinency to life, I think.

Susskind: As writers . . .

Laurents: I don't even think affirmation is—I agree; I happen to feel affirmative, and I think people want to hear it, but since *Gypsy* is what I'm involved in now, and it's what I think of, I didn't want to just do another musical, nor did Ethel Merman, and this is a play about something that I think has always been important, namely, that parents who try to live their children's lives destroy themselves and their children, and they have just got to let go. And when Lorraine was talking about watching an audience—it's very interesting to see them in Philadelphia where they come in expecting to see a big razzle-dazzle, that same old Ethel Merman show. And they don't see it. They see her giving an extraordinary dramatic performance. But then when it gets down to the basic facts that she is a mother who is destroying her child, you can feel the change in the audience. It isn't a question of whether the play is good or bad. It is something that is directly related to their own lives. And that's what they care about. I think when you were asking about Tennessee Williams and the so-called aberrations, it may be that he has gone too far in the sense that people can't find anything to identify, but I don't think any subject should be ruled out merely because it's an aberration. [*several people speak at once*]

Hansberry: Absolutely. May I just say something about Tennessee Williams?

Susskind: . . . focus on that in recent years.

Laurents: . . . we can't connect with it personally. Because the interest is too much in the aberration rather than in the human circumstance that makes for the aberration.

Glenville: But you can't say . . . I was going to say you cannot say that the audience cannot identify with Tennessee Williams's plays. I happen to like them very much but the audience identify with *Raisin in the Sun*, they identify with *The Majority of One*, but also they identify very much with *The Sweet Bird of Youth*. You can't say that there was a . . . [*several people speak at once*]

Hansberry: May I say something about the nature of that . . . I'm interrupting everyone. [*several people speak at once*]

Hansberry: The entire Tennessee Williams question interests me very much, because there's a natural tendency on the part of people to assume that I am arbitrarily on the other side. That I am saying one thing about the human race, and he is saying something else—which I don't happen to feel. I think that he continues—whatever the problems in his work which I think are there—but whatever the problems in his work, he continues to do a service for American drama. And by that, I mean that I think that it has always been valid, very much in the way Mr. Schary was saying, for the writer to take what is ill, what is sick in our culture, any culture for the last two thousand years, and say this is the way it is, and you see it thus and so forth, you see it with a façade, and here's what is underneath—and that this is always valid, and important, and necessary. Now, in specifics, because—to narrow it down to American life—I think we've had not so much too much Tennessee Williams, but we've had a reverse kind of thing in America.

We've had the glorification of this dying culture. We've had it till it comes out of our nostrils practically, you know, beginning with certain famous motion pictures . . . [*laughter*]

Schary: Why are you laughing, Arthur?

Laurents: I won't mention any more than Lorraine will!

Hansberry: Well, I have in mind things like *Gone with the Wind*, where one would suppose that the foundation, you know, of the thing that Williams continues to examine and expose, was somehow very beautiful, which of course it wasn't; it was sick. And in the twentieth century, it is possible to turn on your television set and see a distinguished congressman from this part of the South and get the idea that this is a man who's given the best years of his life to something very fine and very wonderful, and Williams takes it, and he exposes it on the stage. Now, whether or not he does it with too much villainy so that we can't recognize of the matter as a human being—that's a problem of art. But I think when we're talking about whether it is relevant and valid, of course it is, and I think it's very important, and it's very . . . It's an affirmation of its own kind that he even bothers and that he understands it, and where objectivity overrides the subjective impulse in art. Because there is something disturbing this man, and I think this is what we should all feel when we sit in the theater. There is something he is saying that, doesn't give the sweet bird a chance in this world. And it needs to be changed. And I'm for that.

Laurents: But you know what's interesting about that play to me is that —I don't think it's the brilliant performance of Geraldine Page that overpowers it, but to me it's like seeing two Blanche Dubois on stage. One is the actress, and one is the boy that Paul Newman plays, but the woman has that very thing you were talking about. She has dignity even though she's a wreck, and the boy doesn't have it, and I think that's basically why the audience goes for the woman so much and is a little thrown out of focus by the second act, in which she doesn't appear, because they expect her, and they want her to be the central character of the play. They want somebody to aspire to more, and I think that character does have enormous dignity. And I think as good as Paul Newman is, he cannot help the character of the boy. I, for one, just didn't care about him.

Susskind: Let me ask you three writers, Dore and Lorraine and Arthur, that as individual writers, do you feel affirmative today about life? I mean, are there positive values in all of your works, in *Sunrise at Campobello* and *Raisin in the Sun*, in your work. There's hope implicit in it. There's love in it, and it isn't invariably dealing with people—forgive me, Peter—but I can't identify with the characters in a Tennessee Williams play. I am fascinated by the writing. It's like watching incredibly interesting little squirmy things under a microscope. You cannot look away. You're just riveted by the power and the talent of the man and the virtuosity of the man, but no identification is possible with the people in those plays, because they don't remind you of yourself or anyone you ever knew . . .

Glenville: Is that necessary?

Susskind: No, but . . . [*several people speak at once*]

Hansberry: First of all, is it true? I don't know why everybody's so removed from the characters—we have enormous problems in our culture, and these people seem to me to be running around, yes. I don't . . .

[*Quintero shares his opinion of* The Iceman Cometh, *after which Laurents and Schary have a lengthy discussion regarding the dreams of mankind appropriate to theatrical representation.*]

Susskind: You two have wandered a bit afield from the point that I labored unsuccessfully to make and that is that when the plays that you write have to do with what you were speaking about, Arthur—to do with truth and freedom and love and so forth, as *Our Town* does, as *A Raisin in the Sun* does—then, the theater for me is not only a wonderful place to be on an exciting adventure, but it has a ring of positive values for me. I mean, I'm tired of going in and seeing . . .

Schary: But David, truth has many faces, and . . .

Susskind: But don't you think . . .

Schary: The theater must concern itself with them all.

[*Glenville, Laurents, and Schary have a lengthy debate regarding legitimate subjects for drama and whether or not it is important that plays be memorable or make you think.*]

Susskind: Can I barrel in on this very specific point now and talk about some of those very slight vehicles that are always cropping up in every theatrical diet each year that I think are just appallingly reminiscent.

Schary: Why should we talk about them? We may be guilty of one of them in the years to come.

Susskind: No, I mean . . . In other words, there is a phase of our theater now that can best be capsuled by the sex comedy. This shows up every year. It generally has one or two big Hollywood stars, and it romps through to critical adjectives like—*hilarious*, I think, is the favorite one, or *delicious* . . .

Laurents: *Titillating.*

Susskind: *Titillating* and *dazzling* are the things mounted above the theater, and they're generally pieces of piffle. They look like each other, and they never change. They have no content, and we have them on Broadway right now.

Glenville: Well, I think that if a sex comedy is dazzling, then let's have it. By all means, I can't wait to go. What you're really saying is that most of the ones—most of the sex comedies—are of a low level. If you say that, then that's . . .

Laurents: Well, they never do it in those sex comedies, that's what matters.

Quintero: They're not sex comedies. [*several people speak at once*]

Laurents: No, they're always getting up to the door, but they never go in.

Glenville: In Paris, you get real sex comedies, and though usually nine out of ten are bad, the tenth is worth having. But you're saying they're not very good here.

Susskind: Yes, well, in the spirit of truth—and you chaps have been deliciously generalized tonight—let's take, for example, *The Marriage-Go-Round*, which has, I think, mounted above its theater, words like *dazzling*, *hilarious*, *titillating*. Now that is a comedy that I think reminds us of every other such comedy. Isn't that true? There's a man and a woman, and a blonde threatens the domesticity and the peace.

Schary: But you have two very good performances by two very good people whom I would certainly not dismiss, as you did, with the quotes, "Hollywood stars." They are very engaging. They bring the show off very well. I grant you that when you leave the theater, you've not seen anything that's deeply moved you or provoked you into any kind of thinking. But you have had an evening's entertainment in terms of an experience of watching two very delightful people come off with two very, very good performances. Now, sure, we like to ask for more in the theater, and during the course of a season you get more, but you have some seventy-five productions every year now on Broadway, about that number, and they're not all going to be up to the standards of the few top plays that come along each year. It's impossible because it's very hard to do. It's very difficult.

Glenville: But Dore, there the question is—admittedly, there are two splendid performances by attractive and adroit actors. So, let us say that as a vehicle, it succeeds completely with two charming people. Then, of course, it isn't a deep play and doesn't make you think, because it doesn't even enter that arena. It doesn't pretend to [*unintelligible*]. What is surely, therefore, the point of discussion, if we're going to discuss that particular play at all, is—does it amuse and entertain you while it's on? Do the lines themselves, do the situations, does the point of view, does the slightly nudging, conniving, domestic identity angle, is it proper and admirable fare for the adult in a relaxed, postprandial mood? Or is it thin?

Susskind: Pretty thin. Pretty thin.

Hansberry: [*laughs*] Well-spoken . . .

Quintero: But are we talking about the play or quarreling with the fact that a play like *The Marriage-Go-Round* should not be put on, or are we talking about if it is put on and played charmingly—I haven't seen it—does it deserve the kind of critical . . .

Glenville: Yes, now you're getting to the point.

Laurents: Now we're getting to a point we should avoid.

Hansberry: No, I think . . .

[*unintelligible conversation*]

Quintero: . . . applause, where a play like *Red Roses for Me*, for instance, when it was put on, there was in the criticism of it, there were enormous reservations, you know. Like, for instance, Mr. Kerr had enormous reservations about *Red Roses,* and where in one play of great merit a critic will have reservations about it and will criticize it on a certain level, then comes a slight comedy, which I certainly—people find it amusing—perfectly fine— they go all out utilizing the same words and giving it the same value that they would give, let's say, to *A Long Day's Journey into Night.* I think there's a confusion there.

Glenville: I think you're absolutely right. The question is—do small, entertaining, and charming plays deserve the indulgence that they are given and sometimes the superlatives? But on the other hand, I think to be fair, if you really read the critical assessment of those plays, if you read the critical assessment of, say, *A Touch of the Poet,* I don't think anybody who really read from the beginning to the end of any given critique of those two plays would be under any misapprehension as to which is the major work and which is the minor. [*several people speak at once*]

Laurents: I think there is a double standard of criticism, and I think it's a question of emphasis. I didn't see the—whatever that play we were talking about was either—but I know in reviews of plays like that they will say in one line, "Of course it is a trifle." Then the rest of the review is two columns full of those adjectives. Whereas a serious play, or a play that—it doesn't have to be serious—a play that is trying to be more, you will find paragraph after paragraph beginning with *but* and *however* and *unfortunately.* And I don't think people read these reviews—we do in the theater. I suspect the audiences don't. They skim it. And they can tell—they look at the first paragraph and the last—you can tell, should I run to the box office? And it's a question of emphasis if they . . . well . . .

Glenville: Arthur, I think there are two separate issues. Obviously, if a play aims very high, aims to be in its own sense an important play, it deserves the flattery. It deserves the compliment, rather, of a very serious assessment on a very high level. Now, a quite separate point is attracting large audiences into theaters by means of excerpts from criticism out of their context, which can be very misleading, and obviously a light play with a notice that starts, "This is a trifle with no particular literary merit, but it's quite engaging." We now come to the question of the performers, say, and then there are two columns of praise for the performers. Naturally, the excerpt can be used commercially, which is not a terribly deep or serious ill in the theater, but it's a commercial embarrassment that . . . [*video blacks out*]

■ ■ ■

Susskind: I suppose what we were really talking about before was whether plays of the size and content of *Marriage-Go-Round, The Gazebo, Make a Million,* and such really merit space in the theater. You know, the theater situation is very crowded now . . .

Richards: I think we can go a little further than that. Not only whether they merit it, but I'd go even further and ask what is the condition of theater today in this country. What are our standards? Are we—now I see a play like—and I don't want to mention any names because I don't know particularly—but I think that as I look at it a comedy of that kind, which you say says very little, that has say mediocre reviews, has a much better chance of running—for those things: hilarious, titillating, whatever they have—has a much better chance of running or receiving an audience than a serious play with faults. And the question arises to me is have we—what is being done with theater to the extent of what do we expect from theater, or what have we educated, in theater, our public to expect? Is it a place where they just go now for entertainment, and it is that the view of our theater? Or is it a place where people go also with the view of probably learning something, questioning something, or some of the other aspects of theater, and it is . . . the appalling part of it to me is that I feel that our theater is becoming a place or has become a place where entertainment just for itself alone is the thing that attracts people. It's not a place where a great many of the theater-going public go to hear an idea, to really learn something, or to as you say, come away thinking of something, really having something . . .

Schary: Well, I'm not sure you're right, because a play such as *Disenchanted* did not get what we call rave notices, and because there's been interest on the part of the public, the play has maintained its run. In the same way that a play that got also indifferent notices but was indicated to be a good comedy, or good evening in the theater, was a good performance by Sam Levine in *Make a Million*, that's also running. I don't think it's true that one excludes the other. There are plays each season that manage to get along for only one reason—because the audience finds these plays, regardless of the notices. They find them. And I think this is the big point, Peter, which I want to make in terms of what you said before about notices. The audience finally determines whether the play gets good notices or indifferent notices—the audience makes up its mind. Last year one play comes to mind, which I thought was a very moving play called *The Rope Dancers* by Morton Wishengrad. It got wonderful notices. The play did not run. Because audiences . . .

Laurents: Dore, I'm afraid you are wrong. It did not get wonderful notices.

Schary: Oh, yes. It did.

Laurents: It got one or two.

Schary: No, it got about four or five.

Laurents: I think the majority of the notices were . . .

Schary: Walter Kerr gave it a good notice, Watts gave it a good notice, and Atkinson.

[unintelligible conversation]

Laurents: But I don't think Kerr did, I'm not sure.

Schary: Yes, I'm pretty sure he did.

Glenville: But in any case, I think that . . .

Laurents: I loved the play, but I really don't think it got—I think most of the notices were against it.

Schary: But there was something apparently about it—it had certainly enough good notices and enough support from important people to have maintained it for quite some time, but the audiences apparently were not satisfied with it as an experience, for whatever the reasons might be. And the audiences are satisfied with lesser plays very often because it provides them an evening's entertainment. Certainly, in this season with a play like *J.B.* and *Sweet Bird* and your play, *A Raisin*, these are plays that are very provocative and very moving and not completely easy to watch.

Susskind: Serious plays do tend to get very short shrift compared to the musical and the comedy. Now you've mentioned some plays, *The Disenchanted* is running, but it's on *two-fors*, which means you get two tickets for the price of one. This is the death throes of a play. You do that just before close.

Glenville: I say to all this, why not? I think the audience have a right to judge what they find entertaining and what they don't. I'd much rather see—I mean, we're talking, and you all, I think, have supplied the audiences with extremely entertaining, satisfying evenings, but you are really talking very gloomily and making the theater sound the most ghastly bore. So, the only subjects that you could possibly allow properly in the theater and nod your heads to are plays of very, very serious . . . [*several people speak at once*]

Laurents: I think what Lloyd said was that the mediocre comedy stands a much better chance of surviving than a play that is trying to be good and has faults.

Glenville: Of course. Yes, and it is true what you said.

Richards: Yes, and I refer to *Red Roses for Me*. Faults though it may have, this is a very important play. And it received a very short shrift. And . . .

Glenville: But do you agree with Dore that it's the audience that—I agree with you—it's the audience that finds the . . .

Richards: But we condition an audience. And I'm questioning to what extent has the audience been conditioned in theater to expect, or to go to the theater, only for entertainment? [*several people speak at once*]

Richards: I don't know that it has always been so.

Glenville: I think that a good . . .

Hansberry: May I suggest that we don't do what we accuse the critics of doing, and that is just lump everything together. There are materials of stature, and there are other things which only have the intent to be entertainment, and I should like to say for myself, in answer to what you say, that I'm very much in favor of entertainment in the theater. There's no contradiction between art and entertainment. There never has been, there never should be.

Glenville: But you can have entertainment without art. And it's not necessarily a bad thing.

Hansberry: Very rarely. I can't think of an example. On those occasions where I have been genuinely entertained, I think there's artistry involved. It doesn't matter if you're talking merely about the variety arts or so-called low comedy or whatnot. It's usually artistry that gets it over.

Glenville: Well, what do you mean by—I don't quite know what art in that sense means. I know what fine arts are; a thing done with adroitness and craftsmanship in the theater, I think, is obviously good, and you can have an entertainment very adroitly performed and charmingly performed that has no seriousness, but whether it's artistic—anything well done is artistic in that sense.

Schary: Exactly.

Glenville: What does art mean, then?

Schary: *La Plume de Ma Tante* is artistic.

Glenville: And a vaudeville, a good vaudeville turn is—is it art? Would you consider it art?

Hansberry: Yes. If it reaches those particular heights, yes. By all means, I don't think there's any other way that you can transmit other than by art. It doesn't matter what the media is. But I was really trying to get to something else, which—I'm very much affected by the point of view that the theater and the entertainment industry, like all other art forms, must be dictated by the circumstances of the given society at the moment. For me, it's kind of pointless to sit and talk about what audiences do or do not demand, so long as we know that our theater has the structure that it has, commercially speaking. We all know and suffer from it, in some cases profit by it—that a good play doesn't necessarily run—we know this. Or that a bad play can. These are limitations outside of what we as participating artists may feel is good or bad about the theater. I don't see why . . .

Glenville: I think a goodish play may not run, but I think a really wonderful play does run. [*several people speak at once*]

Hansberry: We have a problem in this country of even doing Shakespeare, and he wrote a rather good play in his day. You know we do. This is a legitimate problem. It has to do with soil erosion to even present it free in New York City; you can't quite do. And I don't think it has anything to do with the quality of the art, frankly, if you understand my point. But what I'm trying to suggest is, I don't think there's any quarrel between the fact that by the very nature of the theater, we need and want everything. I'm very much addicted to certain popular American forms. I'm a great movie-goer, and there's nothing quite as entertaining as to go see an old American movie either on television or in the theater. Or certain kinds of materials on television. They're enjoyable, and they're delightful, and sometimes they're very bad—well, they're bad. But what I'm saying is there's no reason to confuse the issue and suggest that pieces of stature are not due their own area, are not due their own reward. And I would like to imply that it sooner or later gets back to something that Dore Schary was saying just a moment ago that I didn't want us to lose. And that is that serious drama, *serious* drama, drama that has at least the objective of making a larger statement about life—I think sooner or later has to become involved in its time. For this reason, I don't think that we can get lost and despair or make abstractions about how man defeats himself, because once we have truth, and I am saying that life has this and that quality, we must also assess it in such a way that we see that there's no blanket group of people called *man*, but there are people who are very arbitrarily trying to do one thing and people arbitrarily trying to resist it. Jules Dassin thinks so, too. Julie Dass. [*laughs*] And that if we could take a lesson from drama, we know that there are conflicts going on very actively so, but they're not abstractions, and that, I think, it isn't so much a matter of wondering if some vague force of fate is going to blow us all up, you know, but who is doing it? And what can we do about it? And how can we participate in it? From this kind of assessment of life, I think you—I'm really back to the other question where you were asking how writers do or do not become affirmative. I think we're obliged, if we're serious, to take a position, and the problem in art and pieces of stature of any given time and period in history has to do with what kind of position you take. I say very often that you'll go to see *Romeo and Juliet* and, fact of the matter is that you, you're not confused, you're on the side of the kids, you want them to get married, you're very sorry. That's why it's a tragedy when they don't make it. And the things that prevent this, the problems with their families and the reasons why their families won't let them make it, are very much of the time, and very important.

Glenville: But when you see *Troilus and Cressida*, what do you think?

Hansberry: I never saw it. [*laughter*]

Susskind: You're all so artistic, and your integrity is shining so brightly that I seem to be the crass introducer of notions . . .

Laurents: Commercials. [*laughter*]

Susskind: . . . that don't interest you much, but what appalls me about our theater is that it is infinitely easy, it seems to me, to raise money for a sex comedy with some big names—I'm coming to Lloyd Richards's point— to get on a piece of trivia than it is to mount a *Red Roses for Me* or *The Visit* or, if you will, *Rachimo*. That there is an onus on the more serious work with backers, with critics, and with the public.

Schary: I don't think it's that. I think that what—I think there's confusion. I think whenever you come in, whenever you have a play or a picture that strikes any kind of a new note, and usually it is the serious play that does that, you always have resistance, particularly when people involved in it are more or less perhaps a little new to the theater, but even to those who have some reputation, and it's always a little tougher when you're striking a new path, and the history is very clear on it. A musical like *Oklahoma!*, which had a new point of view about a musical, found it very, very tough to raise money. A play like *Life with Father*, which we now look back on and say, "What should have been the problem?" They had a lot of trouble to get the money. I remember years, many years ago, when I was just breaking into the theater, *Broadway*, which again had appeared to be a new form of telling a play, had an awful lot of trouble getting its money.

Laurents: We had a great deal of trouble getting a producer for *West Side Story*.

Schary: Of course, it must have been an enormous problem, and I heard that that was so. [*several people speak at once*]

Schary: *Raisin in the Sun—Raisin in the Sun*, I understand, had a lot of trouble. There are many people who didn't know about the play. I like to believe that if I had known about it, if anybody had come to me with it, it wouldn't have been any question at all about doing the play, but many people found resistance because it was new. I know we had enormous trouble getting money for a *Sunrise at Campobello*. We didn't have the money until we started rehearsals.

Glenville: Do you think this is a problem connected with the theater specifically?

Schary: No, I say it's true in any medium. I know in motion pictures that it's very difficult.

Richards: It may be, but I think this is what's unfortunate—that we have created a theater or an art form which is an exploratory form, supposedly, wherein just the act or the fact of exploration is suspect.

Hansberry: Yes, yes.

Richards: If we are not doing something that has been done and has been proved, we are immediately suspect. Now, the thing that appalls me and the thing that I'm talking about is the fact that we have a theater or an art form that should be an exploratory form, where new ideas could exist, where new concepts can exist, that has this kind of resistance, and that's what I mean when I say I'm questioning theater and what have we made of theater. I think it's a commercial repetition of things.

Schary: I don't think that's what we've made of it, though, Lloyd.

Richards: When you find people in theater . . .

Schary: I don't think we've made that . . . I think, again, the audiences made that.

Richards: No, I don't think so. [*several people speak at once*]

Glenville: It's the same with books. It's two things. It's not only whether it's exploratory or not, but it's also whether it's very serious or not. A historian can work for five years on a book which may be absolutely magnificent, and then you write a sexy novel or a very comic book, very light, the sales are obviously going to be greater for one than for the other. I mean it's a basic—it's an inevitable—and it seems to me a not too distressing thing that the people don't want to think too profoundly or perhaps whose education has not afforded them the enjoyment out of the more serious things, that more serious things can provide people who have had the benefit of a perhaps more careful or more classical education, say. But they're obviously in a minority, and more people will be buying tickets at six dollars or whatever it is to see a light entertainment that's going to amuse them and keep . . . [*unintelligible*] [*several people speak at once*]

Quintero: The theater, to look at it just as an art form and one experiment in it, that's marvelous. I believe that, and I love to do it, I've tried to do it downtown, but there is an enormous financial aspect to this, the theater. And I think that what we best do is really look into it—try to as much as we can to—for instance, if I were to do *Mother Courage*, a play that I love . . .

Richards: You'd have a rough time.

Quintero: Not if I could find somebody that could play it. And still have a big name to carry it. Because that is something that I—we—you have to— [*several people speak at once*]

Richards: And that's what I'm talking about. You have to have a big name to carry it. You have to have the play itself, and the fact of what it's about cannot carry. To talk about a big name, or something else, these are things that we've run into.

Glenville: But you're selling a popular medium. You're selling something that you—in order to make it financially possible . . .

Richards: Well, we've made it popular is what, uh . . .

Glenville: But you're never going to make what you want popular. I think you're overly idealistic [*unintelligible*].

Laurents: I think you are over-accepting, because I do think that the standards of taste have grown, and forgive me, I think the attitude should not be that this is the way it is, about anything, and therefore this is how it will always be. I don't say you have a duty, but I do, in a way. My back goes up a little at this attitude—you people don't want entertainment in the theater, and the public will always like the cheap—I don't believe they will. I think . . .

Glenville: More of the public will like the cheap is what I say. And not necessarily the cheap: the light, the frivolous. More will. It's only a question . . . [*several people speak at once*]

Glenville: I agree with Dore when he says there will be good plays—and you said it too—there will be plays of stature, and if they're good, and they'd better be good and well done, otherwise of course, there's no point in discussing. But if they're well done, there will be a public who will enjoy it and who will give it great praise. And I don't think that there are great masterpieces wonderfully done because [*unintelligible*].

Schary: You know, in answer to what you said before, I think your show last season, *West Side Story*, was a very good indication. You had no stars. You had no stars at all. And the show was an enormous success.

Glenville: And so is yours.

Schary: Well, they have a star, they have a star. Sidney Poitier. [*several people speak at once*]

Schary: But in terms of what we're talking about, we're not talking about the talents. You know, the town. We're talking about the stars you put up on the marquee.

Laurents: First of all, Dore, it was a musical. And musicals, generally, tend to run longer.

Schary: It was also a very good show, Arthur! [*several people speak at once*]

Laurents: Yes, it was, and it is not going to run nearly as long as *Music Man*.

Glenville: Would you quarrel with that?

Laurents: Yes, because I think it's a much better show than *Music Man*.

Glenville: Yes, but that's where we disagree. In pure numbers, in pure numbers, there will always be more people, but if more people go to a lighter entertainment than to a more serious one— [*several people speak at once*]

Richards: That is because they have not been exposed to the other . . . [*laughs*] and found out that they can get just as much enjoyment out of *Romeo and Juliet* or out of some of the more serious things in life. These things have not been presented to them. As a matter of fact, they've been presented to them in a negative way in terms of the fact that they will not, or they might not, or you will not, and people have been conditioned to expect that I'll go to Shakespeare and be bored, or I'll go to [*unintelligible*] and be bored.

Schary: But that's not true. But that's just not true. Shakespeare is produced more than any other playwright. He's constantly being produced.

Glenville: More played than any playwright's ever been.

Hansberry: Where?

Glenville: Everywhere.

Schary: All over! All over.

Hansberry: No, I'm quite serious. Where?

Schary: Yes, on Broadway, too.

Hansberry: Where is . . . no.

Susskind: On Broadway and next week we'll see an eight-week engagement of one of the great—I saw *Much Ado about Nothing* . . . [*several people speak at once*]

Susskind: . . . eight weeks is all it can take in the largest and richest city in the world. I would like to say this . . .

Schary: But I would like to say this: I would hazard a guess that if you take an American theatrical season all over the United States and add up the playing time of all plays, you'll find that Shakespeare, at the end of the year, has been played more than any other playwright who ever lived. Every year in America he's played all the time.

Glenville: In England he's considered the most commercially sure author.

Schary: If you look over the long runs, the plays that have run the longest, over long periods of years, there are very serious plays and very important plays that have run a long, long time. Audiences have been exposed to them.

Richards: I am not saying that this does not exist, but I am decrying the fact that *West Side Story*—and the presentation of *West Side Story*, or the trouble in getting on *West Side Story* suddenly makes *West Side Story* a problem and an exception. It makes our play a problem and an exception.

Glenville: I think you're being ungrateful.

Richards: Goodness.

Glenville: The play got on, and it's a great success. What are you bellyaching about? I don't . . . [*unintelligible*].

Susskind: They were near misses, they were near misses. It almost didn't get on. Peter, really. They were desperate . . . [*unintelligible*] [*several people speak at once*]

Glenville: . . . the most long and serious play, and you can't quarrel with what happened to it. I suppose more people saw *South Pacific* than saw any of the things we're discussing, but they are there, they are put on, and the public go, and they can be successful. You had a success with *Long Day's Journey into Night*, than which nothing can be more serious. You've just had a great success with *Raisin in the Sun*. *West Side Story* is no flop. So, you're quarrelling about the few extra people who want to go in for lighter entertainment. [*several people speak at once*]

Susskind: No, something deeper.

Hansberry: We're talking about something deeper than that . . .

Laurents: I'll bring up another play. My first play, *Home of the Brave*, which people think of now as being a success, was an outright flop. It ran sixty-nine performances. It got generally vague reviews from the critics. It was my first play, and it taught me a lesson about the theater, which is simply that you must write what you believe, and care as you care, and not have yourself be depressed and discouraged by what happens either in the papers or with the audience. I hesitate bringing up the play because it's my own, and you can certainly say it has faults—it does. It is now considered quite a good play. You said before a goodish play will run. That play didn't run— didn't run at all. And in the subsequent reviews of plays of mine, the critics have said it is not as good as the memorable *Home of the Brave*, which they slammed the first time around.

Glenville: That is . . . most unfair.

Susskind: I would like to give you a parallel. Last night, I did the *Browning Version* on television with Sir John Gielgud. I woke to find that we had half the public—that something called *Mark of Zorro* and *The Real McCoys*, which is a real cornball, family Western presided over by Walter Brennan. *Mark of Zorro* is a show in which something remotely resembling Superman flies down and performs little good deeds. We had the *Browning Version* with Sir John Gielgud, Margaret Layton, Cecil Parker, and Robert Stevens. Half the American public tuned to us that tuned to this other junk. [*several people speak at once*]

Schary: How many people were tuned into you? Millions, weren't they?

Susskind: Well, I'm not—I'm only attempting to draw this kind of parallel in the theater, too. *The Visit* and *The Entertainer* and *The Waltz of the Toreadors* are first, not produced as often as *Marriage-Go-Round*, and *Once More with Feeling*, and *Make a Million* and *The Gazebo*.

Glenville: How often can they produce them?

Susskind: And they don't run nearly as often.

Glenville: You can only produce them once.

Susskind: But producing them is a labor.

Glenville: Anything worthwhile is a labor. Anything. If a thing aims high, you're going to have more trouble with it. The real thing I think you're discussing shouldn't be discussing the inequities of the theater, because it seems to me that things aren't perfect, but at least good plays get a chance and can be a success that are good. But you're talking about education. You're talking about the conditioning of the public—not only of America, but of anywhere—educating people to the point where they will actually derive more pleasure out of something of more substance than out of something of less substance. As long as the people in the population are so conditioned or educated, they will have actually derived more pleasure from a light comedy, sex comedy, than from something of serious substance, it seems to me that that will always be the case.

Richards: Yes, but our attitude is to accept this as so, and I don't believe that it is so.

Schary: I don't think we do accept it.

Richards: I think we do. I think that there are problems in putting on any play—be it a light comedy or whatever. But the nature of the problems is the thing that upsets me. I don't know what problems you had with *West Side Story*. I know what problems we had with *Raisin in the Sun*. And it's the nature of the problems. It isn't that it's a play, it's that it's controversial, it's that it's Negroes, it's that . . . should a Negro play be directed by a white director or a Negro director, because it was last directed and a bit successful with a white director. It's the nature of the problems that bothers me, and the nature of the fact that this will not be commercial because it has ideas in it, or that will not be commercial because it is controversial . . .

Glenville: But, is your play controversial? I don't think it is.

Richards: No . . .

Laurents: Peter, I tell you . . .

Hansberry: I think we are trying to say something on a slightly different level, if I may say so. Really, I think part of what some of us are saying, Peter, is as artists, we have a responsibility to be concerned beyond the specific problems of the theater. In other words, we want our people, our American people, to constantly move up, and you can't just reverse the question and say that because certain of our traditions haven't committed them to enjoy what is really the fruit of world, culture in perhaps its highest level, that therefore we accept this and that we respond always to the fact that they prefer lighter things. What we're suggesting is that the artist in society always has the responsibility to constantly be trying to explore something that is a little deeper, a little more profound for our time, so that we can't afford the snobbish attitude of sitting back and saying, "Well, you know, give them dog food." [*several people speak at once*]

Quintero: . . . from the artist's point of view in the theater, whom I consider a serious, dedicated worker in the theater, I think in some way, in different degrees, is really, desperately trying to do that.

Laurents: Besides, there's another point about what people really want. Now, *Home of the Brave*, which, as I said, was a failure. Since then, I doubt there's a day when that play is not being performed someplace in this country and around the world. And to go to a much higher level, you asked before where Shakespeare was being performed. In small festivals all over the country but not on Broadway.

Hansberry: And the universities.

Laurents: And the universities. My point is if, perhaps, the audience that has the money to spend six to ten dollars for a show—that's the audience that wants the frivolous theater. I don't know.

Hansberry: Thank you.

Laurents: But there seems to be some kind of dichotomy between what, quote, "people," unquote, want and what the Silver Fox Trade wants. I don't know.

Schary: I think there's something happening in the theater—

Susskind: Can I interrupt us just a moment?

Schary: Not another commercial.

■ ■ ■

Susskind: Shoot, Dore.

Schary: The point I wanted to make about serious plays and their reception by the audience: we forget that in recent years the runs of plays have changed enormously. It's quite true, Arthur, that probably a majority of those six-dollar-ticket buyers will want to go to see perhaps a musical comedy or comedy or a light play that doesn't move them. But the other plays are more successful. The serious plays are more successful than they've ever been. If you go back into the record of some of the serious plays of years ago, including some O'Neill, you'll find runs of 180 performances, two hundred performances. And because of the economics of the theater they were considered highly successful. That's no longer true. You can look at the list and see very important plays by Tennessee Williams and Arthur Miller and Bill Inge and yourself that have run on and on and on.

Laurents: That's the point we're trying to make, Dore, that you can raise the level of taste.

Schary: Of course! This is what—well, this is what we're all saying.

Glenville: Peter says no.

[*unintelligible conversation*]

Glenville: I never said any such thing. I said that you're making an over-tragic statement as to the situation. If you read the theater lists of 1920 to 1930, I think you would find, in the way you've been speaking, you find that list of productions much more discouraging than you would if you read 1940 to 1950 or '50 to '60.

Quintero: I also think that there's been a growth in them. But there has been a slow growth in every phase of the theater, too. You have acting—this whole style of acting has progressed and changed in the question of what—thirty years, forty years? The quality of production . . . and audiences are more willing to accept a stylized set, or a play on the platform and a back-drop today than they were . . . than the plays of the sets of Belasco some years ago. I do think there has been a movement to do exactly what they, you, they are saying. You can have a play of O'Neill that runs four hours and a half and run it to sell out houses for a year and a half. I don't say that it's perfect, but you do continue working in the theater, and in some way, you do have some control in, through the work that you do, into bringing a . . .

Glenville: Bettering.

Quintero: Yes, a better production, better plays . . .

Glenville: And better taste.

Schary: That's right.

Susskind: You skillfully avoided—all of you—a discussion on this season, and I'd like to ask a few questions about this season and see what we can come up with. This season, I think everyone will agree, the musical has been notably unsuccessful. We've had some rather lavish musical productions that open and close rather quickly: *Whoop-Up, Goldilocks,* and *Juno.* Those that are running could hardly be compared with *My Fair Lady, West Side Story,* or any of the really wonderful musicals in recent years. What, in your opinion, accounts for the lackluster level of musicals this year?

Glenville: Chance.

Susskind: Chance?

Glenville: It's just that in one given year—I think that talents may be not at their best or brightest—the best writers in the world or the best actors and the best producers may do a very good work one year and not so good the next. I think that will change, and one year will be a little better than the other.

Hansberry: Plus, another aspect, if I may, which is, I'm afraid, very much related to what we were discussing. Perhaps the impulse to write something like *Whoop-Up,* which with all apologies, I did not see, but the title somehow connotes it's kind of . . . [*laughter*] The impulse of a young composer to sit down and write for something called *Whoop-Up*, commercially speaking, was probably far greater than for him to set out to do something that might emulate the stature of *Fair Lady* or *West Side Story*.

Glenville: There I really disagree with you completely. I think if you write *Whoop-Up* it's because [*unintelligible*].

Hansberry: I don't think anyone sits down and really gets inspired to *Whoop-Up*.

Glenville: Yes, but I don't think you'd find that to say Mr. Laurents or yourself or—however the conditions from year to year, which I don't think change all that rapidly from year to year, but supposing they did—that you would never or Mr. O'Neill would never find himself, because of the conditions, writing *Whoop-Up* instead of *Long Day's Journey into Night* or [*unintelligible*].

Laurents: How does the title *Gypsy* strike you?

Hansberry: Peter, may I say that I think you're being . . . [*unintelligible conversation*]

Laurents: I'm being serious, because it didn't strike me as something I ought to do until I found a way of saying something that I wanted to say through that material.

Glenville: Exactly. Well, then yes—but it wasn't because of the conditions were such that he was cheapening himself. It's because it was something he wanted to do, and he had something to say. Not because the conditions this year didn't look very promising, so I better do a musical rather than a serious play.

Hansberry: Or a certain kind of musical [*unintelligible*].

Susskind: There's a great responsibility on *Gypsy*. It could rescue the musical season, you know, Arthur.

Laurents: I know.

Susskind: Which is [*unintelligible*] pretty dreary.

Glenville: When there was a very much beloved and extremely adroit showman in the English theater for years, and a very nice man, and a man who did wonderful things in the theater in the sense that he gave great, simple, innocent, romantic pleasure to a great number of people, and his name is Ivor Novello. Ivor Novello wrote a succession of romantic, wedding cake-y musicals. Nobody would consider them today a very high standard. But to write one that ran three years, you would have to write sincerely. You would have to be a sincere Ivor Novello. You couldn't say—Aldous Huxley couldn't sit down and say, "I need some money, I am going to write an Ivor Novello show and run three years." It's not possible. You have to write sincerely in your own media, and I don't think conditions will alter that.

O'Neill will still write O'Neill. He may make a little less money one year than in another, but he won't write *Whoop-Up*.

Quintero: We have that choice. I think that we do have a choice as workers in the theater. We have a choice to either accept something that we don't want to do but we—

Glenville: We don't do it.

Quintero: [*unintelligible*]

Laurents: I don't think you really do have the choice.

Hansberry: I don't either.

Laurents: I think it's the kind of person you are. [*several people speak at once*]

Glenville: No, that's going too far. [*laughter*] We've all known for years that little cheap bedroom farces, little cheap plays are, on the whole, attended by a greater public than more serious ones. But I don't think any of them . . .

Schary: [*unintelligible*]

Glenville: For other reasons. [*laughter*] For other reasons. But I don't think any of us, because we've all known for many years that this type of play plays to a greater audience, and I think we're not overflattering ourselves to say that we do not find ourselves necessarily preoccupied with promoting, directing, writing, acting in those productions. We don't. We have the choice of doing what we want to do; we do our own level to the best of our ability, and I think we'll continue to do that.

Richards: That's after you've established a level.

Hansberry: Yes, and a name.

Richards: If you look at—and I'll go a little further—to young playwrights, coming up faced with a theater in which this is the kind of thing that succeeds, then what do whatever talents they have bend toward? And this is a very formative stage. I think that people who are . . . who may have gone ahead and set an idea and set a way of working for themselves have a greater opportunity to continue in that way than the young person who's coming up as a young writer and takes a look at our theater and what is successful. What is it going to end? And goes around trying to find out what should I do or trying to get a job? What are these talents going to be led into? I am not as concerned about our O'Neills because he's going to write O'Neill. Tennessee Williams is going to go on writing Tennessee Williams, and Mr. Miller undoubtedly, and Miss Hansberry, because I know her, is going to write on.

Hansberry: Thank you for the company.

Richards: And Mr. Laurents, let me include everybody. But say, even eight years ago, in a time in this country when controversy was something to be abhorred, controversy was something to be stayed away from, and please write me a play that says nothing or as little as possible and as hilariously as possible. What are young writers going to write?

Quintero: But obviously it didn't stop the people that you mentioned from writing what they wanted to write.

Richards: Because they had been writing before. This is what I—they had been. I'm talking about a young writer.

Glenville: You would prove your point much more if you could show that very talented people could only get into the theater and succeed in the initial stages by cheap work and then proceeded to do serious work. And I don't think the facts bear that out.

Schary: No.

Laurents: I'll tell you, Peter, I think it comes in . . .

Susskind: I'll bring you back to this year if it takes me . . . [*laughter*]

Schary: David, I'll go back to this year. I still say that a season that produced *Touch of the Poet, J.B., Sweet Bird, Rachimo, Raisin in the Sun*, and, with all due deference to Leonard Spigelgass, *Majority of One*—I think that's a very good season. I don't think anybody has to see the theater is in bad shape.

[*Susskind, Glenville, Schary, and Laurents discuss their opinion of the Tony Awards.*]

Susskind: Let me ask you about this. The other day, a very interesting event took place in New York: the Integration Showcase, in which I think it was Windsor Lewis staged an afternoon of excerpts from plays in which Negro performers and white performers played together. And the Negroes played roles that had previously been undertaken only by white performers. Do you know about that?

Richards: I did one of them.

Hansberry: Directed . . . *Tea and Sympathy*.

Schary: And so did I. I directed one too . . .

Quintero: Oh, you did?

Laurents: What did you do, Dore?

Schary: *Caine Mutiny* . . . I did Maryk as a colored man.

Susskind: What do you think will be the outgrowth of that experiment? Do you think it was meaningful? Will it be productive?

Richards: I hope it was—I think it was meaningful. As to whether or not it will be productive, I sincerely hope it will be. I think as slowly as we are moving, and regrettably slowly, but there is step-by-step greater acknowledgement of the Negroes' position in our place, our actual fact of existence,

and in our society through theater. I have been tremendously appalled by—
and I refer to the films now—the fact of, you look at a film in a college, and
there's never a Negro student. You walk down the streets of this country
in all the straight shots, and you hardly ever see a Negro present on the
street. It's very difficult to believe that these people form 10 percent of the
total population of this country and exist in many, many ways and function
in many, many ways in this country. Our art forms just failed, for one reason or another, commercial or otherwise, to accept it. And I hope that the
Integration Showcase brings to mind to many of the people who do control
theater or art forms that Negroes can be and should be integrated into our
theater and our films not particularly as a problem. And one of the things
that I attempted to do in doing *Tea and Sympathy*, or attempted to show,
was that the introduction of a character, a Negro character, in the situation
and in this play would not necessarily change a thing that the author has to
say. I think that we are swamped with the concept or overrun with the concept that anytime a Negro runs on stage, we've got to have a Negro problem.
And we've accepted the fact that our audience is going to accept this fact,
which is not true.

Glenville: Not in the musical field, though.

Richards: The musical field has been . . . performers . . .

Hansberry: Not on an integrated basis, no.

Schary: I think this is true, though. I know, and I speak now with some
experience in motion pictures. During the years that I did run production at MGM, we made a very real and sincere effort to have integration in
motion pictures. And in film after film that I did personally and others that
I could bring some influence to bear, we put the Negroes in all the sections
of the pictures where they should have been—in railroad stations, in railroad cars, in army pictures, and service pictures without indicating any kind
of problem. They played characters without any reference to any particular
problem. We did make, of course, a couple of pictures that dealt specifically with the problem, such as *Intruder in the Dust* or *See How They Run*,
and I think there's been a greater awareness on the part of people in motion
pictures, particularly since World War II, to attempt to reflect more of the
general society of America. If you were to watch most pictures within an
American scene, not particularly localized, I'd say, into a Western, but in
pictures that have metropolitan background—I think you'd find that there's
been a real effort to do that.

Richards: I think that I am cognizant of the effort. I think that the effort—
and this was the purpose, I believe, of the Equity Integration Showcase—to

make it even a greater effort, because there is an effort doesn't mean that it is enough, or that it is accepted, or that it is done, and I think that the Showcase has a tremendous point in exposing this to people who do control the industry and making them more and more and more aware.

Schary: I wish myself, in the show that was done . . .

Richards: I think you're an exceptional person in this respect . . .

Schary: No, no, I think in the show that was done, my only criticism about the show that we both participated in—I wish there had been a better selection of material. I think your scene was a very good one to have tried, but there's so many plays where you could have taken the central character and made him a Negro, and the sequence could have played perfectly.

Laurents: Do you really believe that?

Schary: Yes. Now it is true. There's no doubt about it that as soon as you introduce—for instance, in *The Caine Mutiny*—the scene we did, there's immediately a different tone that comes into that scene, and it doesn't necessarily mean—the point of the Showcase wasn't that now the trick was to take *Caine Mutiny* and have Maryk a Negro—that wasn't the point, that Wouk should have done that, or that Bob Anderson in *Tea and Sympathy* should have made that character Negro. What the point was that those scenes played with the same intensity, the same point of view, the same integrity, even though by having a Negro in that part, there was a different tone that came into it without any reference to it. There's no doubt about that.

Glenville: May I ask . . . ?

Laurents: I'm probably saying something I shouldn't . . .

Glenville: What parts . . . ? Was it all the parts?

Richards: No, no, it was the part of Al. Not Tom, not the lead boy. The roommate.

Glenville: The roommate? Ah, I see. [*several people speak at once*]

Hansberry: The principal character was played by a young Negro actor [*unintelligible*]. The scene that was selected put focus on him, and it was really interesting. Extremely well done.

Susskind: Could I ask you a question which arrests me very much? Have you discovered—you as a playwright, Lorraine, and you as a director, Lloyd—that you had a substantially greater burden to break through theatrically for the fact of being Negro as opposed just to the odds against breaking through? I found a wonderful democracy in the theater. Now, it's hard for a director to get to do his first Broadway play. It's hard for a playwright to get her first play launched. In any circumstances. Do you think that there was an additional real important hurdle?

Richards: I cannot say that they weren't hurdles. I've had many hurdles to jump in the theater. Many, many hurdles to jump because of being a Negro. In radio, too, as an actor before I was a director and an actor along with being a director, but I have faced this in radio. There—when I first came to New York and worked in radio—there were many directors that were very, very delighted with the fact that somehow, I didn't come over on radio as sounding like a Negro and wanted to use me. Some did; others were frightened of their sponsors and told me so. And it has had an effect, certainly. I took an attitude long ago when I was going to college, and I decided to go into the theater against everybody's wishes because—and the wishes were against it, because the Negro has no place to work in theater, that you will never make a living now, and all of the things that they tell you, but I took an attitude that, okay, the time will come. And when the time does come, I will not be kept out because I am not prepared. I may be for a while kept out because I'm a Negro, and yes, I did have problems. But I already worked— the thing you're doing now, or the thing you're trying to impress people now with the movies, twelve, fourteen years ago, we had integrated theaters, and they have them now in all parts of the country, in universities. There are integrated theaters, which go far beyond what we represent in commercial theater, and are successful. We had a very integrated Repertory Theater in which I directed *Oedipus*, did things in the Gibson, did things in all of the classics which were accepted by our audiences. Yes, we had problems when we thought about it. We found an audience willing to accept a performance, and there may have been a reaction in the first ten minutes to adjust to the fact that this man's skin is dark, but if they get involved with the character and get involved in the situation, these things were finally accepted. We had wonderful success with it. But it is just in this commercial area where we get so frightened by sponsors, where we get so frightened by public, that we are again unwilling to try, or we have to make some special conciliatory efforts.

Quintero: Do you—may I ask a question? Do you believe that if you had, let's say, a play like *Ghosts*—you would have Mrs. Alvin played by a white woman and the son played by a Negro? I mean . . . would you do it?

Richards: I have seen it done. I have seen it done successfully. In one of Ibsen's plays, in *Hedda Gabler*, I played Judge Brock. I happened to be the only Negro in the cast and played Judge Brock. This was what . . .

Glenville: Where was this?

Richards: This was in Detroit.

Quintero: Somehow, I can't accept . . .

Richards: Yes, you can't accept it because . . .

Quintero: No, I'm just closing my eyes to something which I don't want to close my eyes to. You know, I mean, there is certainly a difference, not for better or for worse. There's a difference between, let's say a Nordic and myself. There is that. And he couldn't possibly be my father, somehow. [*several people speak at once*]

Laurents: I think the problem is one for the writer, because I did not see the scene from *Tea and Sympathy*, but it seems to me that that play . . . is presumably a play about tolerance. And if you had a boys' school that had—first of all, the class of boy that goes to a school like that, they have to pay; it's not a public school. And if they had a Negro there, then I would assume as an audience looking for truth in the theater that that school had more tolerance, and then therefore, I think what the play would be trying to say would be thrown out of balance. To me, what should be done is to—for example, if you write up a play and show that people have friends, some of whom happen to be Negro, some of whom happen to be white—that makes sense to me. But if you were really seeking truth in the theater, then I think it's a distortion to cast—it would be the same thing as casting, in my terms, a fifty-year-old woman as Juliet. I admit it happens . . . [*several people speak at once*]

Hansberry: Yes, it becomes the point, doesn't it? We're inclined to judge the performance on how she plays it, on whether or not we believe it's Juliet.

Note

1. Editor's note: Self-prepared transcript. The original video version of this interview is available for download at www.historicfilms.com.

The Protest, Part I

Rev. William Hamilton / 1959

Broadcast on *Look Up and Live*, CBS-TV, May 3, 1959. Printed by permission of CBS News.[1]

Announcer: The CBS television network presents *Look Up and Live*. Today, "Part I: The Protest," an examination of what might be the religious nature of our contemporary culture. Our narrator, Reverend William Hamilton, professor of theology at Colgate Rochester Divinity School, Rochester, New York.

William Hamilton: Why should a religious program concern protest? Particularly since some of the most powerful protests of our time are against religion and against God? And even more, many of the critics of our conformist culture tell us that there is no capacity for protest or dissent or rebellion in our times today. Could we be examining something that does not exist? We think there is a kind of protest that's important that we find in our culture today, and we want to examine its shape and direction. We want to see what it is protest against, and we want to see what it is protest for, on behalf of. We will hear it on its own terms as humbly and sympathetically as we can, and we will try, if possible, to speak a Christian word, perhaps, of interpretation and criticism as well. So, this morning, we will hear from four people, have four conversations with protestors or observers of this protest of our time. They will help us clarify our protest, I think. They will also, in their words, speak to us a word of power. For behind their words is real religious power, even if they do not use the word God at all. This power may come through, and we may find that their words are words of divine discontent that will hurt us and perhaps even transform us.

[*Hamilton interviews Nat Hentoff, writer and critic of jazz.*]

WH: Lorraine, we are talking about protest in our time today. What do you see, as both an artist and a person who lives in the midst of contemporary culture, what do you see as the shape of protest in our time?

Lorraine Hansberry: Well, it's there in many diffuse ways. I think we are trying very hard, with some very negative ways even, to set up protest. I think some of the so-called "Beat" is a reflection of a kind of protest. I think some of us are a little more articulate in being specific about our protest.

WH: What are the forms of specific protest that you think are alive today?

LH: Well, with regard to something I feel very close to, the Negro question, for instance, there have been very clear and pronounced movements among Negroes to protest that which is actively against us in society, and other things. I think there is the beginning of some sort of feeling about the right to survive that is not as outspoken as it should be, but it's getting there.

WH: The problem of weapons.

LH: Mmm.

WH: And yet, don't you feel that in a sense there is more feeling about this than any coherent action in our time.

LH: Definitely, but presumably that feeling has to come first.

WH: Yes.

LH: And I think that the feeling is beginning to be there.

WH: And yet, surely, in the world in which you live, the capacity for protest is as often silent as articulate. It is not . . .

LH: That's terribly true, and I don't quite understand it, simply because there is so much to protest, and people who feel that the lack of protest or the absence of it is sophistication, I think, are kidding themselves and are doing no service to our problems.

WH: Then you would emphasize the distinction between simply an emotional identification with causes and actual action on behalf of causes.

LH: Yes, I'm afraid the real rewards in life and in literature come when you do something—when you participate actively—and I think we're going to see that in America.

WH: How rare, though, political protest of any lively kind is.

LH: Well, we've been told that it wasn't nice for eight years to have a political thought that had any element of protest and that this was very unwholesome for America, and I think we're getting over it.

WH: And we're still living on that fear, I suppose

LH: In many ways.

WH: Your play has been sometimes described as a play without protest, and some people have even tried to compliment you by saying that it's not a Negro play at all but a play about people. Do you consider that a compliment?

LH: It's a misstatement. It's very much a play about people [*laughs*], but it's also a play about Negroes in the first place. I've said very often that I think that you achieve the universal through the specific.

WH: Yes.

LH: And it certainly is a protest, perhaps not in the traditional form. That's what they mean, I hope. But it is more than a protest in that I did try to suggest that there is something to do—that it is possible to take principled positions in our life.

WH: Yes, and it's not really a question of fighting against something, but actually fighting on behalf of something.

LH: Always for. Always for. And that doesn't mean that you diminish anything down to slogans; it means that you elevate it up to a very large statement.

WH: And that really the personal relationships at the end of the play between persons are the kind of secret of the . . .

LH: Yes and . . . it transcends interpersonal relationships. They begin to speak to all of us. I think. I hope. [*laughs*]

WH: Thank you very much, Lorraine.

[*Hamilton interviews Gilbert Millstein of the* New York Times *and novelist John Clellon Holmes.*]

WH: We've heard about protest today, a number of different kinds and in a number of different places. We've heard about protest embodied in jazz—not just a protest against our culture here, but a protest on behalf of human integrity and human dignity. We've heard about the kinds of protest possible in regard to the race issue, in regard to the problem of mass destruction weapons today. And we've heard about the kind of protest—very largely negative, we're told—in the very unlikely place of the nightclub comedians. What is the relationship of the Christian faith to all this protest? Does it simply say *yes* to it and give it a word of encouragement? Well, it certainly must do this. But there is something more. John Holmes just mentioned that there is a spiritual *yes* that may be said. And Christians would certainly say this. Say *yes* to human dignity and human integrity and all that this means. But I think that the Christian faith in its depth even has a deeper word to say. A word deeper even than the affirmation of human love or human dignity or human integrity. And that is a word of protest first against God. Biblical man didn't ever get to God easily. It was not easy for him to say *yes* to God. And you can trace that thin red line throughout both the Old and the New Testament, where man was not able to get to God until he argued with him. And whether we look at Jacob having to wrestle with the angel before he could be blessed, whether we look at the psalmist who was hounded by God into submission, whether we look at Job who had to argue impatiently and almost blasphemously with God before he could say *yes* to him, or whether we look at Christ in the Garden of [Gethsemane] turning away from the terror that was to follow, or even more horribly whether we listen to that imponderable word from the cross, "My God, why has Thou forsaken me," we see that at the heart of the biblical message is the statement that one cannot be a man, one can know no human dignity until one dares to protest against God, for only by this vicious kind of arguing with God, can man ever know Him.

Note

1. Editor's note: Self-prepared transcript. The original audio version of this interview is located in the Lorraine Hansberry Papers located in the Moving Image & Recorded Sound Division of the Schomburg Center for Research in Black Culture, New York Public Library.

Unaired Interview with Lorraine Hansberry

Mike Wallace / 1959

Conducted May 8, 1959. Printed by permission of the Bentley Historical Library, University of Michigan, on behalf of the Mike Wallace papers.[1]

Mike Wallace: This is Mike Wallace with another television portrait in our gallery of interesting people. Our guest was an unknown, unpublished writer until earlier this year when her play *A Raisin in the Sun* came to Broadway. She is twenty-eight-year-old Lorraine Hansberry whose powerful story about the struggles of a poor Negro family in Chicago was voted by the New York Drama Critics as the best play of the year, better even than plays by Tennessee Williams, Archibald MacLeish, and Eugene O'Neill. We'll talk with Miss Hansberry about playwriting and about people in just one minute.

■ ■ ■

MW: And now to our story. There is a story that one night, Lorraine Hansberry, a girl who had dabbled in writing, made a brash announcement to her husband. She was going to sit down and write an honest and accurate drama about Negroes. Miss Hansberry exceeded her own expectations, perhaps, because she wrote *A Raisin in the Sun*, the Broadway hit which has been hailed as an important new play by an important new writer on the American scene. Miss Hansberry, first let me ask you this: recently the New York Drama Critics voted that you had written the best play of the season, better than plays written by Tennessee Williams, Archibald MacLeish, Eugene O'Neill. As a heretofore unknown writer, a twenty-eight-, or is it twenty-nine-year-old girl, what was your reaction to that kind of a claim?

Lorraine Hansberry: Well, I received it happily. I felt that our piece was substantial and honest, and the craft of it rather satisfies me. I think I would have liked it as a play if I had just walked in.

MW: John Chapman, the drama critic for the *New York Daily News*, wrote that he has great respect for your play, but he feels perhaps that part of the acclaim may be a sentimental reaction—"an admirable gesture," I think, is the way that he put it—to the fact that you are a Negro and one of the few Negroes ever to have written a good Broadway play.

LH: I've heard this alluded to in other ways. I didn't see Mr. Chapman's piece. I would imagine that if I were given the award because they wanted to give it to a Negro, it would be the first time in the history of this country that anyone had ever been given anything for being a Negro. I don't think it's a very complimentary assessment of an honest piece of work . . . or of his colleagues' intent.

MW: He says that *A Raisin in the Sun*—well, let me quote him. He said, "If one sets aside the one, unusual fact that it is a Negro work, *A Raisin in the Sun* becomes no more than a solid and enjoyable commercial play."

LH: Well, I've heard this said, too. I don't know quite what people mean. If they are trying to speak about it honestly, if they are trying to really analyze the play dramaturgically, there is no such assessment. You can't say that if you take away the American character of something then it just becomes, you know, something else. The Negro character of these people is intrinsic to the play. It's important to it. If it's a good play, it's good with that.

MW: Is it fair to say that even in proportion very few Negroes have distinguished themselves as playwrights, novelists, and poets? There have been a few, including yourself, but not many. How come?

LH: Well, whether they have distinguished themselves is kind of difficult to discuss, because we always have to keep in mind the circumstances and the framework that Negroes do anything in America, which, of course, is a hostile circumstance. We have been writing poetry since the seventeenth century in this country and publishing, been writing plays that simply never see the light of day because the circumstance, as I say, is hostile.

MW: But the same is not true in the case of Negro athletes, Negro entertainers. I think in proportion there are more of them who become hugely successful.

LH: Yes, of course, because one of the features of American racism is that it has a particular place where it allows Negroes to express themselves. We're not very warm to the idea of Negro intellectual exploration of any kind in this country. We presume, or at least the racists do, not me, that it's all right to display physical or musical or other features like that, but don't go writing, and don't go trying to suggest that anything cerebral is within our sphere, you see.

MW: But it is possible that there is another reason or an additional reason, anyway, and that is that Negro dramatists—well, let me quote what you have said yourself. You say, "Negro dramatists burn to fight the cause, they show the Negro as all good and the white man as all bad, and that isn't truth. Compared with Negro poets who have transcended the color question and presented in sophisticated terms, most of our playwrights are retarded." You said that according to the *New York Times* about a month ago.

LH: I'm extremely glad that you asked me about that, because there was an exchange on this question between myself and the *New York Times*. I was interviewed by a very capable young woman who, however, certainly misunderstood this. What I feel happens to be exactly the opposite. Negro dramatists—there's a whole illusion, and I've seen it again and again in reference to our play, where people say this is the first time that the Negro dramatist has broken through and presented the Negro character full scale and many sided and so forth, where we haven't been hit over the head with a message, etc., etc. Well, I'm very glad for the compliment, and I think it's true, and I react very warmly to it. At the same time, I don't really know what they're talking about, and I don't know what that statement out of my mouth could possibly have meant, because, if anything, we haven't had the benefit of enough Negro writers on Broadway to know what they would say about anything. The only other play that I can think in recent years that was the work of a Negro dramatist—people get confused, I'm talking about a Negro dramatist—happened to have been a play about a boy achieving adolescence where I don't even think the word *Negro*, let alone *problem* entered into it, which was *Take a Giant's Step*. There are any number of professional playwrights who simply don't get their scripts read by Broadway producers. I'd be the last person to say that it's because they write poorly. An awful lot of poor scripts get to Broadway, and I don't think that's the reason why theirs don't.

MW: What is the reason why theirs don't?

LH: Racial discrimination in the industry, of course. Broadway simply reflects American life, and American life does not accept Negroes in their full equality yet.

MW: You mean to say that if a first-class Negro playwright were to write a commercial play about white people, let's say, that the very fact . . .

LH: I think he would—up to this point at least—have enormous difficulty even getting it read.

MW: Just for the fact of being Negro?

LH: Oh, yes. I attended a Negroes' writers' conference a few weeks ago where this question was dealt with at length, where a number of very fine Negro writers, Bill Branch, Alice Childress, Langston Hughes, were addressing themselves to the fact that one of the primary problems of the Negro writer is to get the producer and the publisher to not assume that he has written something that isn't going to be interesting because it is going to be limited to the Negro question or problems and so on. Read their scripts.

MW: You do not feel then, or perhaps you do feel, that a good many Negroes themselves grope their way through life in a kind of a color-blinded state? That they do not see the world basically in terms of race conflict and prejudice instead of in terms of human beings?

LH: Of course we do. I do, too. And certainly, my play is actively a protest play, actively so. There is no contradiction between protest and art and good art. You know, that's an artificial argument. You either write a good play or a bad play. It doesn't have too much to do with what it is about. And I should hope that Negro writers would maintain this character. As a matter of fact, I am very fond of noting that people say that this or that minority group is so preoccupied with a problem that this diminishes their art. Well, I have always been very pleased—and my husband also—to note that for the last two hundred years the only writers in the English language which we have had to boast about are the Irish writers, who reflect an oppressed culture.

MW: I saw your play the other night and read the *Status Seekers* by Vance Packard a few days before. Packard writes that the more successful Negroes in America are trying to become ersatz whites. He writes this: "They speak softly and precisely to show they are not noisy, low-class Negroes. They prefer to shop at higher-class white stores, they are more desperately absorbed in surrounding themselves with limousines and mink coats, even than their white counterparts."

LH: Well, that's a very primitive and unfortunate way to characterize the aspirations of the Negro middle class, which certainly are distinct and are different, I think, from Negro working people. To call anybody ersatz any kind of human being is a lot of nonsense. I think a much more intelligent discussion of this is the kind Dr. Frazier of Howard University does in his discussion of the Negro bourgeoisie. There is nothing peculiar or unique or exotic about people having middle class aspirations. We are about to drown in them in America in terms of our total culture, not with regard to Negroes, but everybody is rather fond of high-powered automobiles and what they consider to be the refinements of a better way of life.

MW: There's a tremendous amount of talk . . .

LH: If you're asking me, though, I would like to speak to that. It happens that my own particular point of view, I do come from the Negro middle class, I do come from people who embody much of typical middle-class aspiration in American life. At the same time, however, I deliberately chose the class background of the people who are the characters of *A Raisin in the Sun*, because my own particular point of view is that most of what we hope for as a people, most of what we hope for, our ultimate stature as a people is going to come from these people who are the base and the backbone of our people.

MW: Is there none of you in your play?

LH: George Mur—the young suitor, you know.

MW: The young suitor?

LH: The college student.

MW: I thought the young college girl, Beneatha.

LH: Oh well, this . . .

MW: Because, in an interview maybe it is, it's the same interview, you said whimsically, "She's a mess, she's me eight years ago."

LH: This is true.

MW: Would you elaborate?

LH: Well, I had a great deal of fun with this character because, first of all I knew that if the play ever got to Broadway she would be the kind of character that people had never seen before. A Negro girl with intellectual pretensions of any sort, it's just unknown to the theater, and I also had just a great deal of fun making fun of her a little bit because it's sort of a pleasure to sit back eight years later and look at yourself as you think you were.

MW: There's a tremendous amount of talk—to come back to what we were talking about an instant ago about the—there's a good deal of talk about assimilationism in her particularly. She's mutilating her hair, I gather, to make it straighter.

LH: This is . . . [*laughs uncomfortably*] Mutilation is not proper. She straightens her hair, yes. What are you asking?

MW: Well, this has nothing to do . . . Huh. You were talking about the . . .

LH: What she reflects, if you're interested in the character really, in terms of symbolically, what she really reflects, is a very legitimate and active sentiment among American Negro intellectuals and among much larger sections of Negro life that repudiates much of what has come to us through a cultural experience, a historical experience, that we think is not necessarily as valid as we have been told that it is. And since the thirties there has been quite a movement that feels that what we want now is a recognition of the beauty of things African and the beauty of things Black and this girl represents part of this development, as I do, I think.

MW: If we can generalize, do you think that Negroes generally set high enough standards for themselves intellectually, professionally, in education?

LH: High enough standards?

MW: Mmm-hmm.

LH: Oh, I think they set extremely high standards.

MW: You mentioned the sociologist, E. Franklin Frazier, whom obviously you respect. He said that the middle-class Negro is less competent than his white counterpart, because he doesn't have to compete with whites. The Negro professional, he said, makes excuses for his deficiencies; he likes to complain to white people: we're a poor race trying to get up in the world, you shouldn't expect us to measure up to your standards.

LH: Yes, well, Dr. Frazier of course is speaking from within the veil and he's speaking with an intimacy that you might not as readily understand. It's impossible to discuss the Negro as an abstraction unto itself in this country, so that what he's saying is basically true, that because of the isolation, because of the separation that our people are forced to endure, this particular group cannot come face-to-face with some of the more acute realities of what they are trying to overcome because they just don't get there, they don't become bankers in the larger sense. They don't get an opportunity to deal with those actual things. That has nothing to do with them not having their sights on it.

MW: Well, what about the note that is struck repeatedly in your play, particularly by the son. He says things like this speaking about the Negroes: "We're all tied up in a race of people that don't know how to do nothing but moan, pray, and have babies."

LH: He's an individual, he's one character in the-play.

MW: Representative of no one?

LH: Oh, representative of a good many people. This is inner-group bitterness, when one can't speak against anything else one indicts one's own, you know. This is very common, people have done this always, and he means this to hurt, and he knows it's a line that's directed to his wife in the play. It's a way of turning the attack within for his own personal reasons. I think if you had a conversation with Walter Lee Younger, he'd have other things to tell you.

MW: I see.

LH: But in that moment he is trying to hurt her.

MW: Lorraine, in a moment I'd like to ask you about this: the young girl, Beneatha, who was you eight years ago, I gather, is a rebel in many ways including religion. She even says this, she says, "God is just one idea I don't accept. I just get tired of him getting credit for all the things the human race achieves through its own stubborn efforts," and in a moment I'd like to find just how much of Lorraine Hansberry is speaking there. And we'll get Miss Hansberry's answer in just a minute.

■ ■ ■

MW: And now back to our story with Lorraine Hansberry. The girl adds after that speech that I read just before the break, "There simply is no blasted God—there is only man and it is he who makes miracles." Is there a lot of Lorraine Hansberry in that?

LH: Yes, yes. I feel that ultimately, most of the mystical ideas that man has had about how and why he's going to change his own life and change the universe will disappear and he will ultimately rely on more concrete things, like science, like intelligence, like reason. And I hope so.

MW: In the play, the mother slaps the girl when she says that.

LH: Yes.

MW: Is there an experience within your own past similar to that?

LH: No, I was never slapped.

MW: Never slapped?

LH: Oh no, not in that kind of exchange. What that represents is a character statement of the mother. This is a very strong woman. This is a woman who keeps her authority in any way that she has to—emotionally, physically, however. I think she's a great woman. I think she can be wrong, terribly wrong.

MW: Your play is performed nightly now to standing-room audiences, most of them white people, at least the night that I was there. Now, aside from the obvious motives that a good many of them have, simply that they want to see a good play, can you think of any other motives that some people may have to want to see a play about a Negro family? This is the first time, as you will agree, that this kind of play has gotten this kind of a reception.

LH: Well, it's really difficult for me to try and guess what other reasons they would have. The tradition has been, and we were told rather often, that people weren't interested in seeing a straight drama about Negroes. So, for some reason it has reversed itself and they are now interested to see it partially because it is Negroes. I don't understand it, can't explain it, and I'm quite glad about it.

MW: When your Negro family finally, in the play, decides to move into the white neighborhood, I think the audience is pleased and proud. Do you think they just want to see it on stage, and it becomes a kind of a catharsis for them, but they don't want to see it for themselves?

LH: Probably both things are true. I suspect and if I have any deep feelings at all as a writer, I have a suspicion of the universal humanity of all people, and I think it is possible to reach it and I believe in the moment when they are sitting in the theater and they murmur in favor of the family and they applaud the particular action, I believe that almost every human being there genuinely wishes this to happen. Now to what extent any member of an audience comes out of a theater at any time and retains the emotion of a moment within the theater, I certainly couldn't begin to guess. I think in a much larger way it may have affirmative effects.

MW: Lorraine, unlike perhaps the vast majority of serious writing in America, your play ends on an affirmative note, and in explaining that you once said, "I think the human race is obviously worth saving, ridiculous as it can be." Would you care to go on about that a moment?

LH: Yes, I think that for me this is one of the most affirmative periods in history. I'm very pleased that those peoples in the world whom I feel closest to, the colonial peoples, the African peoples, the Asian peoples, are in an insurgent mood and are in the process of transforming the world, and I think for the better. I can't quite understand pessimism at this moment unless of course one is wedded to things that are dying out which should die out like colonialism, like racism, and so forth. Walter Lee Younger and his family are necessarily tied to this international movement whether they have consciousness of it or not. They belong to an affirmative movement in history. Anything that he does that is the least positive has just implications that embrace all of us. I feel that his moving into the new house, his decision, is in a way a reply to those who say that, you know, all guilt is equal, all questions lack clarity, that it's hard to know what you should fight for or against, that there are things to do, that the new house has many shapes, and that we must make some decisions in this country, as this man does, I think.

MW: Isn't there another side to this coin of racism though? Isn't there a danger?

LH: Of what?

MW: Of—

LH: Racism is always a danger, any kind.

MW: Yes, but isn't there a danger of—I don't know whether you've seen some of the meetings that go on nightly in Harlem.

LH: Oh yes, I have.

MW: Black Nationalists?

LH: Yes.

MW: Do you think that's a good idea?

LH: Oh, at this moment I do, yes.

MW: You do, really?

LH: Absolutely. I think it's absolutely necessary that people who are just coming into their own in the world must be as dramatic about it as they possibly can, must embrace all causes, must embrace all methods.

MW: You know, when the Rev. Martin Luther King was stabbed, it was said that one of the reasons that there was so much feeling about him up there was because he had decided to autograph his book in a Jewish store on 125th Street rather than in a Negro store. Were you aware of that?

LH: No, I don't even know who said that.

MW: And there have—I don't know whether you've gone up to any of these meetings up there . . .

LH: I've lived in Harlem and I go to Harlem often, and I've heard Nationalist meetings.

MW: Well, there's talk of Black supremacy, there's talk against any kind of integration, there's considerable anti-Semitic talk that takes place in these street corner meetings.

LH: The anti-Semitism I have never heard as part of these meetings. Antiwhite, which is quite different if the Jewish merchant in the community is thought of as an enemy—

MW: And exploiter?

LH: Right, he's thought of as a white person and this is the personification. . . . Anti-Semitism is not a part of this, and it is unfair to impose it on it. It isn't true, I don't think.

MW: Well, I can give you book chapter and verse on it and there's a good deal of talk about the Zionist Communist axis up there. As a matter of fact, one of the tenants of Black Nationalism as I, as we, have begun to find out about it, is it is very anti-Zionism, linking, trying to link Zionism to Communism, and a considerable amount of anti-Semitic talk that goes on nightly.

LH: Well, that I would actively disassociate myself from, actively. I find no excuse for anti-Semitism anywhere in the world, I would have been eager to say so publicly when our friends from the African countries couldn't find their way clear to invite Israel to a cocktail party and so on.

MW: But even Black racism you do understand?

LH: I don't, I'm not talking about Black racism, let's keep in mind what we are talking about. We are talking about oppressed peoples who are saying they must assert themselves in the world. Now, personally, I hope that I believe most of all in humanism. I'm not interested in color. I've fought against color prejudice all my life. I'm not interested in having white babies murdered any more than I can countenance the murder of Kikuyu babies in Kenya. I hate all of that kind of thing. But let's not equalize the oppressed with the oppressor in saying that when people stand up and say that we don't want any more of this that they are now talking about a new kind of racism. My position is that we have a great deal to be angry about, furious about, you know. It's 1959 and they are still lynching Negroes in America, and I feel, as our African friends do, that we need all ideologies which point toward the total liberation of the African peoples all over the world.

MW: Miss Hansberry, I surely thank you for coming and spending this very short half hour. I wish we could go on about this at some length and perhaps I can invite you back to do that some time. I'll be back with a footnote to the story of Lorraine Hansberry in just a moment.

■ ■ ■

MW: One of the things that Lorraine Hansberry would seem to be saying in her play is that Negroes are not primarily members of a minority race but human beings. Something that propagandists both for and against the Negro sometimes forget. We thank Miss Hansberry for adding her portrait to our gallery—one of the people other people are interested in.

Note

1. Editor's note: Self-prepared transcript. The original audio version of this interview is available in either the Lorraine Hansberry Papers located in the Moving Image & Recorded Sound Division of the Schomburg Center for Research in Black Culture at the New York Public Library, or the Mike Wallace Papers in the Special Collections Research Center, Syracuse University Libraries and Bentley Historical Library, University of Michigan.

Interview with Lorraine Hansberry

Studs Terkel / 1959

Broadcast on WFMT Radio, May 12, 1959. Printed by permission of Studs Terkel Radio Archive, courtesy Chicago History Museum and WFMT Radio Network.[1]

Studs Terkel: We're seated in the apartment of a Mrs. Hansberry. I believe this is the apartment of the mother or the sister of Lorraine Hansberry, whom we can rightfully describe as a distinguished young American playwright. This may sound like a strange thing to say. An artist has written one play and we call her a distinguished American playwright. But it isn't one man's opinion. The winner of the Drama Critics' Circle Award which in itself may be unprecedented. I'm not sure, we'll ask Miss Hansberry about this. Lorraine Hansberry, originally of Chicago.

Lorraine Hansberry: Very much so.

ST: Back home for a week or so visiting your family.

LH: Mmm-hmm. Until Sunday.

ST: If we could sort of make this a rambling kind of conversation and dig as much as we can out of you. Your thoughts, how you came to write it, and your feelings about the play, and theater generally. This afternoon you gave what everybody there felt was an inspiring—not a speech—an inspiring piece of conversation at Roosevelt University about drama, generally. And if we can touch on that, it'd go a long way fine. I su—Lorraine? May I?

LH: Sure.

ST: A question—

LH: I'm going to call you Studs.

ST: A question is often, I'm sure, is asked you many times. You may be tired of it. Someone comes up to you and says, "This is not really a Negro play, *A Raisin in the Sun.*" I'm sure you've been told this many—what's your reaction? They say, "This is a play about anybody." Now what do you say?[2]

LH: That's an excellent question because invariably this has been the point of reference. People are trying—I know what they're trying to say.

What they're trying to say, and mistakenly as a matter of fact, which I'll speak about, what they're trying to say is that this is not what they consider the traditional treatment of the Negro in the theater. They're trying to say that it isn't a propaganda play. That it isn't a protest play—

ST: No message play.

LH: And that it isn't something that hits you over the head, and the other remarks, which have become clichés themselves, as a matter of fact, in discussing this kind of material. So, what they're trying to say is something very good. They're trying to say that they believe that the characters in our play transcend category. However, it's an unfortunate way to try and do it because I believe that one of the most sound ideas in dramatic variety is that in order to create the universal you must pay very great attention to the specific. In other words, I've told people that not only is this a Negro family, specifically and definitely culturally, but it's not even a New York family or a southern Negro family. It is specifically South Side Chicago. That kind of care, that kind of attention to the detail of reference and so forth. In other words, I think people will, to the extent they accept them and believe them as who they're supposed to be, to that extent they can become everybody. So, I was—it's definitely a Negro play before it's anything else.

ST: The universality itself is italicized when you say something specific about a specific human being or a group of human beings as you did here.

LH: Universality, I think, emerges from truthful identity of what is.

ST: Something you said as you were breaking down this cliché, this well-meant, this well-meant—

LH: Yes.

ST: —point that these are well-rounded people they meant could be anybody. When you say, when people say that, forget that—you wrote this play. You wrote this play for a certain reason, too.

LH: Yes, yes.

ST: You wrote—Not a certain reason, now, a certain need to write this play. How did you come about? This is a rather—

LH: Before I say that, though, I just want to say the other part that I said I would refer to, which is that I don't know what everybody is talking about when they talk about drama in American theater that has been hitting them over the head on the Negro question. They keep alluding to some mysterious—a body of material which allegedly did this. I, for one, can't recall that we have had anything approaching a great number of protest plays or so-called social plays about Negroes. And, as a matter of fact, the last play on

Broadway that was a Negro play dealt with a boy coming into adolescence. In other words, it seems to me—

ST: *Take a Giant Step.*

LH: Yes. You know, where the Negro question, as such, was not the paramount issue at all. It seems to me there's a preoccupation and a sense of guilt for something that some elements are so afraid of what they feel that they're already anticipating something that hasn't been true.

ST: This is a very interesting comment [*unintelligible*] here.

LH: We need a few protest plays as a matter of fact. [*laughs*]

ST: But the last protest play, as such, with a capital P, I believe, was something called *Stevedore* which was years and years ago as I remember.

LH: The thirties?

ST: One of the very few, really. Now, *Take a Giant Step* . . . Now, I suppose, somebody might have said Louis Peterson's play . . . this could be . . . Or could they have said it about that as they did of your play?

LH: And also, the one play of which this description is true, as a matter of fact, was *Deep Are the Roots*, which happens to have been quite a good play. It wasn't a sloppy play. I would treat all dramatic material differently, myself, but that's irrelevant. In terms of ordinary Broadway fare, it was as good as any other play. What they're sensitive about is the material that's used in it, obviously.

ST: I'm thinking of Walter Lee Younger. You call him the focal character, the protagonist of the play, Walter Lee Younger. And for those, the great many listeners who were not fortunate to hear you this afternoon at Roosevelt, you spoke of Walter Lee Younger as an affirmative hero in contrast to many of the heroes of theater such as we see today of very excellent plays. Would you mind explaining that a bit?

LH: Well, as I went on at length about it this afternoon because, you know, I wanted to develop it in terms of what I think are some general patterns in contemporary drama but, specifically, in terms of the play itself, Walter is affirmative because he refuses to give up. There are moments when he doubts himself and even retreats and goes back into something that obviously, to the extent that the point of view of the artist, the author, is clear in this play, that I don't agree with, the things that he decides to do. But in the end—

ST: You mean investing the dough, you mean?

LH: Well, beyond that point, when he says not only was he cheated but the solution is to go out and cheat everybody else.

ST: Oh, yeah. That's right.

LH: Because this is the way life is. What he means, of course, is that this is the way the life around him is. But I suppose, thematically, what he represents is my own feeling that sooner or later we're going to have to make principled decisions in America about a lot of things. And any number of these decisions are going to seem contrary to things that we think we want. In other words, we've set up some very materialistic and overtly, uh . . .

ST: What we think solid values?

LH: Yes, overtly . . . limited concepts of how the world should go. Sooner or later I think we're going to have to decide on them. In other words, I think it's just as conceivable to create a character today who decides maybe that his whole life is wrong so that he ought to go do something else altogether. And really make a completely, a complete reversal of things that we think are very acceptable. This to me is a certain kind of affirmation. It isn't just rebellion because rebellion rarely knows what, you know, what it wants to do when it gets through rebelling.

ST: Even if this affirmation against what you—

LH: It's a little revolutionary.

ST: No. What may be considered accepted values, generally. Conventional values, let's say, within a framework.

LH: Yes, yes.

ST: Which is what Walter Lee does.

LH: Yes.

ST: As you say, nothing is solved, nothing completely solved in the play as they move to a new neighborhood—

LH: Right.

ST: Or a new home.

LH: You know, it would be just as well, though, to say that I chose Willy. I chose Willy Loman because I was making a point. But there was another affirmative character to emerge in the last eight years who, interestingly enough, also chose death. And who was affirmative rather than negative. And this was John Proctor in *The Crucible*.

ST: In *The Crucible*.

LH: In other words, the point becomes what did he choose death for? He chose death for life in this case, you know. This is the story that involves a man who stands up against the Salem witch hunts in the seventeenth century. This is choosing death for a reason that's going to substantiate life or to make it bigger—

ST: For life as a man rather than as a cipher.

LH: Exactly.

ST: John Proctor! I hadn't thought about the connect—this is remarkable, because Walter Lee Younger may have physical trouble as he leaves, you see. As John Proctor—

LH: He probably will! [*laughs*]

ST: —did, yeah. But Walter Lee Younger—

LH: If he's moving anywhere in Chicago! [*laughs*]

ST: —found himself as a man, as John Proctor . . . I hadn't thought about this. I think of, now, Mrs. Younger—that is, Mrs. Big Walter Younger, Walter Lee's mother. Here is a remarkably strong, per—a question I want to ask—you've probably been asked this many times—in many cultures the mother, the woman, is very strong, you know?

LH: Mmm-hmm.

ST: Now, Steinbeck used it with Mrs. Joad in *The Grapes of Wrath*.

LH: Yes, yes. Someone wrote a beautiful analogy—

ST: Now, in Negro families, through the years, the mother has always been a sort of pillar of strength, hasn't she?

LH: Yes, yes. Those of us who are to any degree students of Negro history think this has something to do with slave society, of course, where she was allowed, to a certain degree, of, not ascendancy, but of, at least control of her family, whereas the male was relegated to absolutely nothing at all. And this has probably been sustained by the sharecropper system in the South and on up into, even, urban Negro life in the North. At least that's the theory. I think it's a mistake to get it confused with Freudian concepts of matriarchal dominance and Philip Wylie's Momism and all that business. It's not the same thing. Not that there aren't negative things about it and not that tyranny sometimes doesn't emerge, you know, as a part of it. But, basically, it's a great thing. These women have become the backbone of our people in a very necessary way. This—

ST: Underground Railway leaders?

LH: Yes, yes. The Irish reflect this, I think. There's a relationship between Mother Younger in this play and Juno which is very strong and obvious. I think there's always a relationship, perhaps, I don't know that much about Irish history but there was probably a necessity why, among oppressed peoples, the mother will assume a certain kind of . . . role.

ST: In a way she's almost—that's not, that's the wrong word I'm using—as if there's almost a front. Not really a front, but the guy, you know, immediately the guy, of any people, under pressure is the prime target to begin with, maybe. I don't know. Possibly.

LH: This has an element of it. Obviously, people who are sophisticated enough to know it say that, obviously, the most oppressed group of any oppressed group will be its women, you know? Obviously. Since women, period, are oppressed in society and if you've got an oppressed group, they're twice oppressed. So, I should imagine that they react accordingly as oppression makes people more militant and so forth and so on then twice militant because they're twice oppressed so that there's an assumption of leadership historically.

ST: I want to come back to Mrs. Younger [*unintelligible*] but you mentioned Juno so, there's something you said in the current issue of *New Yorker*: your feelings about O'Casey.

LH: Yes.

ST: O'Casey, the playwright. You were talking about—

LH: Yes. I love Sean O'Casey.

ST: What is it about O'Casey? Of course, your play has a certain life to it now. What do you think about O'Casey?

LH: Well, O'Casey is divided, first of all. When I speak of the O'Casey that I love, I mean things like *Shadow of a Gunman* and *Juno* and—I've never read *The Plough and the Stars*. I want to. But this area—and *Red Roses for Me*. This, to me, is the playwright of the twentieth century accepting and using the most obvious instruments of Shakespeare. Which is the human personality and its totality. I've always thought this is profoundly significant for Negro writers: to use. Not to copy. There's no reason to copy. The material here is too rich to copy anybody. But as a model, as a point of departure. O'Casey never fools you about the Irish, you see. You've got the Irish drunkard, the Irish braggart, the Irish—

ST: Liar.

LH: Liar. Who is always talking about how he's going to fight the revolution when the English really show up, you know. He runs and gets under the bed and the young girl goes out to fight with the Tommies, you see, and so forth and so on. And the genuine heroism which must naturally emerge when you tell the truth about people. This to me is the height of artistic perception. And is the most rewarding kind of thing that can happen in drama because when you believe people so completely, you know, that they're so recognizable because everybody has their drunkards and their braggarts and their cowards, then you also believe them in their moments of heroic assertion.

ST: Heroism, too.

LH: You know. You don't doubt them. You don't feel like, well, this is soap opera.

■ ■ ■

ST: Then Walter Lee: What you said can be directly applied to your own work, really, because you showed Walter Lee's frailties throughout. And when he did emerge in that heroic moment we believed.

LH: That was the hope. That was the intent. Also, the other thing about O'Casey is that, in other words, what I believe in, for instance, if we're really going to talk technical dramaturgy, what I do not believe in is naturalism. I think naturalism should die away a quiet death. I do believe in realism.

ST: By naturalism you mean the tape-recorded kind of—

LH: Precisely. That this is not art.

ST: If we were to say Chayefsky, in a way.

LH: Not because—the only reason I say that is because I'm talking about it negatively at the moment, and there are things about Chayefsky which I think have been very important for American television drama. But naturalism is its own limitation, you know. In other words, if you just repeat what is, you can go and show a murder and say, "This is the whole of life," because, after all, there it is: you've made a photographic reproduction of it. Go deny it. It's true, it's real. Realism demands the imposition of a point of view. And the point of view of O'Casey is always the wonder, of the nobility of people. And he literally imposes it on us. It's the additional dimension always of the humanity of people. And he literally imposes it on us [sic]. And he uses something which I can't imitate because I'm not equipped to. He uses poetic dialogue which moves it out of the realm of what I'm able to write into this field of great art. I wish I could. I think, as a matter of fact, there are parallels between Negro speech, even urban Negro speech in America, and urban Irish speech which should make it very easy, but it doesn't happen. [*laughs*]

ST: There is a great deal of poetry, I felt. I'm not buttering you, now.

LH: Well I'm glad to hear it. [*laughs*]

ST: There is a great deal of poetry in *Raisin in the Sun* because it, to me, again, not naturalism, as you say, but—and not realism, as such—but larger than life. Isn't that what you meant? Theater should be larger than life?

LH: Always. Always. There used to be a ballet in this play. [*laughs*]

ST: There was a ballet?

LH: There used to be a ballet—I had a letter from Max Lerner. I don't know if that means anything to Chicago listeners.

ST: Yes, it does. I think there are many Max Lerner readers here.

LH: And he said to me that—oh, excuse me. Rather, he wrote a column on the play, you know. In the column—

ST: In the *New York Post*.

LH: In the *New York Post.* And he said—it was a very good column—and he said that he liked the play very much, however, it was a little too literal for his taste and those places where Miss Hansberry almost let go her imagination she suddenly remembered that she was a nice, proper girl and then got back to this very literal play, you see. He was very much enamored of the African scene for instance, you know. Walter gets up, which, and so forth, is—

ST: Walter as the warrior, that one where he—

LH: Yes. And where he speaks in open poetic declarations about the coming time when we're going to march and so forth and so on, which is a half of the man, which only realism could impose on the scene. Not naturalism, because in naturalism it would never happen. Nobody would believe it. And I wrote him a note and I said, that was a very interesting remark because I was the one who was tamed, you know. I think that imagination has no bounds in realism, that you can do anything which is permissible in terms of the truth of the characters and that's all, that's all that you have to care about. And I told him that there had once been a ballet, a modern ballet in this play.

ST: [*unintelligible*] as you, when you originally wrote this?

LH: That's right. When the motifs of the characters were to have been done in modern dance. It didn't work. [*laughs*]

ST: It may not have worked [*unintelligible*] but the fact is, that you had a ballet in mind indicates that there was a poetic feeling, you see?

LH: Right. It indicates some of the directions that I feel I would go.

ST: There's something you said a moment ago, and I know Bill Leonard of the *Trib* interviewed you briefly this afternoon. The play, some will ask you, "Is this autobiographical?"

LH: Yes. They keep asking.

ST: Yet, your background is not—your background, culturally, may be the place—to some extent, background—but it is not specifically.

LH: No, it isn't. I've tried to explain this to people. I come from an extremely comfortable background, materially speaking and, yet, I've also tried to explain we live in a ghetto, you know? Which automatically means intimacy with all classes and all kinds of experiences. It's not any more difficult for me to know the people that I wrote about than it is for me to know members of my family because there is that kind of intimacy. This is one of the things that the American experience has meant to Negroes: we are one people. I also tried to tell the people at the *New Yorker*, you know, in that interview that you read, that I had a reason for choosing this particular class. I guess at this moment the Negro middle class may be from 5 to 6 to 7 percent of our people. The, you know, comfortable middle class. And I believe that they are atypical of the more representative experience of Negroes in this country. Therefore, I have to believe that whatever we ultimately achieve, however we ultimately transform our lives, will come from the kind of people that I chose to portray. That, therefore, they are more pertinent, more relevant, more significant, and most important, most decisive in our political history and our political future.

ST: This is, here again is the mark of a playwright, if I may interject this—outside your own. Within your experience and yet outside it in the material sense.

LH: Yes.

ST: Of course, you sensed here was the more dramatic—

LH: Yes.

ST: —figure. The little girl, if I may, I want to bring up a personal thing: the very charming and alive little sister. Is this slightly autobiographical? [*unintelligible*]

LH: Oh, she's very autobiographical, my sister. My brother would tell you that. This, as a matter of fact, it's an expression of conceit, really, because the truth of the matter is that I enjoyed making fun of this girl, who is myself eight years ago, you know. I enjoy making fun of her because I have that kind of confidence about what she represents. I'm not worried about her, you know. She's precocious, she's over-outspoken, she's everything which tends to be comic, and, you know, people sigh with her and they have one at home like that, and they enjoy her for this reason.

ST: She's very much alive.

LH: Yes. But I also feel that she doesn't have a word in the play that I don't agree with still today. I would say it differently today.

ST: That's it—she doesn't have a word in the play you don't—you would say it differently, in a more mature way today?

LH: I hope it's more mature.

ST: But, basically, the kid is right.

LH: Oh, I think so, yes. She's suspect of many things that Walter Lee accepts, you see. He has the energy and he has the will at the moment to make the decisive decisions. That's why I say that he's a pivotal character. As a matter of fact, if I could just digress, people have—I've been interested in some of the criticisms of the play. We had one letter in the *New York Times* from—you could tell by the tone and quality of the letter—from a very sophisticated young man sitting somewhere who said that he regarded it as soap opera, you know, which amused me. Because if anyone wanted to discuss this play in terms of soap opera, they'd have a great deal of trouble because soap opera implies melodrama, and melodrama has a classical definition. If you can prove that there are no motivated crises in this play, I would be astonished. So, I don't think it qualifies as melodrama. I think it's a legitimate drama. Or a happy ending. If he thinks that's a happy ending, I invite him to come . . . [*laughs*]

ST: [*laughs*] Well, he's welcome . . . to go to Trumbull Park.

LH: . . . go live in one of those communities where these people are going. However, so that character of criticism I am inclined to be contentious of because it's based on a snobbery that doesn't understand things, that doesn't understand the profundity of things that are deliberately simple.

ST: Lorraine, you hit a very tender point with me—I won't go into this—on this very, on the letter written by that young man. I'm very well acquainted with it—

LH: What I do want to say, though, is that I'm not hostile to legitimate criticism. And one other thing that's been very interesting to me is that no one has picked out something that I think is a very genuine criticism of the play. That is that it lacks a central character in true classical sense. There is no central character in this play.

ST: Do you mean—

LH: There is a pivotal character.

ST: In Walter Lee.

LH: Yes.

ST: But he isn't, because some will say, some will tell you Mrs. Younger is the pivotal character, isn't that it?

LH: That's right.

ST: [unintelligible]

LH: People come out and they think it's the mother, or they think it's the son, and some people are so enamored of the daughter they're not sure that she isn't really more relevant in some way or somehow. Well this is, to me, a weakness of the play.

ST: Is this really a weakness? I mean, must it be about a single—you see, this is a play in a sense of—maybe you're right—a play about a—I think of *Awake and Sing!* for the moment, you see. Who was the central character in what was a very excellent play of a Jewish lower-middle-class family? There was no central—any more than in yours, really, was there?

LH: Well, obviously when you start breaking rules you may be doing it for a good reason, and you may find something else. And since people are able to hold on to the play and become involved in a way that the central character is supposed to guarantee then maybe you don't really need it.

ST: Yeah. I wonder if—

LH: But, for me, all I'm saying is that, in my view of drama, the great plays have always had a central character with whom we rise or fall no matter what. The Greeks through Shakespeare—

ST: [*unintelligible*] or Hamlet or—

LH: —through Ibsen. And so. The aura—

ST: The African suitor, you know, I've come to something now, has always intrigued me very much, if may I ask?—

LH: It's my favorite character.

ST: Sidney Poitier [sic]. He's a remarkable figure. Who is he? What is his meaning in this particular play in contrast to the others?

LH: He represents two things. He represents, first of all, the true intellectual. This is a young man who is so absolutely confident in his understanding and his perception about the world that he has no need for any of the facade of pseudo-intellectuality, for any of the pretenses and the nonsense which is why he can laugh at her. She's just getting to a point of understanding where he's been already, you know. He can already kid about all the features of intense nationalism because he's been there, and he understands it beyond that point. He's already concerned about the human race on a new level. He's a true, genuine intellectual. He's a man who's involved in concepts so that he doesn't have time or interest, except for amusement, in useless passion and useless promenading of ideas. That's partially what he represents, that's one part of it. The other thing that he represents is much more overt. I was aware that on the Broadway stage they had never seen an African who didn't have his shoes hanging around his neck, you know, and a bone through his nose or his ears or something.

ST: The stereotype.

LH: And I thought that, even just theatrically speaking, this would most certainly be refreshing, you know. And, again, it required no departure from truth because the only Africans that I have known, of course, have been African students in the United States—who this boy is a composite of many of them, as a matter of fact, no one guy. And what they have represented to me in life is what this fellow represents in the play. And that is the emergence of an articulate and deeply conscious colonial intelligentsia in the world. I'm very much concerned and caught up in the movements of the African peoples toward colonial liberation, liberation out of colonialism, and he represents that to me. He also signifies a hangover of something that began in the thirties when Negro intellectuals first discovered the African past and became very aware of it.

ST: Garveyism and everything else at the time, maybe?

LH: Yes. That was part of it in a different sense—

ST: Right, yeah, mmm.

LH: —but I meant particularly in poetry and the creative arts.

ST: Well, the culture that was there.

LH: Yes. Hughes did this and Africa this and Africa that. I still feel this way, I want to reclaim it.

ST: The great culture of—

LH: Not physically, I don't mean I want to move to—

ST: But I think this is—I'm glad you mentioned this—so many anthropologists agree. I mean, the great culture that is there, that has been, and that was stolen, too.

LH: Oh, sure, sure. And which may very well make very decisive contributions to the development of the world in the next few years.

ST: There's a point—

LH: I suspect it's going to.

ST: I'm sure it will. There's a point—

LH: Asagai is an angry young man who can be very quiet in his anger.

ST: This is the young student?

LH: The African student.

ST: You say he is an angry young man?

LH: Yes. Who can be quiet in his anger.

ST: There's a point I want to raise. Now, you may get a kick out of this and disagree. When Sidney Poitier and Leon Bibb, his friend, the singer, you know, were interviewed . . .

LH: Mmm-hmm, mmm-hmm.

ST: They spoke of the young student. They say he's an idealist. He would have a rough time—now, see whether you agree with this, this is a very interesting point—they say Nkrumah and Kenyatta are very practical men— is the point they were making—and he, your friend, would have a rough time, uh, in the power battle, as such. He might be—

LH: With—

ST: —sort of a hamburger squeezed between two forces. This was the inference—I hope I haven't misinterpreted them. I bring this up—

LH: They were saying that Asagai—

ST: Yeah.

LH: The African student in the play, as opposed to men like Kenyatta and Nkrumah—

ST: That's right.

LH: Is an idealist?

ST: Yeah, that's right.

LH: Oh that's—

ST: And that they admire—

LH: That's interesting.

ST: They admire the two men they were talking about. They were saying that he may be just taken—he might be victimized by, in a rough and tumble battle, being the idealist he is, you see?

LH: Except that this man has an ideological preparation for that. In fact, in one sense, he gives the statement of the play, you know? I don't know how many people get it, but he does. He says—she says to him, "You're always talking about independence and freedom in Africa but what about the time when that happens and then you have crooks and petty thieves who come into power and they'll do the same things only now they'll be Black," you know. "So, what's the difference?" And he says to her that this is virtually irrelevant in terms of history, that when that time comes there will be Nigerians to step out of the shadows and kill the tyrants, just as now they must do away with the British. And that history always solves its own questions, but you get to first things first. In other words, this man has no illusions at all.

ST: This is a wonderful answer. This, this—

LH: He just believes in the order that things must take. He knows that first, before you can start talking about what's wrong with independence, get it. And I'm with him.

ST: That's wonder—will you tell that to them when you get back there?

■ ■ ■

ST: Again, if I may come back now and be personal in my reactions to the play when it opened here in Chicago. I was so completely taken with the direction of Lloyd Richards, incidentally, too.

LH: Yes. It's brilliant, I thought.

ST: Of course, the cast but the play's the thing. We'll come back to that again, and you. And the next question: We've sort of talked of *Raisin* now and you have, I imagine, a number of projects in mind. If—I don't want to dig here unless you feel free, yourself. What projects you're thinking of tackling?

LH: Well, of all things in the world I have become involved in doing an opera libretto. Which I do hesitate to talk about because I'm—

ST: All right. This is certainly exciting.

LH: —just getting into it and terrified of it. I don't know a thing in the world about writing an opera but I'm going to do one with a young Negro composer in New York who I think is enormously talented and imaginative in his music.

ST: We'll let that rest for a moment, and we'll see it. That's it—we'll see it. But since you mentioned opera there was a—perhaps you were misquoted, or I want to get—the *New York Times* quoted you. You spoke of a certain irritation in seeing plays, so called, plays about the Negro, as such, written by people wholly removed—

LH: Yes, yes.

ST: From the situation. What was the crack? It was rather wonderful—about *Carmen Jones*—something you said about it that was very funny.

LH: Well, as you know, I probably alluded to the fact that I've been struck that the whole concept of the exotic, you know, that in Europe they think that, well, the gypsy is just the most exotic thing that ever walked across the earth because he's isolated from the mainstream of European life. So that, obviously, the natural parallel in American life is the Negro [*laughs*]. You know, very exotic. So, whenever they get ready to do something like a Bizet opera which involves the gypsies of Spain, it's translated, they think, very neatly into a Negro piece. And I just think this is sort of a bore by now. That this is—it's very fine music, but, you know.

ST: The clichés are there.

LH: I'm bored for the clichés.

ST: It's pretty worrisome by now.

LH: I don't think very many people realize how boring, aside from being nauseating, that stereotyped notions are also very dull. You know, I think this is said far too—not often enough that—it isn't only a matter that *Porgy and Bess*—I'm talking about the book now because once again this is good music, this is beautiful music. I mean this is great American music in which the roots of our native opera are to be found. Someday. But the book—the Dubose Haywood book—not only is that offensive, you know, it isn't only that it insults me because it's a degrading concept and a degrading way of looking at people, but it's bad art because it doesn't tell the truth, and fiction demands the truth. You have to give a many-sided character. In other words, there is no excuse for stereotype. Now I'm not talking socially or politically. I'm talking as an artist now.

ST: Aesthetically now [*unintelligible*].

LH: Exactly. That if someone feels that this is a lie, you know, because it's just one half of me then the artist should shudder for reasons other than the NAACP. The responsible artist.

ST: Something you just said: art must tell the truth.

LH: I think so. It's almost the only place where you can tell it.

ST: What about writing today? Whether it be drama—I'm thinking of, more specifically, I'm—young Negro writers today, I mean, any hit you? There's John Killens's *Youngblood*, perhaps? Or—?

LH: Well, there isn't a great deal happening. I've just started to read Frank London Brown's book and—

ST: *Trumbull Park.*

LH: I'm not equipped to talk about it because I'm just starting to get into it. There's a young guy in New York who's been one of the exiles who's come home, we're starting a new movement against the thirties. Some of the American kids are coming back now from Paris and Rome. Jimmy Baldwin, you know.

ST: Well, he'd gone away.

LH: Who had got—he left. He went. Enough.

ST: Did Baldwin do that, too? Yeah.

LH: Baldwin is who I'm talking about.

ST: Oh, James Baldwin?

LH: James Baldwin. Who is back and who I think—I don't read novels that much, I'm ashamed to say, for somebody who wants to write one—but I think, from what I read of his essays, and some of his fiction, that this is undoubtedly one of the most talented American writers walking around. And if he can wed his particular gifts, I think, which are just way beyond most of us trying to write—at many levels—to material of substance, then we have the potential of a great American writer. He's one that I think of.

ST: He came back. This is interesting. I'm thinking, of course, of someone very definite: Richard Wright, of course.

LH: Yes. Who didn't come back now?

ST: And what a talent.

LH: And who has not been [*unintelligible*] impressive in his output, in my opinion.

ST: Would you feel, since you said this—this last thing you just said—do you feel—this may sound like a cliché, what I'm saying—away, away from roots—I hate to use the word—and yet, Richard Wright, who was so close and strong.

LH: No.

ST: Go ahead.

LH: You know.

ST: Why? Go ahead.

LH: Because—and I said this on television in New York recently—this thing of being away from one's roots. I was making a different point, what I was saying is somebody, people are always talking about how, "Don't get lost in a cause," you know, because this is what destroys art. And I've been obliged to remind people who have—for two hundred years the only writers in English literature we've had to boast about have been the Irish, who come from an oppressed culture, you know? Shaw, O'Casey.

ST: Joyce.

LH: From Jonathan Swift to James Joyce and so forth and so on. You name them in the last two hundred years, and they've been Irishmen. Which I don't think is an accident even though they aren't protest writers in the sense that we think of in the United States. But, also, most of them have been writing outside of Ireland. In other words, O'Casey is writing his Dublin plays, you know, in Devonshire in England and they still ring and have good Irish flavor and the Irish don't seem to reject them in terms of being false so I guess it's good. No, I think there must be some other reason why Wright deteriorated.

ST: Well, you've answered my question right there. That's beautiful. That's right. What—

LH: I don't know what the reason is because I think he had within him the possibilities to have been the greatest American writer. Because what he had, I think, would have made William Faulkner seem just peculiar. Which, of course, is what he seems, anyhow, in my opinion.

ST: Go ahead. You just said—what do you mean by that?

LH: [*sighs*] Well, I haven't even read that much Faulkner, but I'm not impressed with obscurity. I think it's easier. For all I know the man could be a genius. For all I know he might be the reverse. I just can't tell from obscurity. Sooner or later I have to be able to get some sense of organization and treatment of material that lets me know that there is skill here, or genius, you know. And I can't tell this from a Faulkner.

ST: Clarity?

LH: Or for that matter, for much of James Joyce. But at least his point of departure was one I could understand. And Wright, of course, belonged to another tradition of American writing. I don't even think it was a conscious belonging but he did. That I think came to flower in things like *Grapes* *of Wrath* and the novel of that nature. If my husband were here, he'd say Theodore Dreiser, actively.

ST: Dreiser. Mmm-hmm.

LH: But I'd like to see that kind of panoramic power reemerge in the American novel. I think, maybe, it may come from a Negro novelist.

ST: Someone like Baldwin who may have been away and has returned?

LH: I don't know.

ST: You don't know?

LH: I don't know if Baldwin's eyes are that wide. The gifts are there, you know.

ST: "If his eyes are that wide." That's a beautiful phrase. I like that. I love that phrase. Well, it's obvious—

LH: He feels. I'm worried about what he sees, you know? That gets to be the problem.

ST: Well, I think it's obvious that it's no accident that *Raisin in the Sun* came to be written by Lorraine Hansberry after we've been listening to her now. And I know this is late at night here at home and I wish, I'd suggest people read the current issue of the *New Yorker* and you can find there, too, the graciousness in Miss Hansberry and the tremendous demands—what about success? This little god of success—what does it do to you? It obviously deprives you of privacy to some ex—well, right now it does.

LH: Yeah. It does.

ST: This one moment here.

LH: It does except it's wonderful. It's wonderful and I'm enjoying it. I think it's important. I think there comes a time when, you know, you pull the telephone out and you go off and you end it. But for the time being I am enjoying every bit of it. I've tried to go to everything I've been invited to. I shouldn't even say this on the air, but so far, I've tried to answer every piece of correspondence I get. Which, as I said in the piece, gets to be about twenty, thirty pieces a day at this point. But this, I don't have the right to be very personal about the reception to this play because I think the reception to this play transcends what I did or what Sidney Poitier or Lloyd Richards or even Philip Rose or any of us connected with it. I think what it reflects at this moment is, that at this particular moment in our country, as backward and as depressed as I, for instance, am about so much of it, there's a new mood. I think we went through eight to ten years of misery under McCarthy and all that nonsense and to the great credit of the American people they got rid of it. And they're feeling like, make new sounds. And I'm glad I was here to make one, you know?

ST: Beautiful. "Make new sounds." That's—the best of jazzmen say that, too. But in this case, certainly, one of the most sensitive of writers says it.

LH: It's a close relationship.

ST: I think it is.

LH: I've often said that the glory of Langston Hughes was that he took the quality of the blues and put it into our poetry. And I think when the Negro dramatist can begin to approach a little of that quality you might almost get close to what O'Casey does in putting the Irish folk song into play. I'd like to.

ST: Well, I think Lorraine Hansberry is on that road. Certainly. Thank you very much. And is there anything you, as sort of a postscript—I always allow this opening. Anything else you care to say? Anything? It doesn't matter. That you haven't said thus far?

LH: You mean quickly or a paragraph?

ST: No, no. As much time as you want.

LH: I can always say something.

ST: We're not bound to the clock.

LH: I'd say this: that I spoke of how I think there's a new affirmative political mood and social mood in our country having to do with the fact that people are finally even getting aware that Negroes are tired and it's time to do something about that question. But beyond that, in terms of the total picture, I'd also like to see a parallel to it in terms of the culture of our country. I can see no reason in the world why the American theater should be lined up on, about, six blocks on Broadway in New York City. I'd like to be, see a little agitation to get a national theater and other art programs in this country so that the kids all over the United States can go see Shakespeare without thinking it's a bore, you know. Or Lorraine Hansberry or Eugene O'Neill. That's all.

ST: Well, a double thank you for that, certainly. Lorraine Hansberry. And you people who have missed the play here during its pre–New York run, go to New York. Well, if you can get tickets, fine. But some day it will return to Chicago. Obviously, it will when the national company comes and the original company. Lorraine Hansberry, playwright, human being. Thank you very much.

Notes

1. Editor's note: The original audio is available in the Lorraine Hansberry Papers in the Moving Image & Recorded Sound Division of the Schomburg

Center for Research in Black Culture, New York Public Library, and at the
Studs Terkel Radio Archive at https://studsterkel.wfmt.com/programs/
lorraine-hansberry-discusses-her-play-raisin-sun.

2. Editor's note: Hansberry's oft-quoted response to this question—"Well, I hadn't
noticed the contradiction because I'd always been under the impression that Negroes
are people," which appears in *To Be Young, Gifted and Black: Lorraine Hansberry in Her
Own Words*—does not appear in the original recording of this interview and was likely
added by Nemiroff, perhaps based on private conversations with Hansberry.

An Author's Reflection: Willy Loman, Walter Lee, and He Who Must Live

Lorraine Hansberry / 1959

From *Village Voice*, August 12, 1959, pp. 7–8. Reprinted by permission of the Lorraine Hansberry Literary Trust.

A man can't go out the way he came in . . . Ben, that funeral will be massive!
—Willy Loman, 1946

We have all thought about your offer, and we have decided to move into our house.
—Walter Lee Younger, 1958

Some of the acute partisanship revolving around *A Raisin in the Sun* is amusing. Those who announce that they find the piece less than fine are regarded in some quarters with dramatic hostility, as though such admission automatically implies the meanest of racist reservations. On the other hand, the ultra-sophisticates have hardly acquitted themselves less ludicrously, gazing coolly down their noses at those who are moved by the play, and going on at length about "melodrama" and/or "soap opera" as if these are not completely definable terms which cannot simply be tacked onto any and all plays we do not like.

Personally, I find no pain whatever—at least of the traditional ego type—in saying that *Raisin* is a play which contains dramaturgical incompletions. Fine plays tend to utilize one big fat character who runs right through the middle of the structure, by action or implication, with whom we rise or fall. A central character as such is certainly lacking from *Raisin*. I should be delighted to pretend that it was *inventiveness*, as some suggest for me, but it is, also, craft inadequacy and creative indecision. The result is that neither Walter Lee nor Mama Younger loom large enough to monumentally command the play. I consider it an enormous dramatic fault if no one else does.

(Nor am I less critical of the production which, by and large, performance and direction alike, is splendid. Yet I should have preferred that the second-act curtain, for instance, had been performed with quiet assertion rather than the apparently popular declamatory opulence which prevails.)

All in all, however, I believe that, for the most part, the play has been magnificently understood. In some cases, it was not only thematically absorbed but attention was actually paid to the tender treacherousness of its craft-imposed "simplicity." Some, it is true, quite missed that part of the overt intent and went on to harangue the bones of the play with rather useless observations of the terribly clear fact that they are old bones indeed. More meaningful discussions tended to delve into the flesh which hangs from those bones and its implications in mid-century American drama and life.

In that connection it is interesting to note that while the names of Chekhov, O'Casey, and the early Odets were introduced for comparative purposes in some of the reviews, almost no one—with the exception of Gerald Weales in *Commentary*—discovered a simple line of descent between Walter Lee Younger and the last great hero in American drama to also accept the values of his culture, Willy Loman. I am sure that the already mentioned primary fault of the play must account in part for this. The family so overwhelms the play that Walter Lee necessarily fails as the true symbol he should be, even though *his* ambitions, *his* frustrations, and *his* decisions are those which decisively drive the play on. But however recognizable he proves to be, he fails to dominate our imagination and finally emerges as a reasonably interesting study, but not, like Arthur Miller's great character—and like Hamlet, of course—a summation of an immense (though not crucial) portion of his culture.

Prior Attitudes

Then too, in fairness to the author and to Sidney Poitier's basically brilliant portrayal of Walter Lee, we must not completely omit reference to some of the prior attitudes which were brought into the theater from the world outside. For in the minds of many, Walter remains, despite the play, despite performance, what American radical traditions wish him to be: an exotic. Some writers have been astonishingly incapable of discussing his purely *class* aspirations and have persistently confounded them with what they consider to be an exotic being's longing to "wheel and deal" in what they further consider to be (and what Walter never can) "the white man's world." Very few people today must consider the ownership of a liquor store as an expression of extraordinary affluence, and yet, as joined to a dream of Walter Younger, it takes on, for some, aspects of the fantastic. We have grown accustomed to the dynamics of "Negro" personality as expressed by white authors. Thus, de Emperor, de Lawd, and, of course, Porgy, still haunt our frame of reference when a new character emerges. We have become romantically jealous of the great image of a prototype whom we believe is summarized by the wishfulness of a self-assumed opposite. Presumably there is a quality in human beings that makes us *wish* that we *were* capable of primitive contentments [sic]; the *universality* of ambition and its anguish can escape us only if we construct elaborate legends about the rudimentary simplicity of *other* men.

America, for this reason, long ago fell in love with the image of the simple, lovable, and glandular "Negro." We all know that Catfish Row[1] was never intended to slander anyone; it was intended as a mental haven for readers and audiences who could bask in the unleashed passions of those "lucky ones" for whom abandonment was apparently permissible. In an almost paradoxical fashion, it disturbs the soul of man to truly understand what he invariably senses: that *nobody* really finds oppression and/or poverty tolerable. If we ever destroy the image of the Black people who supposedly do find those things tolerable in America, then that much-touted "guilt" which allegedly haunts most middle-class white Americans with regard to the Negro question would really become unendurable. It would also mean the death of a dubious literary tradition, but it would undoubtedly and more significantly help toward the more rapid transformation of the status of a people who have never found their imposed misery very charming.

My colleagues and I were reduced to mirth and tears by that gentleman writing his review of our play in a Connecticut paper who remarked of his pleasure at seeing how "our dusky brethren" could "come up with a song and hum their troubles away." It did not disturb the writer in the least that there is no such implication in the entire three acts. He did not need it in the play; he had it in his head.

For all these reasons then, I imagine that the ordinary impulse to compare Willy Loman and Walter Younger was remote. Walter Lee Younger jumped out at us from a play about a largely unknown world. We knew who Willy Loman was instantaneously; we recognized his milieu. We also knew at once that he represented that curious paradox in what the *English* character in that *English* play could call, though dismally, "The American Age." Willy Loman was a product of a nation of great military strength, indescribable material wealth, and incredible mastery of the physical realm, which nonetheless was unable, in 1946, to produce a *typical* hero who was capable of an affirmative view of life.

I believe it is a testament to Miller's brilliance that it is hardly a mis-statement of the case, as some preferred to believe. Something has indeed gone wrong with at least part of the American dream, and Willy Loman is the victim of the detour. Willy had to be overwhelmed on the stage as, in fact, his prototypes are in everyday life. Coming out of his section of our great sprawling middle class, preoccupied with its own restlessness and dis-playing its obsession for the possession of trivia, Willy was indeed trapped. His predicament in a New World where there just aren't any more forests to clear or virgin railroads to lay or native American empires to first steal and build upon, left him with nothing but some leftover values which had forgotten how to prize industriousness over cunning, usefulness over mere acquisition, and, above all, humanism over "success." The potency of the great tale of a salesman's death was in our familiar recognition of his entrap-ment which, suicide or no, is *deathly*.

New Typicality

What then of this new figure who appears in American drama in 1958; from what source is he drawn so that, upon inspection, and despite class differ-ences, so much of his encirclement must still remind us of that of Willy Loman? Why, finally, is it possible that when his third-act will is brought to bear, *his* typicality is capable of a choice which affirms life? After all, Walter Younger is an American more than he is anything else. His ordeal, give or take his personal expression of it, is not extraordinary but intensely famil-iar like Willy's. The two of them have virtually no values which have not come out of their culture, and to a significant point, no view of the possible solutions to their problems which do not also come out of the self-same culture. Walter can find no peace with that part of society which seems to permit him and no entry into that which has willfully excluded him. He shares with Willy Loman the acute awareness that *something* is obstructing some abstract progress that he feels he *should* be making; that *something* is in the way of his ascendancy. It does not occur to either of them to question the nature of this desired "ascendancy." Walter accepts, he believes in the "world" as it has been presented to him. When we first meet him, he does not wish to alter it; merely to change his position in it. His mentors and his associates all take the view that the institutions which frustrate him are somehow impeccable, or, at best, "unfortunate." "Things being as they are," he must look to *himself* as the only source of any rewards he may expect. Within himself, he is encouraged to believe, are the only seeds of defeat or victory within the universe. And Walter believes this and when opportunity, haphazard and rooted in death, prevails, he acts.

Huge Obstacles

But the obstacles which are introduced are gigantic; the weight of the loss of the money is, in fact, the weight of death. In Walter Lee Younger's life, somebody has to die for ten thousand bucks to pile up—if then. Elsewhere in the world, in the face of catastrophe, he might be tempted to don the saffron robes of acceptance and sit on a mountain top all day contemplating the divine justice of his misery. Or, history being what it is turning out to be, he might wander down to his first Communist Party meeting. But here in the dynamic and confusing postwar years on the South Side of Chicago, his choices of action are equal to those gestures only in symbolic terms. The American ghetto hero may give up and contemplate his misery in rose-colored bars to the melodies of hypnotic saxophones, but revolution seems alien to him in his circumstances (America), and it is easier to dream of personal wealth than of a communal state wherein universal dignity is supposed to be a corollary. Yet his position in time and space does allow for one other alternative: he may take his place on any one of a number of frontiers of challenge. Challenges (such as helping to break down restricted neighborhoods) which are admittedly limited because they most certainly do not threaten the basic social order.

Not So Small

But why is even this final choice possible, considering the ever-present (and ever so popular) vogue of despair? Well, that is where Walter departs from Willy Loman; there is a second pulse in his still dual culture. His people have had "somewhere" they have been trying to get for so long that more sophisticated confusions do not yet bind them. *Thus, the weight and power of their current social temperament intrudes and affects him, and it is, at the moment, at least, gloriously and rigidly affirmative.* In the course of their brutally difficult ascent, they have dismissed the ostrich and still sing, *"Went to the rock, to hide my fare, but the rock cried out: 'No hidin' place down here!'"* Walter is, despite his lack of consciousness of it, inextricably as much wedded to his special mass as Willy was to his, and the moods of each are able to decisively determine the dramatic typicality. Furthermore, the very nature of the situation of American Negroes can force their representative hero to recognize that for his true ascendancy he must ultimately be at cross-purposes with at least certain of his culture's values. It is to the pathos of Willy Loman that his section of American life seems to have momentarily lost that urgency; that he cannot, like Walter, draw on the strength of an incredible people who, historically, have simply refused to give up.

In other words, the symbolism of moving into the new house is quite as small as it seems and quite as significant. For if there are no waving flags and marching songs at the barricades as Walter marches out with his little battalion, it is not because the battle lacks nobility. On the contrary, he has picked up in his way, still imperfect and wobbly in his small view of human destiny, what I believe Arthur Miller once called "the golden thread of history." He becomes, in spite of those who are too intrigued with despair and hatred of man to see it, King Oedipus refusing to tear out his eyes but attacking the Oracle instead. He is that last Jewish patriot manning his rifle in the burning ghetto at Warsaw; he is that young girl who swam into sharks to save a friend a few weeks ago; he is Anne Frank, still believing in people; he is the nine small heroes of Little Rock; he is Michelangelo creating David and Beethoven bursting forth with the Ninth Symphony. He is all those things because he has finally reached out in his tiny moment and caught that sweet essence which is human dignity, and it shines like the old star-touched dream that it is in his eyes. We see, in the moment, I think, what becomes, and not for Negroes alone, but for Willy and all of us, entirely an American responsibility.

Out in the darkness where we watch, most of us are not afraid to cry.

Note

1. Editor's note: Catfish Row is the fictional setting of *Porgy and Bess*, based on Cabbage Row in Charleston, South Carolina.

Five Writers and Their African Ancestors, Part II: Lorraine Hansberry

Harold R. Isaacs / 1960

From *Phylon* 21, no. 4 (1960): 329–36. Reprinted by permission of *Phylon*.

James Baldwin was six years old when the Depression set in, but by the time Lorraine Hansberry was six, the Depression was nearly over. This was a divide great enough in itself to mark off two quite different generations. But the difference between the two is marked by more than time, for Lorraine Hansberry came of a comfortably situated family, and though she knew what life was like for most people on Chicago's South Side, in the department of economic well-being, her pangs were all vicarious. Miss Hansberry, born in 1930, is old enough to have footholds of memory back in the world of pre-1945. She remembers newsreels about Italy's invasion of Ethiopia and the strong feelings in her home over that event. She was nine when Europe went to war in Poland and eleven when Pearl Harbor was bombed, and she remembers her father's ambivalent emotions over the conflict between the nonwhite Japanese and the white Americans. Her adult years did not begin until after that war ended. When she came from two years in college in Wisconsin to make her way in New York, it was 1950. All of this makes Lorraine Hansberry old enough to feel some share in the experience of her elders, but leaves her young enough to accept the present climate of great change as her natural environment. She is also so new as a writer that her hit play of 1959, *A Raisin in the Sun*, was the first and only work of hers that anybody knew. It is precisely because of her youth and her newness, and the way in which the subject of Africa appears in her play, that Lorraine Hansberry turns up here at the end of our progression of Negro writers and our scrutiny of the ways in which they have dealt with the matter of their African ancestors.

Lorraine Hansberry took the title of her play from a line by Langston Hughes: "What happens to a dream deferred? / Does it dry up / Like a raisin in the sun?" Her success was the winning of a dream that first came upon her in her young girlhood when she first read the poetry of Langston Hughes and others. Much of this poetry, as we have seen, was about Africa, and on this subject too, curiously enough, Miss Hansberry also in a way completes a circle begun by Hughes. In a new and much more realistic setting, she too has had a vision of a romantic reunion between Negro American and Black African. But her vision is shaped by new times, new outlooks. It is no longer a wispy literary yearning after a lost primitivism, nor does she beat it out on synthetic tom-toms. Nor is it any longer a matter of going back-to-Africa as the ultimate option of despair in America. In Lorraine Hansberry's time it has become a matter of choice between new freedoms now in the grasp of Black men, both African and American.

This idea appears only glancingly in *A Raisin in the Sun*, going largely unnoticed by raving critics and applauding audiences alike. The play is about the drive of the members of a poor Negro family to better their estate. Against this strong and sober central theme, the subtheme of Africa appears only in incidental passages and is used mainly to lighten the play's main emotional burdens. The action turns on the use to be made of the insurance money of the hard-working father who has just died, the son's ill-judged and costly effort to get ahead quick, and the mother's intentness on lifting them out of the Black slums. The daughter of the family, oddly named Beneatha, is the real symbol of its passage from lower-classness; she is already at the university and wants to become a doctor. She has two beaux, one the son of a successful Negro businessman, the other an African, a student from Nigeria. On these two the author's biases are laid with a heavy hand, for the rich man's son is presented as a well-advanced case of bourgeois American decay who offers the girl a future of mink coats and Cadillacs. The Nigerian, by heavy contrast, brings a new look and a new sound to the African theme in American Negro life. He is the most literate, the most self-possessed, the most sophisticated, most purposive, I-know-where-I'm-going character in the play. He offers the girl a life of dedication, work, and self-realization in emergent Africa.

The imminent arrival of this young African brings on this colloquy between mother and daughter:

MAMA: I don't think I never met no African before.
BENEATHA: Well, do me a favor and don't ask him a lot of ignorant questions about Africans. I mean, do they wear clothes and all that—
MAMA: Well, now, I guess if you think we so ignorant 'round here maybe you shouldn't bring your friends here.

BENEATHA: It's just that people ask such crazy things. All anyone seems to know about it when it comes to Africa is Tarzan—

MAMA: (*Indignantly*) Why should I know anything about Africa?

When the young African, also oddly named as Asagai (which sounds more like the Zulu word *assegai*, a sawed-off spear, than like a Nigerian name) finally appears, Mama acquits herself, as always, with dignity. He comes bearing a Nigerian robe as a gift for the girl. He teasingly reminds her that she had first approached him at school to say: "I want very much to talk with you. About Africa. You see, Mr. Asagai, I am looking for my *identity!*" It is clear that this is no joking matter to the girl, and it becomes even less so when he gently but sharply reproves her for "mutilating" her hair by trying to straighten it. She hotly denies that she is "assimilationist," which is one of Miss Hansberry's favorite words.

In a later scene, Beneatha appears in her Nigerian robe and headdress. She flicks off the "assimilationist junk" on the radio and goes into what she imagines to be a Nigerian tribal dance. Brother Walter comes in drunk, full of the angers and confusions arising out of the main business of the play. He enters into her mood. "And Ethiopia shall stretch forth her hands again!" he shouts, and together they go into a wild and noisy and hilarious caper punctuated by what are supposed to be African shouts. Walter leaps on the table and begins to address his imaginary tribesmen, summoning them to battle. In the stage directions we discover that he is seeing himself as "a great chief, a descendant of Chaka," the great Zulu chief—and the creator, incidentally, of the weapon called the *assegai*. It is hard to tell from the text how seriously the author intended all this to be taken; the night I saw the play it convulsed the house with laughter. At its height, George, the rich man's son, walks in. Walter holds forth his hand: "Black brother!" he cries. George looks amazed and disgusted. "Black brother, hell!" he says, and demands that Beneatha go in at once and change to go out. She accuses him of being "ashamed of his heritage," and when she is asked to explain, she goes on:

BENEATHA: It means someone who is willing to give up his culture and submerge himself completely in the dominant, and in this case, oppressive culture!

GEORGE: Oh dear, dear, dear! Here we go! A lecture on the African past! On our great West African Heritage! In one second, we will hear all about the great Ashanti empires, the great Songhay civilizations, and the great sculpture of Benin—and some poetry in the Bantu—and the whole monologue will end with the word *heritage!* (Nastily) Let's face it, baby, your heritage is nothing but a bunch of raggedy-assed spirituals and some grass huts!

Beneatha retorts that he is slandering the people who were "the first to smelt iron on the face of the earth" and who "were performing surgical operations when the English . . . were still tattooing themselves with blue dragons!" But she changes all the same and dutifully goes out with George.

The last act also opens on a relieving bit about Africa. The main action of the play has just come to climax, Walter has stupidly lost the money, and Beneatha sits in crushed defeat and despair, when young Mr. Asagai again appears. He tries to comfort her with philosophy, and she turns on him in anger, predicting that things will be just as bad in Africa when the Black man takes over. He retorts that for better or worse, it will be the Black man's own fate, determined by himself. Then abruptly, he invites her to come home with him. At first, she misunderstands.

> ASAGAI: I mean across the ocean, home—to Africa
> BENEATHA: To—to Nigeria?
> ASAGAI: Yes! (*Smiling and lifting his arms playfully*) Three hundred years later, the African prince rose up out of the seas and swept the maiden back across the middle passage over which her ancestors had come—
> BENEATHA: (*Unable to play*) Nigeria?
> ASAGAI: Nigeria. Home. (*Coming to her with genuine romantic flippancy*) I will show you our mountains and our stars; and give you cool drinks from gourds and teach you the old songs and the ways of our people—and, in time, we will pretend that you have only been away for a day . . .

Beneatha is shaken and confused by all that has been happening and wants time to think. Asagai, gently and sweetly understanding, looks back at her from the door: "How often I have looked at you and said, 'Ah—so this is what the New World hath finally wrought . . .'" and makes a graceful exit.

In the play's last moments, the main issue happily resolved, again after a scene of the highest tension, the unresolved subject of Africa reappears to help break the strain. To make talk to cut in on the insupportable emotion of the moment, Beneatha announces that Asagai had asked her to marry him. Mama is barely able to hear what she says.

> BENEATHA: (*Girlishly and unreasonably trying to pursue the conversation*) To go to Africa, Mama—be a doctor in Africa . . .

MAMA: (*Distracted*) Yes, baby.

WALTER: Africa! What he want you to go to Africa for?

BENEATHA: To practice there—

WALTER: Girl, if you don't get them silly ideas out of your head! You better marry yourself a man with some loot . . .

And the two of them go out, still arguing, George versus Asagai, as their voices fade away, leaving the issue, America or Africa, hanging in the air, rustling and sounding there after they'd gone, like the theme of another play to come.

In *A Raisin in the Sun*, the new form of an old fact, the new shape of the African idea in the American Negro universe, made its first appearance, I believe, in any play or story of wide public notice. If it appeared only incidentally, as a secondary theme to a much more moving main story, this too was appropriate, since this was just about where the subject of Africa stood in the thinking of Negroes at the time the play was produced. The play's audiences were moved by its dramatization of an American problem, by the classic figure of the strong mother, by the son's struggle to find his manhood, by the endurance of the son's wife, and by the fresh forthrightness of the daughter. But few, it seemed, were quite ready to tune in on the new sounds and sights of Africa that also came into view in Miss Hansberry's play. They will no doubt reappear at higher and stronger levels, as time goes on, and will be counterposed to something more substantial than Miss Hansberry's idea of decadent bourgeois affluence in America. Still, she had opened the subject to a new and higher visibility than it had yet enjoyed, and I found, when I sought her out to talk about it, that she was grateful to have someone notice it. She was being praised so highly for creating "real" people in the play that hardly anybody had given her credit, she said ruefully, for also trying to deal symbolically with some important ideas.

These ideas, I found as we talked on, had been assembled out of a series of sources and exposures going back to her childhood and were sometimes expressed in a string of broad generalizations somewhat eclectically tied together. Thus Miss Hansberry described herself as "a strong Negro nationalist" who also believed that all peoples and cultures must eventually merge in a common humanity: "It will be a great day when people merge biologically and in culture," she said, "but until that day, oppressed peoples must express themselves," and this has to be done by stressing one's special identity. "I want all to assimilate in all," she said at one point, "but now one must identify." It sometimes seemed during our conversation that a kind of shape-as-you-go quality had been imposed on Miss Hansberry's thinking by the need, in her sudden celebrity, to answer a lot of questions about herself that she had never been asked before or, for that matter, asked herself. Because she had so successfully created some "real" people on the stage, she was having the wonderful but rather unseating experience of discovering that her opinions about all sorts of things had overnight become important. Inevitably, some of her opinions and perhaps some memories had to be put together on the spur of the moment. But Lorraine Hansberry was not only a polite and decent young woman trying hard to keep her balance in the storm of a Broadway success. She was also a bright and thoughtful person, and almost every thread of her thought did lead back to some significant life experience.

Talking about the changes in the world, she described how sometime after World War II she had begun to feel not so much a member of an American minority as of a "world majority" of oppressed people who were beginning to throw off the systems that oppressed them. "As a fairly self-conscious Negro," she said, "I began to feel this kinship, the feeling from the past summed up in 'Aren't we all miserable' passing to a new and happier feeling: 'Aren't we all moving ahead!'" For herself, she thought, this was not a change, "just a logical progression. Why, ever since I was three years old," she exclaimed, "I knew that somebody somewhere was doing something to hurt Black and brown peoples. Little as I was, I remember the newsreels of the Ethiopian war and the feeling of outrage in our Negro community. Fighters with spears and our people in a passion over it, my mother attacking the Pope blessing the Italian troops going off to slay Ethiopians. When the Pope died that was the thought of him that came to my mind. I didn't know a thing about Spain, but I certainly did know about Ethiopia. I didn't know about Hitler, but I certainly did know about Leopold cutting off the hands of the people in the Congo. Japan's war in China? Vague, very vague. I don't remember people talking about it. In 1941, though, many people saw the Japanese as a colored nation, and this affected their feelings, certainly in Chicago, and this was reflected even in my own home. But we just expected that things would change. We had been saying for a long time: 'Ethiopia will stretch forth her hands!' This always meant that *they* were going to pay for all this one day."

Miss Hansberry said she remembered the verse about Ethiopia's hands "because I am the granddaughter of an AME minister." She was also the daughter of a strong-minded man who evidently devoted himself, with considerable success, to winning just the kind of bourgeois affluence she deprecates in her play. Besides being a well-to-do businessman and a power in the Chicago Negro community, her father was also a strongly race-conscious man. "My father was a student of history," said Miss Hansberry, "and we were always taught pride in our Negro heritage." Her father gave her a strong sense of the positive virtues of Negro-ness, but these all had to do, she remembers, with Negroes in America. "It was all in terms of the United States," she said, "nothing in particular about Africa." At the same time, her family also had certain prejudices about color. "My people had the stereotyped attitudes," she said. "They thought blacker people were less attractive, and we were a dark-skinned family! Nowadays nobody would admit ever having such feelings. We assumed, of course, that *our* color was the marking off point. . . . The prejudices in my family were very, very complicated. We were never proud of its attitudes." Some combination of these factors, involving attitudes about Africa and color, doubtless had something to do with the odd fact that by her own account Lorraine Hansberry had never even heard about Marcus Garvey until after she came to New York in 1950. But little Lorraine took in a great deal about Africa nonetheless. Her father's house "was full of books," and when she was about nine she started reading the Negro poets, and got some of her first and more enduring images of Africa from their lines, so much so that when I first asked her what came to her mind when she thought of Africa she instantly said, "Beautiful mountains, plateaus, beautiful dark people." And these pictures came, she added, "from the poets I grew up reading, Langston Hughes, Countee Cullen, Waring Cuney. I was deeply influenced by them, and their images of Africa were marvelous and beautiful."

Out in the hard world of the Chicago South Side, in its schools and on its streets, Lorraine had ample opportunity to summon up the resources of pride she had acquired from her father and from Langston Hughes's poetry. She ran into all the familiar hateful images and she fought them back with all she had:

"In school in the lower grades, primitive peoples, hot, animals, mostly negative, how good it was we were saved from this terrible past. Most of the kids reflected this. To call a kid an African was an insult. It was calling him savage, uncivilized, naked, something to laugh at. A naked Black savage with a spear and war paint. It was equivalent to ugliness. Everything distasteful and painful was associated with Africa. This came from school, from the movies, and from our own people who accepted this. In common talk, the term was always derogatory—'you are acting like a wild African!' This meant heathen, un-Christian. Most children absorbed this and acquired a deep shame of their African past. But I resented what I saw in the movies and I resented the teachers who couldn't give a more positive view. This too was mainly about our own American Negro past. We were very sensitive to such things as how the slavery issue was discussed, even in grade school. I resented all of it. I was very unique in that I extended this [resentment] to the African thing too. The others didn't do this, but I made the connection. . . . I really don't know why this was so, but I was very aware, and even when kids said 'you look like an African' as a form of insult, this hurt me, it brought me pain. At the movies when one white man was holding off thousands of Africans with a gun, all the kids were with the hero, but I was with the Africans. When I was thirteen or fourteen, I was more sophisticated. I had begun to read Carter Woodson. My brothers and I talked about Hannibal, we had passion, if not information, and we thought Africa was a great thing in the world. . . ."

Lorraine Hansberry, then, got her early defensive race-consciousness from her father and her romantic view of Africa quite largely from the poems of Langston Hughes. These two influences in her young life were further linked by a curiously arresting set of coincidences that I mark here because of their obvious relevance not only to our grasp of these two individual writers, but also to our general subject. I can do so, however, only in scantiest outline, for they involve the two fathers about whom neither writer has yet told us quite enough.[1] Lorraine Hansberry's father and Langston Hughes's father were evidently in many ways very similar men, both hard-driving and ambitious and intent on wealth and recognition. As the reader will recall from our brief account of Hughes, his father quite early in his life quit the United States because it did not allow a Negro to be a man and migrated to Mexico where he made his fortune in business. Lorraine's father made his fortune here, in Chicago, after coming up empty-handed out of Mississippi. He fought personally to wring recognition of Negro rights out of the white world. At his own expense he carried a restricted covenants case right up to the Supreme Court, and he won. But he came finally to the despairing conclusion, like Hughes's father and others before him, that the United States was no place for a self-respecting Black man to live out his life, and he decided to migrate. It was not Africa, however, that he had in view. As Miss Hansberry's own account intimates, her father had something less than a romantic view of Africa. Remember, she never even had heard of Marcus Garvey in her father's race-conscious home— the only version of back-to-Africa that had ever reached her, she told me, was Senator Bilbo's race-baiting bill in Congress to ship all Negroes back where they came from—and there were also the elder Hansberry's views about Blackness. These views and attitudes were somehow linked, but we will not ever know their inwardness unless Miss Hansberry one day chooses to explain why her father's color attitudes were so "very, very complicated." In any case, when he planned to migrate, the elder Hansberry fixed his eye not on Africa, but like the elder Hughes some forty years before, on Mexico. In 1945 he took the step, actually bought a house in a Mexico City suburb, and put Lorraine and her sister in school there. But he had waited too long. Within a short time, Mr. Hansberry died, and the family resumed its life in the United States.

Her brothers, Lorraine Hansberry told me, have been moved to follow in their father's path, and they now see West Africa, not Mexico, as a more promising land since, with the changing times, they have been able to develop business interests there. But Lorraine herself chose quite differently. Like Langston Hughes in a far-gone year, she decided that she was not Africa, or Mexico, but Chicago and New York. She went even further and by marrying a non-Negro added to her vision of the far future the ultimate end of all troubling race distinctions. At the same time, she has clung hard in her near view to a strong insistence on racial and national identifications. She thinks it an absurd idea that persons of African descent should return to Africa because of that; Africans have their own national identities, and American Negroes have—or must now shape—their own. And this, again, is the rub. Here Lorraine Hansberry in her turn arrives, behind Ralph Ellison and James Baldwin, at the new edge of time and looks with them out over the same confusions: as he emerges from his second classness, what does the American Negro become? And in this process of new becoming, what is he to Africa, and what is Africa to him? "I don't know about the future," answered Lorraine Hansberry, "or what role Africa will have in it. One thing, though, the shame about Africa among Negroes is actively disintegrating. I don't think this change should be so difficult. Most people are glad to replace a negative view with an affirmative view."

Note

1. My information about Hughes's father comes entirely out of Hughes's autobiographical volume, *The Big Sea*. I know about Hansberry Senior only what Miss Hansberry herself told me. Essentially the same details appear in the autobiographical account she gave of herself in the *New Yorker*, May 9, 1959. [note by Harold R. Isaacs]

The Negro in American Culture: Interview with James Baldwin, Emile Capouya, Lorraine Hansberry, Langston Hughes, and Alfred Kazin

Nat Hentoff / 1961

Broadcast on WBAI-FM, January 10, 1961. Printed in *CrossCurrents* 11, no. 3 (Summer 1961): 205–24. Reprinted by permission of Wiley.[1]

The accompanying article represents a useful commentary on the Civil War commemorations now taking place in various quarters.

The text represents, with only minor editing, a discussion broadcast early this year over WBAI-FM, the invaluable listener-supported radio station of New York. The moderator was Nat Hentoff, former editor of *Downbeat*; participants included James Baldwin, author of *Notes of a Native Son* (Beacon), *Go Tell It on the Mountain* (Universal), and *Nobody Knows My Name* (Dial); Alfred Kazin, author of *On Native Grounds* (Anchor), *A Walker in the City* (Grove), and *The Inmost Leaf* (Noonday); Lorraine Hansberry, author of *A Raisin in the Sun*; Emile Capouya, an editor at Macmillan & Co.; and Langston Hughes, whose many books include *Simple Stakes a Claim* (Rinehart), *Selected Poems* (Knopf), and *A Langston Hughes Reader* (Braziller).

The relaxed and spontaneous form of the remarks of these distinguished writers provides a candid presentation of attitudes often neglected in the glow of our easy denunciations of southern racists or that cheap statesmanship which calls for "moderation" in regard to elementary human dignity.

Nat Hentoff: To begin the subject, which sounds rather alarmingly vague, I'd like to start with the end of the book review that James Baldwin wrote for the *New York Times* a couple of years ago. The review was of poems of Langston Hughes, and you concluded by saying that "he is not the first American Negro to find the war between his social and artistic responsibilities all but irreconcilable."

To what extent do you find this true in your own writing in terms of the self-consciousness of being a Negro and a writer, the polarity, if it exists?

James Baldwin: Well, the first difficulty is really so simple that it's usually overlooked: to be a Negro in this country and to be relatively conscious, is to be in a rage almost all the time. So that the first problem is how to control that rage so that it won't destroy you. Part of the rage is this: it isn't only what is happening to you, but it's what's happening all around you all of the time, in the face of the most extraordinary and criminal indifference, the indifference and ignorance of most white people in this country.

Now, since this so, it's a great temptation to simplify the issues under the illusion that if you simplify them enough, people will recognize them; and this illusion is very dangerous because that isn't the way it works.

You have to decide that you can't spend the rest of your life cursing out everybody that gets in your way. As a writer, you have to decide that what is really important is not that the people you write about are Negroes, but that they are people, and that the suffering of any person is really universal. If you can ever reach this level, if you can create a person and make other people feel what this person feels, then it seems to me that you've gone much further, not only artistically, but socially, than in the ordinary, old-fashioned protest way.

I talked about Langston not being the first poet to find these responsibilities all but irreconcilable. And he won't be the last, because it also demands a great deal of time to write, it demands a great deal of stepping out of a social situation in order to deal with it. And all the time you're out of it you can't help feeling a little guilty that you are not, as it were, on the firing line, tearing down the slums and doing all these obviously needed things, which in fact, other people can do better than you because it is still terribly true that a writer is extremely rare.

Hentoff: Miss Hansberry, in writing *A Raisin in the Sun*, to what extent did you feel a double role, both as a kind of social actionist "protester," and as a dramatist?

Lorraine Hansberry: Well, given the Negro writer, we are necessarily aware of a special situation in the American setting. And that probably works two ways. One of them makes us sometimes forget that there is really a very limited expression in literature which is not protest, be it Black, white, or what have you; I can't imagine a contemporary writer any place in the world today who isn't in conflict with his world. Personally, I can't imagine a time in the world when the artist wasn't in conflict; if he was any kind of an artist, he had to be.

We are doubly aware of conflict, because of the special pressures of being a Negro in America, but I think to destroy the abstraction for the sake of the specific is, in this case, an error. Once we come to that realization, it doesn't get quite as confusing as sometimes we tend to treat it.

In my play I was dealing with a young man who would have, I feel, been a compelling object of conflict as a young American of his class of whatever racial background, with the exception of the incident at the end of the play, and with the exception, of course, of character depth, because a Negro character is a reality; there is no such thing as saying that a Negro could be a white person if you just changed the lines or something like this. This is a very arbitrary and superficial approach to Negro character.

But I am taking a long way around to try to answer your question. There really is no profound problem. I started to write about this family as I knew them in the context of those realities which I remembered as being true for this particular given set of people; and at one point, it was just inevitable that a problem of some magnitude which was racial would intrude itself, because this is one of the realities of Negro life in America. But it was just as inevitable that for a large part of the play, they would be excluded. Because the duality of consciousness is so complete that it is perfectly true to say that Negroes do not sit around twenty-four hours a day, thinking, "I am a Negro." [*laughter*] They really don't. I don't. I don't think he does or anybody else. And, on the other hand, if you say the reverse, that is almost true. And this is part of the complexity that I think you're talking about, isn't it?

Baldwin: Yes, I agree completely. I think we are bound to get to this, because white men in this country and American Negroes in this country are really the same people. I only discovered this in Europe; perhaps it was always very obvious, but it never occurred to me before. The only people in the world who understand the American white man are American Negroes [*laughter*]—nobody else.

Hentoff: Langston Hughes, you have a large continuing body of work, and I wondered if you had felt in the course of your long development as a writer, a change in your feeling of this duality as the conditions around you changed, as the struggle for equality became more militant, and the status, to some extent, of the "Negro writer" began to change.

In other words, to what extent did the society around you change the kind of tension under which you wrote?

Langston Hughes: I must say that I don't notice any changes as yet. [*laughter*]

I happen to be a writer who travels a great deal because I read my poems in public and almost every year I travel over most of the country, south and north. I do, of course, see appreciable changes in some areas of race relations, and I trust that my recent work reflects that to some extent, but by and large, it seems to me not really very different from when I was a child. There are still a great many places where you can't get a hamburger or a cup of coffee, or you can't sit on a bench in a railroad station, something of this sort—and not just in the South. Those problems exist in Washington, on the West Coast, and in Maine, you know.

I am, of course, as everyone knows, primarily a—I guess you might even say a propaganda writer; my main material is the race problem—and I have found it most exciting and interesting and intriguing to deal with it in writing, and I haven't found the problem of being a Negro in any sense a hindrance to putting words on paper. It may be a hindrance sometimes to selling them; the material that one uses, the fact that one uses, or that I use, problem material, or material that is often likely to excite discussion or disagreement, in some cases prevents its quick sale. I mean, no doubt it's much easier to sell a story like Frank Yerby writes without the race problem in it, or, yes, like Willard Motley, who also happens to be Negro, but writes without emphasizing the sharpness of our American race problem. Those writers are much more commercial than I or, I think, Miss Hansberry, or James Baldwin, who to me seems one of the most racial of our writers, in spite of his analysis of himself as otherwise on occasion.

Baldwin: Later for you. [*laughter*]

Alfred Kazin: Emile Capouya, from what you've observed in publishing as a whole, do you think that Langston Hughes's point has validity, that the degree of sharpness in which the racial problem is written about is a deterrent to sales, let's say, in the book field? I wonder if there isn't a distinction between magazine writing and book writing here.

Emile Capouya: No, I think not. From an editor's point of view, somebody who's professionally interested in buying or selling literary material, an artist and a writer are two different people.

First of all, he's an artist, and as such his claims are absolute. But he's also a commodity, and as a commodity he has no rights at all. He just has a market value.

So to come directly to your question: do I think that the material that a Negro writer may find readiest to hand is questionable from a market point of view, I'd say that each writer is an individual case.

Mr. Hughes suggested that it's been a stumbling block on his road to riches, but that wouldn't be the case obviously for Mr. Baldwin whose business as a novelist is largely with that material. And Miss Hansberry has had a great success, I think partly because of what that great public that went to see that play thought of as exotic material.

Hughes: May I say that from long experience with publishers, and many of them—I have about six now—it has been my feeling that if a publisher has one Negro writer on his list or two at the most, he is not very likely to take another if the Negro writer is dealing in Negro themes? And it's not prejudice, it's simply, "Well, we have a book, a Chinese novel on our list. We don't want any more Chinese novels."

And the same thing is true in the theater. Once in a blue moon, there's a hit like *Raisin in the Sun*, but the Broadway producers will tell you quite frankly, "No more Negro plays. They're not commercial, we can't sell them. People won't go to the box office."

So if you want to make money out of writing, being a Negro writer, I mean quickly and easily, I would say become a Willard Motley, become a Frank Yerby.

Capouya: I don't think that's the whole truth in relation to the way in which the question was originally posed. Suppose there were two plays about the Jewish East Side—

Hughes: Yes, it's not a matter really of racial prejudice; it's a matter of the economy we're dealing in.

Hansberry: Well, I wouldn't be so quick to decide whether it is or isn't prejudice. There are so many different ways of saying the same thing. It would be more than wishful thinking to me to exclude prejudice regarding Negroes in any area of life. I just don't think that's realistic.

It's prejudice when you can't get an apartment; it's probably prejudice when a skillful writer cannot publish because of some arbitrarily decided notion of what is or is not, as they tell me all the time, parochial material, of narrow interest, and so forth.

In a culture that has any pretensions towards sophistication or interest in human beings, there shouldn't be any designations of kinds of material. A good book should find a publisher.

Hughes: Since the problem of the writer as a commodity has been brought up, I think it is by and large true to say that for the Negro writer to make a living is doubly hard due to the prejudice that Miss Hansberry has spoken about in other areas related to writing.

For example, I told you that I'm a lecturer and I read my poems. I have been with two or three of the top agencies. Those agencies cannot, as a rule, book me at women's clubs. Women's clubs have teas; they do not wish to mingle socially with their speaker apparently, and they do not wish to invite their speaker's friends in whatever town he may be speaking on the program, because it's followed by a social event. Therefore, it's a rare occasion when I read my poems to a women's club.

If you want a job in the publishing industry, try and get it. How many editors of color can anyone name on any of our New York publishing houses? You may find an occasional girl secretary at the switchboard or a typist or a stockroom boy, but for the writer himself to get some sort of work related to his actual writing in publishing is well-nigh impossible, I think.

Until very recently, in the last few years, Negroes did not write for Hollywood. Nothing was really sold to Hollywood. That's sort of a new development. I have been writing for thirty years and I've had one Hollywood job in thirty years. Prejudice doesn't keep a writer from writing; if you're colored, you can write all you want to, but you just try and sell it, that's all.

Kazin: May I go back a moment to the point that Mr. Baldwin began with, this alleged conflict between the social and the artistic in American life?

You know, words like social and artistic are easy to use, and I'm sure that if I had to go through the daily humiliations that certain of my friends go through, I would feel this way.

But let me for a moment, put it on a purely theoretical plane, where art may be discussed. America itself has always been a social question. All that's good in American writing, American art, comes out of the profound confrontation of social facts. It was true of *Moby Dick*, of *Leaves of Grass*. It comes out of what I consider to be the driving force behind all things, which is human hunger, human desire. Only it's a question, of course, not of how much you desire or how bad you feel, but how artistically you can realize your desire.

We have to consider two things. One is the current fashion to believe that art is somehow created apart from society, on the basis of purely individual will, as opposed to the marvelous books published in this country between, I would say, 1911 and 1934 or '35, many of which, like Faulkner's and Steinbeck's, Mr. Hughes's and other such books, are based on very real and agonizing social problems. And I must say that in this centenary year of the Civil War, it's hard to forget that the Negro is the central issue in American history, has been the central issue all along, has been the real crux of our history and our aspirations as a people, and that, therefore, the question that comes up is always how deeply, how profoundly, how accurately do we recognize this social kind of drive in our literature right now?

And one thing that's happening right now in middle-class writing everywhere is what's happening to Negroes too: people don't have as many beefs as they think they have; they often have no real beefs; they are very often led by purely arbitrary problems, and consequently, a good deal of the tremendous whiplash of hunger, hunger in the widest sense, the deepest sense, has been forgotten here.

I think—to put it very bluntly—that in America there cannot be any conflict between the so-called social and artistic impulse; that one must recognize that what we call art is the most profound realization of some social tendency, and that wherever you don't have this social awareness, social intelligence, then, it seems to me, you don't have art either.

In other words, the Negro has been not merely a writer, he's also been a character, and he's been one of the most profound characters in American literature. I don't mean Uncle Tom, either. I mean a character from Faulkner, a character from many, even, pre–Civil War novelists, who were always aware of the Negro as a force, a human being, as a problem, as a challenge, as a lover, as many things. And one must not forget that this problem goes to the very essence of our life of civilization.

And that's why I'm so troubled when Mr. Baldwin, for reasons which I can well imagine, but which I want, for once, to pretend I don't understand, opens by bringing up this whole question of the conflict between the social and the artistic.

I think that art is never created when it is too aware of this kind of conflict. I also don't believe in conflicts that are realized. Once there is a conflict, the thing to do is bypass it and go on to a third force, as such.

I'm thinking, for example, of Mr. Baldwin's *Notes of a Native Son*, which for me, in many ways, is the most brilliant of Negro books, even though it's a collection of essays, of modern American writing. And I've been struck, in rereading it, by the power, the brilliance, and the vividness of it.

Hughes: You know what I would say about it? I would say it's the *Uncle Tom's Cabin* of today. [*laughter*]

Kazin: Well, I happen to like this *Uncle Tom's Cabin*. I think it's a masterpiece.

And the reason it's a masterpiece is because the broken glass of the '43 Harlem riot, the miseries of personal friends—all these things have been captured and realized as a piece of art. And the minute one tries to break away from this, tries to get away from this enormous passion, then one is lost.

The other thing is that one must recognize that art is a word that people use, but the ability to create is something which is utterly God-given, accidental, and capricious. And I think, for example, to speak of something I know rather intimately, when the Jewish immigrants, from whom I come, arrived in this country fifty, sixty years ago, there was a whole hoard of sweatshop poets and they were miserable people. They worked eighteen, nineteen hours a day; they lived horrible lives. None of this poetry that I have seen, in English, in Hebrew, or in Yiddish, is any good at all. And then suddenly in the last fifteen years, we've had a group of writers, like Saul Bellow and Norman Mailer and Bernard Malamud and others, who, with enormous surprise to themselves, I think, have suddenly created five or six really good books, which are as fresh as anything can be.

Now, one reason they've done this is that they've come to recognize their fate as being universal in some sense, and not merely accidental or parochial. I don't mean that they shouldn't write about parochial things, on the contrary, but they've come to recognize the universal in this.

And I ask myself, what is the difference between those lovable, dear people sixty years ago, with their awful sweatshop poetry, and a writer who to my mind is as first class as Saul Bellow in one or two short things?

I can only say it's a question of the welding together at a certain moment of all these impulses, without for a moment forgetting that intelligence and social passion come into play here. And one mustn't ever try to divide the two. Otherwise, it becomes a problem in the economic history of the writer; it becomes a problem in the social history of the writer; it does not become a problem of art, as such, which is something very different.

Baldwin: There isn't any conflict between what you said and what I mean. I should clarify my terms some more.

In that particular book review, I was using the conflict between social and artistic responsibility in a very limited and specific way. I know that art comes out of something much deeper than anything that can be named. I know it is always and must be social, because what are you investigating except man and the ways in which he lives, and the ways in which he tries to remake his world, and the ways in which he sometimes fails and sometimes succeeds?

Perhaps I was using the wrong word there; perhaps I should have said propagandistic. Because I don't think there's any point really in blinking this fact and I don't think it can ever be used to defend oneself or excuse oneself for failure, which after all has to be personal and private failure.

Now, there's no point in pretending that being a Negro writer in this country doesn't present certain particular hazards which you would not have if you were white. It is perfectly true, as Langston says, that anybody with his comparable reputation and body of work, who was white, would have much more money than Langston does. This is a fact. But the Negro writer is not as interesting a subject to me as the Negro in this country in the minds of other people—the Negro character, as you put it—and the role that he's always played in the American subconscious, which has never really been dealt with. It has always been there, almost like a corpse which no one knows what to do with, floating in the waters of the national life. And really everything in America can almost be defined by the presence of the Negro in it, including the American personality.

To deal with this, I think, is the real challenge one faces. Somehow actually to unify this country—because it never has been united—and to make a wedding for the first time really, between Blacks and whites. Because, this is really the history of a very long love affair, and it's this, much more than anything else which Americans are afraid to look at and don't want to believe.

Kazin: To use a cryptic phrase, the presence of the Negro in America, in the whole imaginative and moral history of this country, is what I call the central fact.

I've been reading Civil War history for the last few months for an article I'm doing, and I'm struck again and again by the enormous effort so many people made in the thirties and forties of the last century in the North to overlook the Negroes, to make sure that their little Unitarian, Abolitionist hopes would get rid of him. But again and again the fact came up, it could not be bypassed, and it couldn't be bypassed any more by the Abolitionists who looked the other way, than it could be bypassed by the southern slave masters. And now, in the midst of this agonizing struggle going on in the South, which the whole world is watching, the fact remains, because of the very nature of American democracy, that never in history has a whole body of former slaves been made the issue of human and civic equality on such a large scale as in this country.

The love affair, which I would say is more a mutual and fascinated awareness of each other, is itself the very incidence of the agony and passion of the Negro's presence in American life. And this is why, when you recognize the social factor, as Faulkner does in his best work—and I'm not thinking here of Joe Christmas—I'm thinking here of the total context he creates—then you recognize the depth of emotion, the depth of commitment out of which art can come.

Now, the economic problem is something else. It is disgusting that a lecturer should have to be banned from a women's tea club because he might have to have tea with them.

But think what a marvelous story this makes, about America: people who think they would like to hear the lecturer, are afraid to have the tea. Note the slightly comic element, not in the sense of being amiable, but in revealing human paradox and hypocrisy.

When I was a professor at a New England college some years ago, there were two Negro boys in the college, a testimony to its Abolitionist background. And, of course, these boys were miserable and about as lonely as a spar of wood on a Cape Cod beach. But the fact remains that out of this kind of experience would come to an artist, white or Negro, a sense of the extraordinary comedy of social hopes and moral would-be feelings of this country, too—which is, I submit, as close to the life of art as the suffering and anxiety of an individual writer who happens to be a Negro here. And this is why I hope that we will not only remember, as we all must, what is happening to each of us who is a Negro down South, but also of the enormous presence of the Negro as a fact in the American imagination, which again and again has created something which is absolutely inextricable—it cannot be lost, cannot be forgotten, cannot be bypassed, in our minds for a moment.

Hughes: Speaking of the celebration of the centennial of the Civil War, I have just written yesterday columns for the *Chicago Defender,* for which I write, using my Simple character as a kind of social protest mouthpiece, and I'd like to read you a section because it involves the very thing that you're talking about.

Simple is in the barbershop and this is what he says:

"I sit in that barber chair, thinking about how God must love poor folks because he made so many of them in my image. [*laughter*]

"You know, as long as I've been poor, I'm not used to it. My papa were poor before me and my grandpa were poorer than that, being a slave which did not even own hisself. So, I was settin in that barber chair thinking, one day the time might come when I will own Old Master's grandson, since him nor none of his white relations won't let me get hold a nothing else."

"What on earth are you talking about," I asked, "reinstating slavery? Are you out of your mind?"

"I was sort of dozin and dreamin whilst he cut my hair," said Simple, "and in snoozin I kept thinkin about how much I been hearin about this here centennial of the Civil War and stuff the white folks has been tellin—intendin to celebrate in honor of the North and South. And they're goin to be on parades and meetins and battles and things like they were one hundred years ago. One way of makin people remember what that Civil War were all about might be to bring back slavery for a month or two, only this time, reverse it. Make the white folks the slaves and me the master.

"I would like to own some of them white Simples on my grandma's side, which were the ones, I understand, that gave me my name. Oh, I would like to own a few white folks just once." [*laughter*] "Maybe I could work out of them some of the money that they owe my great-grandfolks and never did pay. Else make up for these low wages which I'm gettin right now.

"I would like to own me some rich white slaves, not used to workin like me for hardly enough to pay income tax when April, let alone Harlem rent and balancing your budget."

"Dream on," I said.

"From dawn to long after dark, I would find something for them white folks to do," said Simple, "if I owned them, and come the end of the week, not pay them a cent. That would be a real good way, I figure, to celebrate the centennial. Make it real, not just playactin, but bring slavery back to its own doorstep. One hundred years, it is time to turn the tables.

"But don't you know, since I was dreamin about all this, the barber cut my hair too short?"

"It looks all right to me," I said, "In fact, I would say, with you, the less hair the better."

"I might have bad hair," said Simple, "But I've got a good-shaped head." [*laughter*]

Well now, I very often try to use social material in a humorous form and most of my writing from the very beginning has been aimed largely at a Negro reading public, because when I began to write I had no thought of achieving a wide public. My early work was always published in *The Crisis* of the NAACP, and then in *The Opportunity* of the Urban League, and then the Negro papers like the Washington *Sentinel* and the *Baltimore American*, and so on. And I contend that since these things, which are Negro, largely for Negro readers, have in subsequent years achieved worldwide publication—my work has come out in South America, Japan, and all over Europe—that a regional Negro character like Simple, a character intended for the people who belong to his own race, if written about warmly enough, humanly enough, can achieve universality.

In fact, I think my Simple character has achieved universality with the very kind of thing that he talks about here in the barber chair, because all around the world poor people have economic problems, all around the world, in almost every country, there is some sort of racial problem. In Japan it's—what do they call them?—the Ainu; in India, it's the Untouchables; in France, it's the *sals Algériens.*

These problems are not limited just to America. But they impose no limitation on the writer one way or another.

Norman Mailer was mentioned—I didn't know he was a Jewish writer until right now—he achieved a universality, in spite of his Jewish background.

And I don't see, as Jimmy Baldwin sometimes seems to imply, any limitations, in artistic terms, in being a Negro. I see none whatsoever. It seems to me that any Negro can write about anything he chooses, even the narrowest problems: if he can write about it forcefully and honestly and truly, it is very possible that that bit of writing will be read and understood, in Iceland or Uruguay.

Kazin: I agree entirely, Mr. Hughes. I was thinking about the difference between two of Richard Wright's books, one of which moved me enormously when I was younger than I am now, *Native Son*, the other, *The Outsider*, which I didn't like at all. I agree with you entirely about the need to be parochial, the need to write out of one's milieu and to one's milieu; in fact, Wright's *The Outsider* is my text to prove it.

When I read about this Negro on a train meeting this hunchback, who made common cause with him because they were both symbols of the outsider, I thought this was weak artistically; I felt it was, as the French say, *voulu*, it was willed, it was not real. What seemed to me to be absolutely legitimate; however, were the profoundly touching scenes in which Bigger was involved in *Native Son*, which still is a very powerful and enormously moving book.

We Americans are very symbolic to ourselves as well as to other people. And very often we think of ourselves as being in the forefront of the world. (I think we still are. I still think we're more revolutionary than any other country in the world, at least implicitly, in terms of the kind of society we're trying to build.)

But the point I'm getting at is that the Negro tends very often today to think of himself as being the symbol of man in the outside world, because of the enormous fact of the race problem in all countries of the world, because of the enormous suffering and wars going on right now. The Negro middle class writer in America, may, if he is in Paris, as Wright was, think of himself as being the symbol rather than the fact. And my point is that only when the Negro thinks of himself as a fact can art begin. The minute he thinks of himself as a symbol, then theory creeps in and the whole problem is dis-social, dis-artistic.

When you're writing out of the actual broken glass of the actual confused heats of that race riot in '43 in the Harlem streets, when Jimmy took his father to the grave, then you have the beginning of what you don't understand too well.

There is a certain law for art: not to know as you're writing what everything means. It's being impressed with the fact, not with the significance of the fact. Too often one tends, because of the enormous centrality of the Negro position today in world experience, to say, "Well, we all know what that means," but we don't. It all goes back to one house, one street, one uncle or grandmother, or whatever.

Hansberry: I don't think that there should be any overextended attention to this question of what is or what isn't universal.

I think that Simple, for instance, is as kin to the Shakespearean wise fool as any other character in literature I've ever heard of, but we don't notice the Englishness of a Shakespearean fool while we're being entertained and educated by his wisdom; the experience just happens. It happens because people have rent problems everywhere in the world and because men are oppressed everywhere in the world. The point of contact is innate to the piece to the extent that it is true, to the extent that it is art, which is what I think that you were saying.

I have been distressed personally, in connection with something that Mr. Kazin was saying, having to do with the traditional treatment of Negro characters in American literature—let's speak now of non-Negro writers. I was perplexed to find, when I addressed myself to that question in two popular essays, that nobody seemed to know what on earth I was talking about—which, of course, could be a matter of delivery. On one occasion I tried to discuss the character, Walter Lee, the young man in my play, in terms of why, as you said a moment ago, in the so-called white mind, he was still an expression of exoticism, no matter how he had been created. Many people, apparently, recognized his humanity, but he was still exotic to them.

In my opinion, since man is so complex and since I disagree with most of the despairing crowd, if you're going to get ridiculous and talk about man being basically anything, you may as well say he's probably basically good. If that is true, then it is also true that man is trying to accommodate his own guilt always, all of us.

And it seems to me that one of the things that has been done in the American mentality is to create this escape valve of the exotic Negro, wherein it is possible to exalt abandon on all levels, and to imagine that while I am dealing with the perplexities of the universe, look over there, coming down from the trees [*laughter*] is a Negro who knows none of this, and wouldn't it be marvelous if I could be my naked, brutal, savage self again?

This permeates our literature in every variation: I don't believe that Negro characters as created thus far have overcome that problem. I don't even believe that the Negro artist has overcome it, because we have been affected by it.

For example, the Emperor Jones is not a man in conflict with the world. He is an arch-symbol that never existed on land, sea, or under it; and to the extent that we recognize something about him, we recognize something symbolized in our own minds. I think this would also be true of Porgy.

The discussion of the Negro character has been so primitive in the past, we've been so busy talking about who's a stereotype and who isn't, we have never talked about it as art. I maintain that the problem is that these characters as they've appeared in literature have never gained full human stature because the writers who have created them haven't thought about them as men in the first place. It isn't a matter of just wanting to change how they speak. Every time you say something about *Porgy and Bess*, somebody says, "Well, you know, Negroes did speak dialect forty years ago." Heavens, they still do. That is not the argument; the argument is that Porgy is not a man.

Kazin: No, he isn't. I think that American literature written by white people is probably 99.9 percent full of these stereotypes and that lately we have been treated to the worst stereotype of all, which is what Norman Mailer calls the "White Negro," namely, the noble savage brought back as an example to the bourgeois white American.

Baldwin: I have some objections to Faulkner's Negro characters. I'll try to tell you what they are. I think the principal one is that not only is there something left out, there is something left out that should be there. Even in the great portrait of Joe Christmas—the only way is to put it as bluntly as possible, then we can go back and modify it—there is something about him which rubs me the wrong way, and it's not his situation and it isn't his dialect, it isn't any of these things at all. What it is is that he's also a kind of apology for an injustice which is really still not being dealt with.

Now Faulkner is a very good example of what I mean. The southern writers who have written about Negroes and have written about them well have all written about them in more or less the same way, essentially out of a feeling of guilt. What is most mysterious is that it is a guilt to which they cling. It's a guilt without which their identities would be threatened. What is so fascinating about this whole Negro-white relationship in America, is what it means in the American personality to have a Negro around. That is why he's always the noble savage in no matter what guise, from Eisenhower to Norman Mailer, nobody can give this up. Everybody wants to have this sort of walking symbol around to protect something in themselves which they do not want to examine.

But what one deals with in the world every day, really, isn't the world's malice or even the world's indifference, it's the world's ignorance. And it's not ignorance of the Negro or the fact of Negro life as such. It's an ignorance of a certain level of life which no one has ever respected, or it's never been real in America. You can almost say—you can say, in fact—that one of the reasons that the Negro is at the bottom of the social heap in America, is because it's the only way everyone in America will know where the bottom is. [*laughter*]

Kazin: Exactly, as you put it, marvelously, to show us where the bottom is, where everything that is fundamental is in our country. But at the bottom, there are people who, understandably because they've been at the bottom so long, will be seen by an imaginative writer like Faulkner in a certain way.

Now, would you want Faulkner to write about the Negro only, so to speak, as he *should* be in our minds, if he were given half a chance, or do you want him out of all these hundreds of years of southern bondage and southern slaveowning and southern prejudice to release that powerful talent and throw it away?

Let me put this in a personal way, if I may—I too come from people who are not altogether unused to prejudice. Now, only fifteen years ago a million and a half Jewish children were put into bonfires by the Nazis just because they were Jewish children. It's a terrible fact, part of the incredible oppression of the Second World War. Nevertheless, if I read Shakespeare's *Merchant of Venice*, with its venomous, unbearable portrait of Shylock, though I think it's false, I have to admit it's a great artistic creation. And it seems to me that over the years, one thing that's happened to me as a writer in America, is that I've learned to say that Shylock is a great character and not worry about him so much.

Don't misunderstand me, though. I'm not trying to sermonize on this question. All I'm saying here is that we do have a handful of books that seem to be written out of the bottom, and one mustn't presume too much here too, for this reason: Joe Christmas is not a Negro. No one knows what or who he is. People think he's a Negro, and the point in that great novel— *Light in August* is a very great book, an extraordinary book—is that because people do not know him, but merely see in him what they think he is, not what he really is (he could be anything)—they do everything to him right up to the end. They murder him, they castrate him, and he becomes the dead Christ on the American cross. Again and again, it's made clear, that the fact of Negro suffering has created this figure.

On the other hand, when Faulkner writes a letter to the *New York Times* about segregation in the South, he writes like a damn fool, he writes like any typical, vulgar Mississippian. When he writes a novel, which has a Negro character in it, he's a great artist.

Hughes: Oh, certainly, he's an amazingly good writer. However, it seems to me that he doesn't really and fully understand even the southern Negro with whom he's lived all his life. Did you see *Requiem for a Nun*, last season?

Kazin: Yes. It was terrible. I hated *Requiem for a Nun*, both as a book and as a play.

Hughes: In that play he has this Negro woman who is going to her death for having committed some sort of murder, I believe, which she felt was justified, and the lawyer or the judge is talking to her, and she says she doesn't mind dying, in essence, because she is going to Heaven. And this southern white lawyer, judge, or whatever he is, says, "What would a woman like you do in Heaven?" And she says, "Ah kin work." Now, that is the most false line in literature regarding the Negro, because no Negro in God's world ever thought of Heaven as a place to work. He just doesn't understand the Negro mind, that's all.

Kazin: But as a writer, and a very good writer, do you think it's necessary to understand something in order to create a good character? Is understanding, in the deepest human, civic sense, the brotherly sense, is this really necessary for artistic creation?

Hughes: To create a believable character, you certainly have to have a certain amount of understanding. And this woman in *Requiem* became so unreal to me.

Kazin: Yes, I agree with you about that case, but let's consider Dilsey. She was also a southern Negro, and a character who would cause me the deepest pain and chagrin if I were a Negro; nevertheless, I believe she is a great creation.

Hughes: Yes, I don't doubt that.

Kazin: Well, you can't understand Negroes on one page and forget them on another. Because understanding is always the same. It's typical Faulkner, who reveals his limitations in nonartistic areas. But as a writer, once in a while, something is created which comes out of the deepest, most unconscious sense of love.

Let me give you an instance: you may remember that the fourth part of *The Sound and the Fury* opens with Dilsey coming out on the porch. She is portrayed in a typical hand-me-down costume of a woman who has worked for fifty years for this rotting family, the Compsons. The costume itself is demeaning, but the description of Dilsey, everything about her, is of such an extraordinary artistic beauty and intensity that I can never read it without being moved to tears. The thing has been made flesh, and she is there, we know her. This is something very different, I submit, from one hundred and one moralizings that you might get from well-meaning northern "liberals."

All I'm saying is on this page—and on many pages of that book—he really created a human being, and even when he sees her without understanding in his mind, there was tremendous understanding in his heart.

Hughes: Yes, and I think another fine southern white writer, Carson McCullers, is also successful in creating character.

Hansberry: I think, Mr. Kazin, that you may be imposing on my earlier remarks a lack of dimension that wasn't there. What I was trying to say is exactly the opposite of what you emphasized. I am not concerned with doing away with the mere traditional paraphernalia of the inexpressive, crude Negro character. That is not the point. I myself, very arbitrarily, after deliberate thought, chose to write about the Negro working class, although I come from the middle class. Eventually, I think more of our writers are going to begin to deal with the Negro middle class, which most white people don't know exists.

But we're not trying to escape from some image of truth. When you spoke a moment ago, you seemed to suggest we would be satisfied if the image were glossier, more dressed-up. That is not the point. When language is handled truly, and Negro speech used with fidelity—which doesn't have to do with the dropping of g's and misplacing of verbs—when the essence of character is as true and as complicated as—as character should be, whatever character you're dealing with, only then ought we to be satisfied.

There is a comedy line in my play, where the young daughter says to one of her suitors, "You think this about women because this is what you got from all the novels that men have written." Obviously, novelists have created some memorable women characters. But I am altogether certain that in regard to the inner truths of character, the woman character will always partially elude the male writer. Of course, women, like Negroes, I'm afraid, accept many images of themselves that come from literature, and start to act those roles, but there are other truths, which can be found only by studying people in depth.

You mentioned Carson McCullers. There's a scene in *Member of the Wedding*, when the young Negro nephew of Bernice is being chased by a lynch mob, and she takes the young white boy whom she has nursed all his life—he's about to die, I think, because of some constitutional weakness—and this woman's preoccupation is with that child. I happen to think that it was a lovely play and I believe Bernice's character, but we are now talking about these extra nuances, and my point is that the intimacy of knowledge which the Negro may have of white Americans does not exist in the reverse.

Kazin: That's absolutely true.

Hansberry: William Faulkner has never in his life sat in on a discussion in a Negro home where there were all Negroes. It is physically impossible. He has never heard the nuances of hatred, of total contempt from his most devoted servant and his most beloved friend, although she means every word when she's talking to him, and will tell him profoundly intimate things. But he has never heard the truth of it. For you, this is a fulfilling image, because you haven't either. I can understand that. Obviously Faulkner is a monumental talent, but there are other dimensions of that character, and as I would create her, or Jim, or Langston, there would be a world of difference, and it's this we're trying to get to. I *want* white writers to begin to create Negro characters. We need it desperately.

Baldwin: Lorraine's point is very important. We have to look more carefully at the characters created by Faulkner, or by Carson McCullers. Lorraine mentioned that absolutely incredible moment when this woman's nephew is being chased by a lynch mob, and she's worried about this little boy. That scene doesn't reveal anything about the truth of Negro life, but a great deal about the state of mind of the white southern woman who wrote it.

Regardless of Faulkner's talent, the thing I will not settle for is that this image is maintained. Southerners have an illusion and they cling to it desperately; in fact, the whole American Republic does. These characters come out of a compulsion. Dilsey is Faulkner's proof that the Negro—who, as Langston points out, has been worked and worked and worked and for nothing, who has been lynched and burned and stolen from for generations—has forgiven him. The reason the walls in the South cannot come down, the reason that the panic is too great for the walls to come down, is because when they do, the truth will come out. And it's perfectly true, as Lorraine says, you can't know what I'm talking about, if you haven't been in a home with all Negroes together, if you haven't listened to Dilsey at home—who might be my mother—and heard what she says about the people she works for—and what is more important than that, not only what she says, but what she knows. And she knows much more about them than they will ever know about her, and there's a very good reason for this.

Faulkner has never sat in a Negro kitchen while the Negroes were talking about him, but we have been sitting around for generations, in kitchens and everywhere else, while everybody talks about us, and this creates a very great difference. It also creates—now speaking specifically for the Negro writer—a very great advantage. While I was living abroad in France, somebody said something—it's something, I guess, the French say all the time—but this day it was said to me and it rang a bell. He said, "If you want to know what's happening in the house, ask the maid." And it occurred to me that in this extraordinary house, I'm the maid. [*laughter*]

Hansberry: Which is a different relationship, because the employer doesn't go to the maid's house.

You see, people get this confused. They think that the alienation is equal on both sides. It isn't. We have been washing everybody's underwear for three hundred years. We know when you're not clean. [*laughter*]

Kazin: I accept everything you say, Miss Hansberry, but I wonder if you would allow me to try to persuade you that it's still slightly irrelevant to the point I was making.

Hansberry: Oh, then I'm sorry.

Kazin: No, no; as I was irrelevant to your point, you're being irrelevant to mine. This is the way people learn to talk to each other.

My point is this: I don't for a moment mean to say that the truth about Negro life has been accomplished, to use the biblical phrase, forever. I'm talking about what has actually been done as art.

This is an artistic question, it's not a social question. I know that Negroes have been maids, they have been the drawers of water and the hewers of wood. They have been the slaves and slaves do all the work.

But my point is this: it's something Edward Hopper, the painter, once said, which has stuck in my mind: "Thought is endless, but the picture exists in space and time."

Every Negro walking the streets, every American, is full of the past, the present and the future. No book, either his book or a white man's book, can satisfy him about the truth. Because the truth is not only about what he has and what he is, but what he wants to become, what he wants America to become. Therefore, there is no book that exists right now that in the deepest sense can be satisfying to him.

But a book does exist in space and time. Those distortions of Shylock, or of Dilsey, or of anyone else, horrible as they are to our conscience, nevertheless exist as such. Dostoyevsky, Tolstoy, Melville, all the great novelists, have written the most frightfully distorted anti-Negro, anti-Japanese, anti-Semitic, anti-French stereotypes.

Do American characters come off much better, in American fiction as a whole? Not always in contemporary American fiction. They are portrayed uniformly as lechers, sadists, masturbators, idiots, bourgeois decadents, and the rest. This is a society that is full of self-disgust. It doesn't know what it wants or what it believes, and it's constantly getting rid of its own guilt about its own unsatisfied wantings in that way.

My point is that a book exists in itself, as such, and perhaps—it's hard for a writer to admit—perhaps, all of us who write books are not so busy mirroring life, as we always think we are, as creating life.

For example, Tolstoy created a great book like *War and Peace* and then looked about him and found out something about the actual conditions of serfdom and contemporary Russia; he discovered, what his wife had told him beforehand, that the two things—the thing he had created and the world around him—had nothing to do with each other in any immediate sense.

This is a terrible paradox. But the fact remains that there are no people anywhere like the people in our books or anybody else's book.

Simple is delicious and wise and right because he is a product of Mr. Hughes's imagination. Many people have gone into making him up. He is no one else, he is Simple. This is true of any true character.

It's even true of a good autobiography like Jimmy Baldwin's *Notes of a Native Son*, where we find that the author himself becomes his own myth, as Thoreau said about himself in *Walden.*

I am not trying to say that Mr. Faulkner is the last word on Negroes in America. God forbid. What I am saying is that something was created, something was not just being talked about, hopeful and wishful, all the time. Something that is true, I think, as such.

Baldwin: We are talking somewhat at cross purposes, because I cannot disagree with what you say.

Kazin: But there isn't any argument. We are reflecting on a problem which has many facets. I don't disagree with you about this thing at all. How can I? What is there to disagree about? Do you think I would say that Dilsey is the truth about Negroes in America? That would be a horrible untruth.

Baldwin: All right, I accept the proposition that perhaps we are not so much reflecting life as trying to create it—but let's talk now not about books but about this country.

I'm talking now about the role of the Negro, and what seems to me to be at stake is that somehow the Negro contains a key to something about America which no one has yet found out about—which no one has yet faced. Contains maybe the key to life. I don't know; I don't want to talk about it in such mythical terms.

My point is that there is a tremendous resistance on the part of the entire public to know whatever it is, to deal with whatever this image means to them.

Hentoff: I wonder how many doors that key unlocks.

Langston Hughes has mentioned the urge to whiteness among some Negro writers. This leads, of course, to assimilationist novels, but I wonder if it doesn't also lead, without complete realization on the part of some Negro writers, politicians, and others, to a desire for equality within the white value-structure. Has there been enough questioning of this within Negro writing?

Baldwin: I feel that there's been far too little.

Hentoff: In other words, equal for what?

Baldwin: Equal for what, yes. You know, there's always been a very great question in my mind of why in the world—after all I'm living in this society and I've had a good look at it—what makes you think I want to be accepted?

Hansberry: Into this.

Baldwin: Into this.

Hansberry: Maybe something else.

Baldwin: It's not a matter of acceptance or tolerance. We've got to sit down and rebuild this house.

Hansberry: Yes, quickly.

Baldwin: Very quickly, and we have to do it together. This is to you, Alfred, speaking now, just as a writer. You know, in order to be a writer you have to demand the impossible, and I know I'm demanding the impossible. It has to be—but I also know it has to be done. You see what I mean?

Kazin: Yes, I see entirely what you mean, but let's talk about this presence of the Negro in American history for a moment, because when we really get into the question of the white writers' portraits of Negroes we're talking about this larger question. Maybe that way we can come back to the difficulty we had earlier.

This presence of the Negro in American civilization, I said before, is the central fact about our moral history. And the conflict in the American heart, which exists in Negroes as well as among whites, comes out of a constant tension between what this country is ideally supposed to mean and what it actually has been as such. The problem has become more and more catastrophic and dangerous because of the growing world anxiety about possible world annihilation. Suddenly you begin to realize that people who don't treat their fellow-citizens well are, in a sense, building up a bonfire for everyone else in the same way, as is likely to happen in Africa before our generation is over.

At the same time, this very tension in America between the ideal moral purpose and the reality, also creates two things. One, it creates the fact that we never know quite what we want, as you yourself admitted before. You said you weren't quite sure you wanted equality to disrupt you. And secondly, it creates the white man's constant bewilderment between what he feels abstractly to be his duty, and the actuality of a society in which human beings were held as slaves, and in which, twenty-five years later, these people were sitting in Washington as senators.

So, you have this enormous comedy of American pretension and American actuality, leaving the white man, who is also here, in a constant bewilderment. But whereas you spoke of guilt, I think it's more a sense of an intellectual paradox. Because in order to justify his own presence in this country, the white American has to understand the Negro's place, but to understand it fully, he has to make a gesture of imagination, morally—even religiously, in the deepest sense of the word; yet very often he is debased by his own culture and kept from making this gesture. But this is what happened again and again. This is what happened with the Civil War.

Let's put it this way: who in American history among the white writers or white men did make the fullest effort of imagination in your point of view?

It wasn't the Abolitionists; it wasn't Colonel Higginson, leading Negro troops in the Civil War. Who was it? Who would you say it was? I think it's been no one. I think it's a fight which has constantly been in process, constantly going on. But nowhere, in no particular point in space and time can you say this has been understood fully and deeply.

Hughes: To go back to Jimmy Baldwin's point, at the First Negro Writer's Conference, a year and a half ago, and published in *The American Negro Writer and His Roots*, is a speech by Julian Mayfield, one of our better young Negro novelists. Speaking of the examination of American values by American Negro writers, this is what he says:

"This new approach is suggested by the Negro mother, who having lost one of her sons in the Korean adventures, was heard to remark, 'I don't care if the Army is integrated, next time I want to know what kind of war my boy is being taken into.'

"In the same sense, the Negro writer is being very gently nudged toward a rather vague thing called the mainstream of American literature. This trend would also seem to be based on common sense. But before plunging into it, he owes it to the future of his art to analyze the contents of the American mainstream, to determine the full significance of his commitment to it.

"He may decide that though the music is sweet, he would rather play in another orchestra; or to place himself in the position of the Black convict in *The Defiant Ones*, he may decide that he need not necessarily share the fate of his white companion, who after all proffers the hand of friendship a little late. The Negro writer may conclude that his best salvation lies in escaping the narrow national orbit, artistic, cultural, and political, and soaring into the space of more universal experience."

Hentoff: In this regard I'd like to bring up one further thing before we conclude, concerning the future.

In an otherwise rather strange book, *The Negro Novel in America*, by Boone, he has statistics showing that of sixty-two Negro novelists writing between 1853 and 1952, forty, or two-thirds, published only one novel, eleven more published only two, and only eleven have published more than two.

Is this largely due to economic discrimination and the like, or is it due to a self-limitation to a single theme, which could only be expressed once?

Hughes: My guess would be that it was largely due to the limitation of thematic material, and secondarily due to the fact of economics, due to the fact that the Negro people themselves, of whom there are now about twenty million in our country, have not one single publishing house.

We discussed a while ago, you remember, the limitation placed upon the number of Negro novels that can be published in a year.

The same thing is true in the theater. Do we have one serious Negro dramatic theater that belongs to us, that is managed by us, that is directed by us? No. The nearest thing we have to it is Karamu Theater in Cleveland, which is a part of a settlement house. Formerly it was largely Negro attended, but it does such beautiful productions that now more than two-thirds of its personnel is white, because white people come from all over to work in Karamu. They used to do plays by Negro writers almost entirely, about Negro life, but not anymore. The trend is to integrate everything, so that you kill yourself with an integrated cast.

The trend toward integration in some cases, particularly in the folk field, in my opinion, can go too far, in that it is damaging artistically. For example, I narrated a gospel song program in Chicago, a winter or two ago, with Mahalia Jackson, and do you know that the people who presented the program integrated the gospel singers? Mahalia listened and gathered her fur coat about her at rehearsal, and went home with the parting shot, "Y'all ain't got the beat."

There is a tendency at the moment, in jazz, to integrate every combo, which is wonderful, sociologically speaking. But very often the white players who may come into a combo will not have that same beat, let us say, that Jonah Jones has, you know what I mean?

Hansberry: Are we just skirting around a larger political question in an effort to avoid it, perhaps? Because, what are we faced with? We are faced with the fact that due to these three hundred years of the experience of Black people in the Western hemisphere—not only in the United States, though it was least successful in the United States—a possible difference of ultimate cultural attitudes now exists as a reality, so that in Mayfield's statement that you read just now, there are the tones of Negro nationalism, articulated in a far more sophisticated and pointed way than years ago. The question is openly being raised today among all Negro intellectuals, among all politically conscious Negroes: is it necessary to integrate oneself into a burning house? And we can't quite get away from it.

There are real and true things existing in the consciences of Negroes today which have to do with why, on two occasions, the American Negro delegate at the United Nations disassociated herself from her government, when we refused to vote for an Algerian Algeria, when we refused to vote for the end of colonialism. When the most compromised element in the Negro population, from which these people are drawn—I mean no offense personally to that lady, I don't even know who she is, but there is only a certain section of Negro life that is allowed to represent us—when they are moved to disassociate themselves in an international hall, and when ten thousand Negroes will come out to greet Fidel Castro in Harlem and wave at him and cheer him every time he shows his head, this is an indication of what is going on. This dichotomy is going to become more articulate and we are going to see it more and more in Negro literature.

Hughes: I would like to say that in Lorraine Hansberry's play the thing that comes through is that, in spite of all these differences and difficulties, *this is our house.* That was their Chicago. This is our country. And I for one am intensely concerned and fascinated by the things that go on here.

Some people have asked me why Richard Wright didn't come home and why he lived in Europe, and why some of our better Negro artists and writers are living over there. My feeling is that they have a perfect right to live wherever they want to, and to get away from the tensions of the American scene, if they wish. It just happens that it interests me, it doesn't upset me particularly. I like to indulge in these racial arguments and fights and discussions, such as we are having here, about what to do about all this. And I stayed here and I live here because I like it, quite frankly, and I think that we can make out of our country something wonderful and quite beautiful, in which eventually we can even integrate gospel songs and have them sung well.

Capouya: I'd like to raise a question regarding the sit-in movements in the South. Certainly, a Negro ought to be able to eat where everybody else does; since he's a brother of mine, obviously, that's the first step, before I can be free to eat where I want, too.

But a couple of years ago, when the March on Washington was made, the Negro leaders were saying, "After all, you people are fighting for your lives, you're fighting against the Russians. Why don't you admit us to that status of citizenship where we can help you? Why don't you admit us to the community so we can pull our weight?"

Well, that's a lot of nonsense as far as I'm concerned, and if that's what they're out to get, if they want to get atomized at the same time we do, we'll all be holding hands in Christian brotherly love when the bomb falls. Well, that is stupid.

I would be delighted if the Rev. Martin Luther King would think one step ahead of himself in this sense, and not feel that civil rights for Negroes in the South is the be-all and the end-all. It may be a tactical first step, but if it isn't to move to a higher plane, then I'm not interested.

Hughes: Well, I heard Rev. Martin Luther King say at a meeting not long ago that perhaps it was the Negro's destiny to save America for itself. And another rather distinguished Negro leader disagreed and said, "Well, first, certainly, we've got to save it for ourselves."

Baldwin: I'm delighted that we've got around to this very thorny area. It has always seemed to me that one of the great handicaps of this country in its dealings with the world is that it doesn't know anything about the rest of the world, not in the sense that a Frenchman doesn't know anything about China, but in the sense that it has always avoided knowing those things—I'm afraid you have to call them tragic or black or deep or mysterious or inexorable—which are at the very bottom of life.

One of the reasons that Cuba has been such a disaster is because people in America do not know that just down the road Mexicans and Cubans, and a whole lot of other people in a place called South America, are not only starving, which you can tell by statistics, but are living there. And they don't like to be mistreated. And one of the reasons that we don't know this is our evasion in the world, which is exactly the evasion that we've made in this country for over one hundred years, to date it only from the emancipation. Ultimately, it's a moral evasion of oneself, which really menaces—and this cannot be overstated—the very future of this country. That is why there is so little time to save this house; after all, one can always jump, that's not the problem. I don't want to be atomized with you or with anybody, and I don't want anybody else atomized, either.

But the price for American survival is really the most extraordinary and speedy metamorphosis, and I don't know if they're going to make it. But we've got to realize that when people say God, they don't always mean the Protestant God. There are people on the other side of the world who have been worshipping somebody else for thousands and thousands of years. I do think that anybody who really cares about this must insist on nothing more or less than a moral revolution. Because nothing can be patched up. It's got to be remade.

Capouya: That's so true, but I want to object to something said before, the notion of the white man's guilty secret, and that the Negro has got to be where he is because we have to know where the bottom of the heap is. That's not true: the Negro is where he is because of the long history of slavery, economic rejection, and so on.

Hughes: At the moment I have a play which I hope will be on Broadway next season. The play was originally entirely about Negroes—about the gospel churches. However, with the current trend towards integration, some backers said that they would not put money into an entirely Negro-cast play.

Well, the leading lady in my play, who makes a great deal of money out of selling holy water, worked up to having a chauffeur; in my script it never occurred to me that he should be one color or another. I thought of him as a Negro chauffeur because most Negroes who can afford chauffeurs have Negro chauffeurs, but not all. However, when the demand came for integration of my cast, I said, "Well, always in white plays the chauffeurs are Negroes; let's make the chauffeur in my play white, which would not be untrue to life." Adam Powell, I believe, has a white or Japanese chauffeur. Jules Bledsoe, when he was star of *Showboat* had a white chauffeur, and when people asked him why he had a white chauffeur, he said, "So people can tell the chauffeur from myself." [*laughter*]

Well, at any rate, it's not too unusual that some colored people do have white chauffeurs, and some have white maids, even in Harlem. And so, I thought that would be nice and a little novel to Broadway. Let's have a white chauffeur. Do you know that everybody said, "Oh, the American public wouldn't accept that." So, my play is still not integrated.

Hansberry: I gather we are close to conclusion, but, Mr. Kazin, I'd like to pick up something that you said, and to try and bring it up to date for myself.

You said, I thought rather beautifully, that the Negro question tends to go to the heart of various missorted American agonies, beginning with slavery itself. I am profoundly concerned that in these one hundred years since the Civil War very few of our countrymen have really believed that their Federal Union and the defeat of the slavocracy and the negation of slavery as an institution is an admirable fact of American life. It is possible today to get enormous books that are coming out on the Civil War and go through to the back of them, and not find the word slavery, let alone Negro.

We've been trying very hard in America to pretend that this greatest conflict didn't even have at its base the only issue that was significant. Person after person will write a book today and insist that slavery was not the issue. They tell you that it was fought for economic reasons, as if that economy were not based on slavery. People spend volumes discussing the battles of the Civil War and which army was crossing the river at five minutes to two and how their swords were hanging, but we have tried to get rid of the slavery issue. Ever since *Gone with the Wind*, it has been an accepted part of our culture to describe the slave system in terms of beautiful ladies in big fat dresses, screaming that their houses have been burned down by the awful Yankees. But when someone asked me to write ninety minutes of television drama on slavery, not a propaganda piece, but, I hope, a serious treatment of family relationship, by a slaveowning family and their slaves, this was considered controversial. This has never been done.

Those millions of Americans who went out only a month or two ago, presumably voted for a Federal president, but our culture does not really respect the fact that if the North had not won, if the Union forces had not triumphed over slavery, this country that we're talking about would exist only in imagination. Americans today are too ashamed and frightened to take a position even on this.

Baldwin: Yes, this breaks the heart; this is the most sinister thing about it. Not that it happened, not that it's wrong, but that nobody wants to admit that it happened. And until this admission is made, nothing can be done.

Kazin: How much time do we have?

Hentoff: Is there anything you want to add?

Kazin: We should begin the interview.[2]

Notes

1. Editor's note: The original audio of this interview is also available in the Pacifica Radio Archives.

2. Editor's note: In the original audio, Hentoff responds by saying, "I was just going to say we're going to end at the beginning. I hope we can talk again," before closing out the interview.

Interview with Lorraine Hansberry, Leo Genn, Reginald Gardiner, and Elizabeth Seal

Mitch Miller / 1961

Broadcast on *The Mitch Miller Show*, WCBS Radio, March 25, 1961. Printed by permission of the Mitch Miller Estate.[1]

Mitch Miller: This is Mitch Miller. Saints and sinners, *A Raisin in the Sun*, and who knows, maybe even talking wallpaper. We may very well be hearing about all these matters and more from my four intriguing supper companions here at Sardi's East. [. . .] Without further ado, may we have their names please?

Announcer: Thank you Mitch. This is the Mitch Miller Show, forty-five minutes of off-the-cuff conversation, from the New York theatrical restaurant Sardi's East. Joining Mitch's private party this evening are these well-known figures of the international stage and screen world. The distinguished British actor Leo Genn currently heading the cast of the smash Broadway hit *The Devil's Advocate*. Lovely Elizabeth Seal, another British performer who has taken Broadway by storm in the long running musical *Irma la Douce*. Lorraine Hansberry, the American playwright whose hit of the 1959 stage season *A Raisin in the Sun* will shortly be opening in a screen version, also written by Miss Hansberry. And yet another British favorite, this time one who hails from Hollywood, the witty and always surprising, Reginald Gardner. You'll meet them all after this message.

■ ■ ■

MM: Lorraine Hansberry, it looks as if the English have us outnumbered this evening. Don't be alarmed. These redcoats are all friendly. . . .

[*Miller talks to Elizabeth Seal, Leo Genn, and Reginald Gardiner about their views of America and baseball.*]

MM: Well, Lorraine Hansberry, one aspect of American life that all of us aren't completely happy about is our race question, but you've gone a long way towards easing it and . . .

Lorraine Hansberry: [*laughs*]

MM: Yes! I know, by writing a great play that depicts a Negro family as people with problems much like everybody else's. And now Columbia is presenting your movie version. Tell me Lorraine, were you able to keep the story intact in the transition to the films?

LH: Yes, basically, I think it emerges well that the . . . what I call the arc of the drama is still there and, in some ways, a little more forceful.

MM: Closeups help.

LH: Yes, yes, Dan Petrie is extraordinary.

MM: Did you have to make many concessions to Hollywood taboos in transposing such a realistic story to the screen?

LH: I worried about it enormously. I . . . was dedicated to the proposition that no freethinking human being ever sells anything to Hollywood. And carried on famously, all of the—anyone who had anything to say. And then after any number of conversations with people that I really respected, we decided that perhaps, with this and that effort on the part of everyone that it would be possible, since it has happened before, to once again make a reasonably good Hollywood film. And I didn't see it until a few weeks ago. And I'm very grateful. I think they did that.

MM: Well, it's most unusual for an author to say that they did right by her.

LH: I know, and I'm glad you asked me now and not two weeks ago when I didn't know.

MM: Well, you've had a number of firsts with *Raisin*, Lorraine, a Drama Circle Critics' Best Play Award with your first produced show. And it was the first on Broadway for a woman playwright of your race. What theme will you be applying your gifted typewriter to next? Do you have any idea yet?

LH: Well, as a theme I don't. I'm very much intrigued with the world. All of it. And what people are doing in it. And the different kinds of situations that we get ourselves into. And I don't know ultimately what will emerge.

MM: That's a broad canvas.

LH: [*laughs*]

[*Miller talks to Leo Genn about his prior career as lawyer, his shift to becoming an actor, his parents' view of his career, and British law.*]

■ ■ ■

[*Miller talks to Elizabeth Seal about* Irma la Douce, *being the only woman in the cast, and the relationship between British and American shows. Miller then talks to Reginald Gardiner about Beatrice Lillie, Eva Gabor, Gardiner's shift to becoming an actor, and his parents' view of his career.*]

MM: Well, Lorraine Hansberry, in *Raisin in the Sun*, as I recall, there is a conflict between faith as represented by the mother and skepticism as voiced by the medical student daughter. Were you as a playwright suggesting that Negroes need both in their struggle in equality?

LH: I was suggesting in terms of these characters. I wasn't suggesting very much about what Negroes need or don't need in that moment. I was dealing with two individuals who were having a problem in that family. And what she is articulating in this instance, the daughter, is not skepticism but pure outright outspoken atheism. She is an atheist. I happen to share her viewpoint. That is pretty much what the scene means that within this family these two people both representing different orientations in life don't agree. And the mother imposes the only thing she knows how to impose, which is a rather tyrannical statement of "this is what I believe, and this is what will be." Because she's a marvelous woman, you see, really, in most ways, it's a very moving moment. It doesn't make her point of view right.

MM: Lorraine, gentlemen, and Miss Seal, I see we have some network business at hand but don't go away because I'll be back in just a few moments with more questions for our visitors.

■ ■ ■

MM: Lorraine Hansberry, we had the star of both the stage and screen versions of *Raisin in the Sun*, Sidney Poitier, on the broadcast a few weeks ago, and he was of the opinion that there have been noticeable breakthroughs for Negro actors away from stereotyped parts. Do you have the same feeling on that situation?

LH: I suppose in some measure. Equity has been very forthright, I gather, from actors, in the question of trying to do a few things. But, frankly, I think that the theater tends to reflect American life, rather than the other way around, which we theater folks sometimes would almost imply, you know, that the rest of the country is following us. And, since things are really rather shabby in American life as regards the Negro question, it isn't much better in the theater. There have been one or two things that are admirable.

[*Miller asks Leo Genn about* Devil's Advocate *and World War II. Miller asks Elizabeth Seal about her husband, Peter Townsend, his name, and whether he gets kidded about her part as a prostitute.*]

MM: Well, Lorraine Hansberry, you're married to a songwriter and music publisher, Bob Nemiroff. How is he standing up under his wife's success as a playwright?

LH: Very well. He's very good at that sort of thing. As a matter of fact, he's a producer now. To be. In September. But he . . . it's admirable in the sense that he didn't think it had any contradiction to what he wanted to do in the world that his wife wanted to write.

Elizabeth Seal: That's nice.

MM: Have you changed your way of life very much, Lorraine, or do you both still occupy that well-known Bleecker Street walk-up in Greenwich Village?

LH: No, we don't, we use it for other things. Sort of a subsidiary place. But the world has changed life for us, you know. You don't get a chance after your name has been in the paper twice, really, to just go on. That's a lot of romance. It hasn't been the same. I would like to say that it has, because I liked it before. [*laughs*]

[*Miller asks Reginald Gardiner about growing up near Wimbledon, what his first imitation was, and whether he minds living away from England. Miller asks Leo whether he's tempted to move to Hollywood and about censorship in the arts.*]

■ ■ ■

[*Miller asks Elizabeth Seal about* Irma la Douce, *the injury that prevented her from becoming a ballet dancer, and her shift to a career as a musical actor. Miller asks Leo Genn about his first meeting of Elizabeth Seal and jokes about Seal's legs. Miller asks Reginald Gardiner about doing another revue with Beatrice Lillie.*]

MM: Lorraine Hansberry, I understand that your early aim in life was to become a painter. How serious were you, really, about painting?

LH: I wasn't serious at all, my mother was—to borrow your experience [*referring to Reginald Gardiner's earlier story about his parents' view of his career*] which happens to be true. It was the only thing I was ever trained for. I've been through most of the art schools in the Western hemisphere [*laughs*] and . . . with nothing to show for it. I don't know why, there was a point in Chicago when they would come around, you know, and say they're giving Saturday morning classes for the high school students at the Art Institute. My mother thought that was terribly uplifting and there I was the next Saturday.

MM: Simple as that!

LH: [*Laughs*]

Reginald Gardner: I have to say, at the moment, Mitch, we're covered with parents, aren't we?

LH: Terribly.

RG: —influencing our careers of what we don't want to do—

MM: Yes, but we all landed on our feet somehow. [*several people speak at once*]

LH: I must say, in all fairness though that I come from a business family, you know. In the middle West. Which means that down to the last genera-tions, that's what you're supposed to do. Even the girls, you find something to do in business if you're going to not just settle down. And they went along rather well to change the story for a change with the fact that I wanted to do something quite as strange as write, ultimately.

[*Miller asks Leo Genn about doing musical parts and coronation broadcasts.*]

■ ■ ■

MM: Ladies and gentlemen, I'm sorry to say that the time has run out on us here at Sardi's East and we have to give our microphones back to the CBS Radio Network. It's been a delight having all of you. Leo Genn, I'm looking forward to seeing you joust with the angels in *The Devil's Advocate* and a long run to you. Come back soon. Elizabeth Seal, give an extra pirouette for me in your next performance of *Irma la Douce* and my regards to the real Peter Townsend. Thank you for coming. Reginald Gardiner, it was wonder-ful to have you back again for this marvelous visit. Don't stay away so long next time. The wallpaper here at Sardi's East has been complaining. And to you Lorraine Hansberry, the loudest of critical kudos to Columbia's screen version of *A Raisin in the Sun* which opens here March 29 and in Detroit March 31. To station WNIF, serving metropolitan Hartford and Manchester Connecticut, welcome aboard the CBS Radio Network as our newest affili-ate. And to our listeners, I'll be back next week at this time with some more people you'd like to meet. Until then, this is Mitch Miller from Sardi's East saying good night and have a good week. Thank you.

Note

1. Editor's note: Self-prepared transcript. The full audio version of this interview is available in the permanent media collection of the Paley Center for Media, New York.

Interview with Lorraine Hansberry

Patricia Marx / 1961

Recorded on March 30, 1961, and broadcast on WEVD-AM, August 4, 1961. Printed by permission of WNYC Archive Collections.[1]

Patricia Marx: Miss Hansberry, I would like to begin by discussing some of the problems you raised in *A Raisin in the Sun*, and I wonder, so that everyone will know what we are talking about, if you would be kind enough to describe the story briefly.

Lorraine Hansberry: Well, what it involves is an examination of a family on the South Side of Chicago, where I was born, who belonged to the lower classes, a family of domestic workers, who, I hope, are fairly typical of people who think that there is something more to do with your life than accept it as it is. The young son becomes what we call the pivot of drama and his ambition is to—accepting American values in their totality—to become a successful businessman. Very simply, the mother and his wife want to simply get a home, so there is a conflict between the two. In terms of a statement, I think what this play tries to say is that we really don't have very much in the world at all if we allow any aspect of money values to transcend the requirements that are necessary for human dignity.

PM: You said that the play is a great deal about dreams—dreams deferred, dreams realized. Are there certain kinds of dreams that are right and certain kinds of dreams that are wrong?

LH: In my opinion?

PM: Yes.

LH: Yes. [*laughs*] Which of course is my opinion. I, for one, simply can't get terribly excited about anyone who wants to commit their lives to just making money as an end in itself. I can't understand it. If someone can give me an appreciation of it then perhaps I would, but at this moment in my life I happen to think a life that has as its end something of service and purpose—it really doesn't matter whether you are making shoes or writing books or plays or being an engineer—but has some end product—is a far more substantial life than someone who has somehow gotten led into the way of thinking that tells him that money is the reason why we live.

PM: The younger people in the family were concerned with material benefits, weren't they—material goods? Yet you were saying that perhaps the message in the play is that this kind of concern is not enough. Is that correct?

LH: Well, I think that all values ultimately come out of a materialistic approach to life, yes. That there is no such thing as simply saying to people, "now be nice." That you can't be nice if you are living miserably and you can't be anything except very much concerned about how to live better. So, to that extent, all life I think has a materialistic base under it. In other words, it is marvelous for people to have a clean home. It is irrelevant for them to have two television sets. There is a vast difference and I hope that kind of materialism isn't linked with what I'm talking about.

PM: So, after the bare minimum is reached then there are other things that are more important.

LH: Yes, I think so.

PM: Is Mama the embodiment of this kind of ideal then? She seems to value principle above profit.[2]

LH: Oh yes, yes, yes. Much of what she has to say and much of her inspiration in this family is toward a principled end of the best kind, I think. That you can't just dismiss everything because you have an objective to do something in the world. That you have to emerge as a human being of stature. That's why I have characterized her in my own mind as a great woman.

PM: Yes, well, with this emphasis on material gain that, say, Walter the central figure has, do you think by necessity there will be a loss of this kind of moral backbone and old-fashioned virtue?

LH: You mean if they become a middle-class family?

PM: Yes.

LH: No, I don't think so. I think there are other dangers, but I don't think particularly that the middle class loses its notion of virtue. [*laughs*] It loses other things. The transition may mean a certain attraction ultimately to a lot of the meaningless parts of comfort. That one must have two cars, or a car of a certain make. That the children must dress a certain way. That— and particularly in terms of Negro questions, of course—a tendency which already exists in the Negro middle class to want to disassociate the middle class from what is really the most exciting and vibrant part of Negro culture, which is that of the working classes: the blues, the spirituals, the great folk art and culture of the Negro people, you see. They have had in the past—it's beginning to diminish. It's now artistic, you see. They get a little arty now and appreciate it in reverse, which always happens, like you know German meter has to become an art song in the concert hall before everyone can universally say, "My word, isn't this marvelous." Well, that happens.

PM: I know that you said that science will bring more rewards for our generation than mysticism. Does this mean that you place faith in a very rational scientific approach to existence now rather than the traditional—[3]

LH: Yes.

PM: —religious believing of the mama?

LH: Yes, I do. I think that—you see, I don't think anything new has happened since rationalism burst forth with the Renaissance and the subsequent developments in rational thought—that the only time we revert back to mystical ideas which includes most contemporary orthodox religious views, in my opinion, is because we simply are confronted with some things we don't yet understand, so we start all over again what people were doing two thousand years ago. Saying well, you see, because we don't know thus and thus, therefore some other agent that we will never find—I don't find how that follows. I think that it's simply a question of things we don't yet know.

PM: Yet, in the case of Mama, she gets so much sustenance from this kind of faith.

LH: Yes, yes. Well, this is one of the glories of man that the inventiveness of the human mind and the human spirit that whenever life doesn't seem to give an answer, we create them. It gives us strength. I don't attack people who are religious at all, as you can tell from the play. I rather admire this human quality to make our own crutches as long as we need them. The only thing I am saying is that once we can walk, you know, then drop them.

PM: Well then, actually, you believe in a kind of increase in moral and philosophical strength by the use of reason, don't you?

LH: Oh, yes. I don't believe there will be ever—I don't think a time will ever come when we will dismiss the human spirit. I don't think there is any contradiction. We don't need mysticism to exalt man. Man exalts himself by his achievements and his power to rationalize—or, excuse me—his power to reason. [*laughter*] His rationalization has its benefits, too. I don't know if he could get along without that either.

PM: It's very interesting because in the play as you write it, the younger generation is no stronger even with their advanced reason. They don't seem as strong as the mama. Is this intentional on your part?

LH: Oh, well. But actually, they are, you see. In other words, I think it would be a very quick inclination of Beneatha to wish to function as a citizen of the world, you know, and to go to the United Nations and try to affect the political life of her nation rather than pray for peace. I think this is an enormous development and a very positive one over the past. I don't mean that Mama wasn't an effective force in the past. She was, obviously. She left the South. She felt she had to do something. But the less dependent attitude on providence I think is a triumph. I couldn't say that too strongly. People say that there is no difference between today and the past. Well, of course there is. Of course, each generation brings a triumph of rationality.[4] There's an enormous difference between the Greeks and the Romans. There was a time when people thought it was perfectly alright to hold slaves. Even though we exalt, you know, so-called Greek democracy today, the fact of the matter was it was a slave society, and today we would not think that this is a proper thing to admit to—even if it was going on secretly as it does, or covertly, in certain parts of the world. Human morality now negates that, you see. You can take much smaller evidences. Forty years ago nobody thought woman should vote. Today they do. You couldn't really run for office today saying that you were going to stamp out the suffrage of women. Those are all achievements, and we rarely think of it that way.

PM: Dubious achievements [*laughs*] in this case.

LH: Dubious? Yeah?

PM: So you have the faith then that, with reason—or you have a reasoned supposition here—that through increased rationality men will behave better toward men

LH: Oh yes, I think there's been every evidence of it in history despite the rise of Germany and Nazism and all of that. Even so.

PM: Well, this Beneatha, who is the sister of the young man who has these dreams of financial success, seems to look to Africa for a sense of identity. Do you find that this is appealing to you?[5]

LH: To me personally?

PM: Yes.

LH: Well, by "look to," that has to be clarified—in what is really almost a philosophical sense, it's true, I think, that Negro intellectuals and Negro artists are profoundly attracted, once again—but this rebirth of that feeling has to do with the reassertion of the possibility that what we currently call the Western world is not necessarily the universe and that perhaps we must take a more respectful view of the fact that African leaders today say that with regard to Europe and European traditions in the world that we will take the best of what Europe has produced and the best of what we have produced and try to create a superior civilization out of the synthesis. I agree with them, and I think that it commands respect for what will be inherently African in that contribution.

PM: Do you think that the tradition of Africa is meaningful to an American Negro born and brought up here knowing very little about Africa, as every American knows very little?[6]

LH: Is it meaningful? Yes, only because of the peculiar history of American Negroes which has been one of oppression. You see, that without intellectual understanding of African culture—and you're quite correct that it just doesn't exist, nobody hardly knows where it is on the map, or didn't until recently—what there was was emotional kinship for obvious reasons. People who really honestly didn't know which part was east Africa, which part was west Africa, you know, would speak of Kenya as being in west Africa, still have this profound emotional kinship, in spite of so many years and years of contrary kinds of information about it.

PM: This affinity still exists and it's strong.

LH: Yes, and it's getting much stronger, I think.

PM: I know that you were twenty-seven when you wrote this play, and you said that perhaps one of the reasons why so many current Negro writers are so young is that they have so much to say they start earlier. What do you feel that they have to say?[7]

LH: Oh, that was a smart-alecky quote to prove that I still have a little Beneatha in me [*laughter*], but I think what I meant, aside from the fun of it, was that the Negro artist and the Negro writer in particular does have a particular vantage point which is a little different from the white writer. We, as so many people have remarked—it isn't original with me—have the peculiar stance of being within and without a culture at the identical moment, you see, of existence—that we're never really quite in the mainstream and yet we obviously are entirely, completely American and in every way conditioned in our thinking as Americans and so on. So that many of the things which puzzle other people, it seems to me, stand out in more bold relief to us—some of the values, some of the contradictions, some of the goodies that we most long for and whatnot in another part of us we have already judged, you know, have already seen their emptiness. And some of the really marvelous things that other people don't pay that much attention to, we know how precious they are. You know, when you speak of civil rights, civil liberties, that we know that these are not things to be toyed with because we're still just barely getting our hands on them.

PM: Miss Hansberry, what are you trying to achieve through your own writing?

LH: Wow! [*laughter*] Trying to achieve . . . Well, I suppose I think that the highest gift that man has is art and I am audacious enough to think of myself as an artist. That there is both joy and beauty and illumination and communion between people to be achieved through the dissection of personality. That's what I want to do. I want to reach a little closer to the world, which is to say to people, and see if we can share some illuminations together about each other.

PM: Miss Hansberry, you were speaking of the desire to communicate— what do you ask of a play, what do you ask that a play do?

LH: First of all, I think I like for it to activate my imagination. I like very much to sit back in the theater and feel that I'm going to be transported out of my own narrow confines as a human being.

PM: In speaking of what you ask of a play, then, it's partly that it move you?

LH: Yes. I happen to believe very much that it should move you. I think you must feel something about what you are consuming. Otherwise you can walk down the street and see any number of pathetic incidents and all of us being calloused as we are by the facts of our lives, don't have any reaction to it because there's been no preparation, no compulsion on our part to participate in the crisis and so, you know, so that you just passed a blind man, so what? But if you are involved on the stage in the fact of how he got blindness, his relationship to other people because he's blind, his needs and dependencies . . .

PM: This ability to involve the audience or viewer in the scene, do you consciously think when I'm writing this, this is going to involve—how do you stage a dramatic moment? How do you sense drama?[8]

LH: That's a very good question and no one else has ever asked it. That's very good. I suppose I would have to think more carefully when I was working to really answer it honestly. I'm sitting here and, to hear it, I'm not that sure.

PM: Do you sense drama in everyday experience as you are walking along the street or wherever it may be?[9]

LH: Yes, but I happen to believe that most people—and this is where I differ from many of my contemporaries, at least as they express themselves—I think that virtually every human being is dramatically interesting. Not only is he dramatically interesting, he is a creature of stature whoever he is. And Mencken said, in journalism, that there are no dull subjects, there are only dull writers. This is probably very, very true in dramatic materials, that most people have within them the core of their conflicts which give them stature if the writer is able to probe it.

PM: Do most people resolve these conflicts in a way that does give them stature?

LH: Oh, no!

PM: Do you believe this?

LH: Well, that's the beauty of the question because it's in the struggle to overcome a problem, whether it ends in failure or what we might call for lack of a better word, success that people exhibit their possibilities as beings. You know, Hamlet fails, but does he?

PM: You would say that most people have the potential for stature, or that they actually have it?

LH: Yes, yes. They have it within them—what the dramatist, what the artist can do that other people won't think to do in the course of a day, is to wonder about all the elements of it. You know, the fact of getting up and going to work every day is a monumental tribute to the average human being. It really is, you see. And if you dissect it and treat it with all the conflicts that the man has, just getting out of the bed, that's a short story. The things that must pass through his mind, the responsibilities, the weights. He may be the worst worker at the office [*laughs*], you know, or at the factory. But if you stop that moment in time, what he has done just to get out of bed and get on the subway [*laughs*] is quite a thing.

PM: Miss Hansberry, I would like to ask a rather large question. What do you get out of writing?

LH: That is large—and it's also valid. In some measure I get what I said before—a sense of participation in my time and in what I call my world. The people that I create give a great deal back. I'm very, very lucky of course to be only approaching thirty-one at the moment and to have had the opportunity to see it put before many people and have their reaction to it. And there is nothing yet that has been written, I don't think, in poetry or song that has quite articulated the gratification of that. I don't know how one can. It probably is the most fulfilling experience a human being can have. I don't mean just to write, but I mean to try and create something and to have it received with any measure of recognition for the effort. So that I can only say it in personal terms, I get enormous sense of personal fulfillment and a slight sense of justification for being.

PM: When you say that people you create give something back to you, how do you mean that? That you're involved with the characters themselves and grow with them?

LH: Yes. Well, they argue with me in the best traditions that writers are always talking. That isn't just an artsy-craftsy thing. They really do talk back to you, get you angry, and they really do have lives and ideas of their own. I suppose what I am trying to say is that to the extent that I have evolved any, what I can only call, grandly, philosophical notions at all, comes from the process of conversation with people in life and also through the struggle of trying to create people who are true. So that it's pretty much the same process, they do argue with you. They demand that you prove your point for a scene to be true.

PM: I want to close with two personal questions, the first a quite simple factual one. What are your plans for the future? What are you intending to work on next?

LH: Three years ago, or four years ago, whenever it was, I had written four little plays. I say little but they were three-act plays, and I started out never having written a play in my life but three-act plays which was a hangover from my painting days when I never could start anything other than the whole thing at one time, you know—just into it—very big. I want to continue the process. I want to continue just tackling things and writing plays all the way out and those that I think have some merit, I will dare to read to other people as I finally dared to read The One. On from there. I can't think of any part of the world—I'm never sure how this sounds, but it's what I feel, I can't think of any part of the world that doesn't intrigue me, and that I wouldn't like to try and deal with. I want to try and deal it with drama and deep in my heart, of course, like every writer, I would like to write a novel.

PM: The final question I want to ask you is, *A Raisin in the Sun* was about dreams—I wonder what your dream is.

LH: My dream is largely outside of myself which is a happy thing to be able to say, but it is. I don't feel especially compulsive about keeping up with anything or anybody in terms of career or anything like that. I really think I am in the process of living my dream. I am able to work freely and with not a great deal of insecurity—materially, to use our word—on what I want to work on and to do the things I want to do in terms of activities so that there isn't anything aspirational in that sense, which is why I said that most of my dream is outside of myself. I would like very much to live in a world where some of the more monumental problems could at least be solved. I'm thinking, of course, of peace. That's part of my dream, that we don't fight. Nobody fights. We get rid of all the little bombs and the big bombs. And then just all the other things that encompass human questions.

PM: Well, I think on that note, I'd like to close and thank you very much, Miss Hansberry. This has been delightful.

LH: You're quite welcome, I've enjoyed it very much.

Notes

1. Editor's note: Self-prepared transcript. The audio of this interview is available in the Lorraine Hansberry Papers located in the Moving Image & Recorded Sound Division of the Schomburg Center for Research in Black Culture, New York Public Library, and also online at the WNYC Archive Collections: https://www.wnyc.org/story/lorraine-hansberry/.

2. Editor's note: This question and Hansberry's response were edited out of the recording and transcript preserved at the Schomburg, but they are preserved in the recording held by the New York Public Library Archives Collection.

3. Editor's note: The Schomburg recording and transcript resume with this question.

4. Editor's note: The Schomburg recording and transcript cut the following exchange.

5. Editor's note: The Schomburg recording and transcript resume with this question.

6. Editor's note: The Schomburg recording and transcript cuts this question and Hansberry's response.

7. Editor's note: The Schomburg recording and transcript resume with this question.

8. Editor's note: The Schomburg recording and transcript cuts this question and Hansberry's response.

9. Editor's note: The Schomburg recording and transcript resume with this question.

Images and Essences: 1961 Dialogue with an Uncolored Egghead Containing Wholesome Intentions and Some Sass

Lorraine Hansberry / 1961

From *The Urbanite*, May 1961, pp. 10–11, 36. Reprinted by permission of the Lorraine Hansberry Literary Trust.

We spoke first of the Presidential Inauguration: "But," he said, "that *was* Marian Anderson and she was singing the Star-Spangled Banner!"

"Yes," I replied, "and she is much revered by me. And I know the butler was wearing most impeccable tails. But there you are; they were *still* doing exactly what their counterparts would have been doing one hundred years ago at the same affair: the brother was openin' doors and the sister was singin.'"

"Oh, please don't get folksy!" he said. "If there is one thing I utterly *loathe*, it is to hear the way you colored intellectuals are always affecting the speech and inflections of the Negro masses!"

"Please be good enough to explain to me," I replied with heat, "just how you, with your first-generation self, who are always, heaven, spicing up your otherwise rather dull and colorless standard English with old worldisms from your mama and papa's language, can have the glittering nerve to say such a thing!"

"Well," he said twice, "that's so different. Those things have such untranslatable flavor and compactness of expression. One feels one is adding something."

"Do tell," I said. "Now ain't you something else! Let me inform you, *liebchen*, that we colored intellectuals lovingly use the idiom and inflection of our people for precisely the same reason. We happen to adore and find

149

literary strength in its vitality, sauciness and, sometimes, sheer poetry in its forms. Why should that confuse you?"

"Because," he said, without looking the least bit doubtful, "everyone knows how guilt-ridden middle-class Negroes are about not wanting to identify with the less educated classes of Negroes. Consequently, one must assume that the utilization of street idiom is a self-conscious and embarrassed effort to re-identify; out of *guilt*, you see."

I really couldn't help it, I simply had to rub my head and roll my eyes at him, "Now, just a minit there, Sapphire—"

He didn't even hear it. He was absently filling his pipe and thinking of the article he would write, I am sure, on the subject for publication in *Dissent*. He was formulating the thesis aloud. "Naturally, given the discrimination against Negroes, it is perfectly understandable. So is the shame."

"Look," I said, rather glaring at him through the red spots before my eyes which gave me an idea, "to want to be free and equal is not to want to be white. You fellows are always making synonyms out of the wrong words. You, for instance, are just dying for us to catch up in the conquest of space; I presume that does not mean that *you* wish *you* were a *Russian*."

I knew that would get him.

"Oh, do stop playing 'Simple,'" he said, "I know the routine. The trouble is that you've become a racial megalomaniac. It happens to most Negro intellectuals and artists. You all end up trying to define the world in entirely racial terms. Very crippling intellectually!"

"But you," I shouted with outrage, "are the one who brings up race every single blessed time we talk!"

Again, he wasn't listening. "You haven't yet found transcendence to more universal human agonies. Four out of five Negro intellectuals and artists tend to have ultra-indifference, for instance, to the problem of world communism, if not pure and simple sympathies. It seems even more true of the new African leadership. A most unsophisticated approach to life."

"First of all," I said, blinking my eyes powerfully, "you don't know four out of five Negro intellectuals. You don't know five Negroes, period!"

He knocked his pipe violently. "Knowledge of the world does not have to imply personal rapport! You should know that, you are capable enough of generalizations! '*Oh, would some power the Giver give us to see ourselves as others see us.*'"

"Must you even take the Scottish folksiness out of Bobby Burns?" I said, holding my head in chagrin. '*O would some p'wer the Gif tie gie us—*'" I began to intone.

"You've become very smug," he said with cold eyes. "And very sopho-moric in the display of culture."

"I had teachers like *you*."

He ignored that and continued: "As I was saying, nowhere today does one find the Negro thinker breaking out beyond his parochial view of the world and adding his voice to the deepest questions of existence. When are you going to start probing the great absurdity of life; when are you going to produce a Camus?"

"That racist," I said blandly sitting back in my chair.

Outrage swam into his cheeks. "That," he said, "is absolutely the end of this conversation! Such unmitigated ignorance. A person who would so categorize the late great thinker of our times is not liable to intelligent discourse!" Afterthought, "Perhaps you didn't understand me. I was speak-ing of the French writer, the Nobel Prize winner, Albert Camus, *Kaimoo*: C-A-M-U-S."

"I know who you mean, Sweetie, I just finished his essays."

"And you dare speak of him the way you do? He who went to the heart of all human desperation, all human despair in his work?"

"What you don't seem to understand," I said, overcome by seriousness, "is that, in your worship of Camus you have merely imagined one parochial-ism to have value that another, mine, does not have. That's all.

"Frankly, I think that Western intellectuals, as typified by Camus, are really most exercised by what they, not I, insist on thinking of as the 'Death of the West.' It is at the heart of all the anguished re-appraising, the despair itself; the renewed search for purpose and morality in life and the almost mysti-cal conclusions of strained and vague 'affirmation.' Why should you suppose Black intellectuals to be attracted to any of that at *this* moment in history?"

"What in the name of rationality are you talking about?" he exploded.

"I am talking about the death of colonialism, that's what!"

"Ah, you see! You see; race, race, race!"

"What, pray tell, do you think Camus is about? Haven't you read him on the Algerian Question? What other than the rise of subject peoples has brought Western Europe and its intellectuals to their present state?

"What has induced the melancholy other than the collapse of empire? Despite his occasional obtuseness on other questions, Camus was remarkably explicit in asserting that the only obligation of the million Frenchmen in Algeria is to grant the eight million Arabs 'justice'—not national independence. He wrote only as a *Frenchman*, despite his Algerian birth. The assumption of the right to nationhood by the Algerians was incomprehensible to him; he was dedicated to the prevention of the 'humili-ating' absorption of Frenchmen into an Islamic culture.

"I am afraid that the colonial question is not solved by Frenchmen or Portuguese claims that other men's lands are parts of 'the metropolitan countries.' France is France and Algeria is Algeria, which is why the Algerians fight yet today. You will accuse me, but it requires a *racist* presupposition to think anything else.

"All of this, of course, grows out of the traditionally irrational conceits of dominant civilizations. In the modern world, 'the West' has mistaken its own self-glorified image for the world. When Camus writes of man, he means subjectively, Western man, as you do. That is the worst provincialism abroad in the world today; it is the most intense parochialism. I am grateful that my evolution in America permits me alienation from its seduction, for at best it is disastrous.

"Perhaps that helps you to understand why the gloom and doom of so much of Western art and thought which so captivates you leaves me cold. Africa and Asia and American Negroes, in their own comparatively decrepit way, are in anything but states of collapse or decay. On the contrary they are in their most insurgent mood in modern history."

"I hadn't realized," he said from the depths of his shock, "that you were a primitivist."

It was my turn to feel depressed exasperation at the chasm between us, but I sighed and answered, "I am not a primitivist and neither are the nationalist leaders of Africa. Peoples and cultures are *not*, to use my favorite phrase, *fixed in time and space*. Nor is anyone remotely interested in dimin-ishing the realities of Western industrial achievement. Kenyatta has written of it so beautifully, why don't you read that! Africa must absorb the best of the world into its techniques for progress. Nkrumah and Touré have already put the idea into practice. They are building hydroelectric power units in West Africa now, they did not fight for independence in order to sit around making bonds and thumping drums, as lovely as much of that may be.

"Besides, why don't you make up your mind about which thing most worries you about Negroes. Didn't I just read an article by you in a 'little magazine' where you were lamenting about how American Negroes were going to lose their souls in suburbia; how we were going to turn out to be just as dull as the rest of the middle class for the mere price of landscaped lawns, Jaguars, and tuberculosis-less babies?"

"Well," he said, glad I could see, to be back in the US, "you have to admit that it is a consideration. Earthiness tends to go unnourished on Madison Avenue or in Suburbia."

"And we are so earthy and abandoned now, eh?"

"I know none of you like to hear it, but it's true. Negroes are different. There is a quality of—"

"*Life*," I said. "I know what you mean. *No offense.* But look, please don't worry about it. First of all, it is not exactly what you could call an immediate problem. And, secondly, we've been warned by George Bernard Shaw— and, forgive me again, in rather better style. Also, we have a few hip people running around ahead of the trouble already taking pot shots at our middle-class foibles. Dr. Franklin Frazier, from the academic stance, and Jimmy Baldwin has let loose in novel and essay with his swinging, brilliant scalpel and some of the rest of us are learning. So please don't worry about *that*; it will continue to be the job of the Negro artist to satire what I *agree* with you is going to be a crowding on the Ludicrous Scene! Oh yes, it is upon us: attaché cases and martinis! We know—but we also know some of the wonderful things; personally, I go for chitterlings with champagne. But above all, we are too close to the horrors of the ghetto to wax romantic over its impending death. You see, the Negro mother *really* would rather have a tuberculosis-less baby—than even the mighty Blues. That is one of the secrets of our greatness as a people. We do aim to taste the best of this green earth. Who else could have made up a song like "O Lord, I Don't Feel Noways Tired"?

"No," I said, "don't you worry about us, child." I had started patting my feet a little, thinking of the song I had just mentioned and its triumphant spirit. "We don't even feel as comparative as we used to. . . . There are overtones still. . . . But they are *just* overtones. Did you see that fine short story by Ralph Matthews in an early issue of *The Urbanite*? Where the Negro hero said that he hoped the Bilbos would never die, but just take their places on a mountain top for a great contest where Bilbo would be on one mountain shouting 'You ain't!' and Charlie Parker would be on another, blowing his saxophone, answering in a million notes, 'I am!'? There is great lyrical imagery in that. . . . But do you know, we are going to go beyond even that eventually; reach on up where our assertions of identity don't require Bilbo's negations. Oh yes! It's going to come gently, and beautiful like the sweetness of our old folkways; going to spill out and over the world from our art, like the mighty waves of a great spiritual . . ."

I could see his lips moving and knew that he was talking, saying something, but I couldn't hear him anymore, I was patting my foot like the old timers and singing my song between the speech I was making. I was *happy*.

I could see the bridge across the chasm, it was made up of a band of angels hurling forth the art of twenty million. I saw Charlie White and

Leontyne and Lena and Harry and Jimmy. There was Johnny Killens and Nina; and, Lord have mercy, Paul was back! Langston and Julian Mayfield corning on the run; there was Odetta and Josh and P. J. Sidney, acting all over the place; and lo, sister Eartha had got herself together and was coming too; and then there was Ralph Ellison and Pearlie Mae and would you believe it Pearlie Mae had Frank Yerby by the hand, bringing him too. Oh, it was a wondrous thing I could see. And they came on and on, the Count and Duke and Cannonball and Louis himself, wearing the crown what Billie give him before she died. Oh yes, there they were, singing and painting and dancing and writing and acting up a storm, all of them, and many more, and the golden waves rose from their labors and filtered down on the earth and brought much heavenly brightness . . .

"You are disgustingly emotional," I finally heard my uncolored friend say, and turned to see the water standing in his eyes as he put his foot in the same tempo as mine . . .

"Yes, darlin'," I said, "sing along now, Honey, just sing along:

'I am seeking for a city,
Halleluh, halleluh!
For a city into the Kingdom
Halleluh, halleluh!
Oh, Lord, I don't feel noways tired . . .'"

Interview with Lorraine Hansberry and Lloyd Richards

Frank Perry / 1961

Broadcast on *Playwright at Work*, National Educational Television Broadcasting System (PBS), WNET/Channel 13 NYC, May 21, 1961. Printed by permission of WNET.[1]

Frank Perry: In *Playwright at Work*, we are exploring the creative methods, the philosophies, and the aspirations of a new group of writers for the theater. Our guest today is Lorraine Hansberry. Miss Hansberry won the New York Drama Critics' Circle Award for her first Broadway play, *A Raisin in the Sun*. Later in the program we'll see a scene from Miss Hansberry's work in progress, *Toussaint*. The scene will be directed for us by Mr. Lloyd Richards who also staged the Broadway production of *A Raisin in the Sun*. Actors in the scene will be Bramwell Fletcher and Miss Marie Andrews.

Lorraine—a pleasure to have you here today. I'd like to ask you why you write plays—why you've chosen to write for the theater?

Lorraine Hansberry: Well, I think it's because I am particularly attracted to a medium where not only do you get to do what we do in life every day—you know, talk to people—but to be very selective about the nature of the conversation. It's an opportunity to treat character in the most absolute relief—one against the other—so that everything, sympathy and conflict, is played so sharply, you know—even a little more than a novel. And I suppose it's my own private sense of drama that makes that appeal to me.

Perry: A desire to talk to people?

Hansberry: A desire to talk to people—and to [*laughs*] I suppose also have them do what you want them to do ultimately. [*laughs*]

Perry: Your characters.

Hansberry: Yes.

Perry: Are there any particular themes which concern you as a dramatist? Or is it more general?

Hansberry: The human race concerns me and everything that that implies, which is the most ambitious thing you can say, and at the same time the most modest too because I can't think of anything that people do where conflict is born that isn't dramatically interesting. . . . And, of course, it's the role of the dramatist to select which part is most interesting. And when you don't, you get a very bum play.

Perry: You said in an interview, I think, that you wrote *A Raisin in the Sun* from a specific intellectual point of view. Is that true? And if it is, what was that point of view?

Hansberry: Yes, I happen to believe that the most ordinary human being—to almost repeat what I just said—has within him elements of profundity, of profound anguish. That there is—you don't have to go to the kings and queens of the earth. I think the Greeks and the Elizabethans did this because it was a logical concept, but every human being is in enormous conflict about something, even if it's how you get to work in the morning and all of that. So that I thought that it would be very interesting in the contemporary American theatrical moment to explore the most ordinary man, say, on the South Side of Chicago, whom we think we know. You know, he drives you to work and you say, well, he's a nice fellow—but see what he's like at home and some of the ordinary events by the time he gets to work. He's a complicated and large person.

Perry: Are you trying to find tragedy in these people? In the smaller people?

Hansberry: Ultimately, I would like to be able—we think in drama that's the highest form of drama. I don't think that the hero in *A Raisin in the Sun* ever achieves true tragic stature—but as drama it's the route that I'm trying to go, yes.

Perry: It's the direction you're going, that's fascinating. Would you call *A Raisin in the Sun* a naturalistic play?

Hansberry: I would not.

Perry: And what would you call it? If you had to put it in words?

Hansberry: I hope that it is genuine realism.

Perry: What's the difference?

Hansberry: It's enormously different. Well, naturalism tends to take the world as it is and say this is what it is, this is how it happens, it is true because we see it every day in life that way—you know, you simply photograph the garbage can. In realism I think the artist who is creating the realistic work imposes on it not only what is, but what is possible . . . because this is part of reality too. So that you get a much larger potential of what man can do.

And it requires a much greater selectivity. You don't just put everything that seems. You put what you believe is.

Perry: In this framework, would you call Shakespeare a realistic writer?

Hansberry: The greatest of them all. This is why, for instance, the ghost and whatnot are not outside of realism in *Hamlet*. Because it is based on the reality of what a man envisions in himself—it's simply a way to embody conscience. I think Shakespeare was the greatest realist. If we could get that element back into contemporary theater, I think we would be closer to drama of stature again.

Perry: The play you're working on now is called *Toussaint* and is about . . . Well, perhaps you might tell us who Toussaint was and briefly what it's about.

Hansberry: Toussaint is the first name of the great Haitian liberator Toussaint Louverture whom most Americans have never heard of, despite the fact that, in my opinion, he was probably greater than even José Mati or Simon Bolivar or even our own Washington. There is this possibility.

Perry: When did he live?

Hansberry: In the eighteenth century. He was a field slave who ultimately organized the Haitian people to throw out the armies of Bonaparte and to create the Haitian Republic.

Perry: Will we see Toussaint in the scene that we are going to see, himself?

Hansberry: No. From my own point of view, I think what is interesting is something that will try to show the nature of the people who are involved in the struggle which is about to envelope Haiti. The first scene deals with the plantation manager and his wife and what the slave society does to all people involved and not merely the slave.

Perry: Good. I think with that introduction we'll have a look at the scene if we can. We'll ask Lloyd Richards to set the scene for us if you would please, Lloyd.

Lloyd Richards: Haiti. 1780, the year of insurrection, the year before major rebellion. The place is the upstairs bedroom of Bayon de Bergier and his wife, Lucie. Bayon is the manager of a plantation, Breda, and they're preparing for dinner, preparing to entertain Monsieur Petion from France.

[*Scene featuring actors Bramwell Fletcher and Miss Marie Andrews (7:36–19:53): The scene introduces two of the main characters in the play, Bayon, the manager of the Breda plantation, and his wife, Lucie. The scene opens with traditional African drumming and singing, which transitions to European classical music as the camera closes in on Bayon, wearing his dressing gown.*

Lucie is reclining in her dressing gown on a chaise behind him. The two go back and forth in a sarcastic argument about a dead woman whom Bayon once loved. It can be inferred that he has been visiting her grave for some time, and Lucie lets it be known that she is aware of this and angry. They also discuss their incoming guests from Paris, who are a courier from Bayon's employer and his wife. Bayon makes it clear that he needs his wife to entertain the guests, so that he will receive a good report, be granted another year in Santo Domingo, and then be able to return to Paris. Bayon and Lucie have another argument about her Creole parentage and about his many enslaved children on the plantation, born of enslaved women.

The screams of a woman being whipped intrudes on the scene, and the two talk about Toussaint, who is employed as Bayon's slave-driver but who is not shown in the scene. Lucie believes that Toussaint takes no pleasure in punishing enslaved people, while Bayon insists that Toussaint is content and complacent in his role on the plantation. Bayon dresses himself throughout the scene, saying that he cannot bear to have a servant "hovering around" while he is dressing. The scene ends with Bayon reminding Lucie to get dressed herself and to be in "excellent humor" when their guests arrive.[2]]

Perry: Lloyd, thank you very much indeed.

Richards: Well. thank you, Frank, and thank you, Lorraine.

Perry: I would like to open the discussion by asking Lorraine what you were working for in this scene and how well you feel it was achieved.

Hansberry: Well, as a preliminary scene, as what will I still hope be the very beginning of the play, it was an effort to set preliminary character of the two principals and to discover some personal aspects of their lives before we see them in conflict with other people in the play so that the audience is able at once to begin to relate to them in what may not be entirely sympathetic roles as the play evolves, but as human beings, which is always a certain measure of sympathy. This is why I want them to be people in our minds first.

Perry: Lloyd, what problems did you deal with in doing this scene, and how well do you think it came off?

Richards: The problems? The problem was to get it all in. The fascinating, absolutely fascinating part of working on Lorraine's work is that there are so many levels of work to get in. It isn't just the obvious. There are things being said about not just the characters. There are things being said about the time, the milieu. And, to suggest those things and to work out of those things, particularly—like in this scene. To me there were the three levels of slavery. The level of slavery that existed or exists with Toussaint and the relationship to Toussaint, the actual slaves which you see in the scene even setting up the table. You don't see it here, but it happens if you see it on the stage. Then there is the level of slavery of the wife. A woman bought. Not a woman loved but a woman purchased really and the effect of slavery on her. Then ultimately Bayon himself—a man who's a slave to the system. He can't break out of it himself. It dehumanizes him. Right down the line. And this effect on each individual and what it causes them to do to the other was the thing that I was working for in this scene and the thing that I think is there and must be realized, and it's fascinating to work on.

Perry: I certainly think it was realized. Did you have those three levels in mind when you wrote the scene, Lorraine?

Hansberry: Yes, I'm so glad to hear that this is what Lloyd feels about it. It grows out of a thought of mind that—as I study history—that virtually all of us are what our circumstances allow us to be. And that it really doesn't matter whether you are talking about the oppressed or the oppressor. An oppressive society will dehumanize and degenerate everyone involved. And in certain very poetic and very true ways at the same time it will tend to make if anything the oppressed have more stature, because at least they are arbitrarily placed in the situation of overwhelming that which is degenerate—in this instance the slave society. So it isn't that . . . it doesn't become an abstraction. It has to do with what really happens to all of us in a certain context.

Perry: And which is what really happened in Haiti with Toussaint. Isn't that correct?

Hansberry: Yes. Exactly.

Perry: Are there any particular problems you found inherent in writing—or working on—an historical play?

Hansberry: Yes. What I think a dramatist has to do is to thoroughly inundate himself—or herself [*laughs*]—in an awareness of the realities of the historical period and then dismiss it. And then become absolutely dedicated to the idea that what you are going to do is to create human beings whom you know in your own time, you see. So that all of us sitting out in the audience feel that, oh yes, we know him, no matter what period. This is the seventeen hundreds but we must feel, I have had this experience, I have known this person. So that once you know the realities of the time, you use them really as residue at the back of the head, so that, you know, you don't have them go out and get into an automobile, but where the human emotion is universal in the time sense as well as the world sense.

Perry: Well you spoke in the first section about the realistic play—the dramatist superimposing his own solution. Aren't you stuck with the facts of history in a play like this?

Hansberry: Oh, you have to be true to the facts of history . . . but within that context, many things are possible about the supposition of human reactions to a situation. But you don't have the French win the Revolution, obviously, because that . . . that would be against realism.

Richards: And wishful thinking. [*laughter*]

Hansberry: On the French part, not mine.

Perry: Lloyd, in a hypothetical situation, if you were putting this play into rehearsal tomorrow, would you ask Lorraine for any changes in this scene?

Richards: If I was putting the play into rehearsal tomorrow . . . No, I wouldn't. I don't think even now I'm completely able to judge. I think this scene as it exists works with minor changes here and there. I know she has some ideas about that. But this scene exists within other scenes that are going on at the same time. This scene is upstairs. Downstairs the slaves are setting the table. You find too many people . . . which is also indicative of a slave society . . . whereas Lorraine said once when we were discussing it . . . forty people to wait on four . . . one only brings in the pickle fork . . . one the napkin rings . . . and that's all he has to do . . . and just people standing around . . . the waste of it. That you see.

Perry: And that will show in the scene, yes, on the stage?

Richards: Yes. And the outside, the waste of human energy . . . the waste of human life . . . and this taking place within it. Now, I'd have to see all that to see what minor changes would have to be made, but I don't think they would be major at this point.

Perry: Lorraine, did you learn anything from seeing the scene performed?

Hansberry: Yes, both in terms of strength and weaknesses. I think it does work dramatically. There are points where it is a little static. And some static quality in this kind of work is desirable. I have toyed with the idea in my head already—which this makes me wonder about again—the possibility of a third character being in the scene . . .

Perry: In the room?

Hansberry: Yes . . . who would be a slave, a male servant who really is dressing him . . . that this would be one of the affections of the aristocracy that Bayon has taken on. And when this man is literally there . . .

Perry: And would they play the same emotions in front of this man?

Hansberry: Exactly. Their most intimate revelations in front of this human being because this again is the dehumanizing character of such a social order. And this would be very theatrical, I think. I may not do it. I don't know. But it's one of the things . . .

Richards: And it's indicative of today, too. Any bellboy can tell you that this is going on.

Perry: Or taxi driver, I suppose.

Hansberry: Or maid. [*laughter*]

Perry: Lorraine, what would you say have been your most satisfying moments as a playwright?

Hansberry: Well, I would think, just immediately, the audience reaction to the one play after all that has been before the public, and that is *Raisin*.

Perry: The audience reaction, how—in what sense?

Hansberry: We were often struck with the fact that as theatergoers, it seemed to us that we had the most responsive—spectacularly so—audiences that I'd seen in a long time in the Broadway theater. Where people literally were almost talking to the actors. I don't think our curtain ever came down where you didn't hear the women say, "Don't forget your plant." [*laughter*]

Perry: You reached them.

Hansberry: And that's what I'm trying to say, that I do feel that it did reach the audience and no writer ever really wants more than that. No matter how we say it, that's ultimately what we want.

Perry: Thank you. Today on *Playwright at Work* we have investigated the working philosophy of two gifted additions to the American theater. Our guests were Lorraine Hansberry and Lloyd Richards.

Note

1. Editor's note: Self-prepared transcript. The original video version of this interview is available in the Lorraine Hansberry Papers located in the Moving Image & Recorded Sound Division of the Schomburg Center for Research in Black Culture, New York Public Library, and in the American Archive of Public Broadcasting at either Thirteen WNET or the Library of Congress, Washington, DC.

2. Editor's note: An expanded version of this scene, which includes the servant character Destine, was broadcast in 1967 on WBAI-FM Radio as part of a series, "Lorraine Hansberry in Her Own Words," and was published in 9 *Plays by Black Women*, edited by Margaret B. Wilkerson (Signet, 1986).

Interview with Lorraine Hansberry

Eleanor Fischer / 1961

The June 7, 1961, Fischer field recording was probably intended for broadcast by the Canadian Broadcasting Company. Portions of this interview are printed by permission of WNYC Archive Collections; the remainder is printed by fair use.[1]

Eleanor Fischer: Lorraine, what inspired you to write *A Raisin in the Sun*?

Lorraine Hansberry: Well, it's very hard to talk about that because it's just something very hard to pinpoint. I suppose that the thing I generally say is true, and that is that I wanted very much to expose contemporary the-ater-going audiences to an ordinary American Negro family who were very much set upon by all the ordinary things of life, the problems, the travail, and, not to be corny, but the joys and the humor, and then suddenly, in the middle of it, introduce and impose willfully this extraneous question which is racism on these people so that the audience might have the experience of seeing how really extraneous it is that the most dreadful day in an ordinary man's life is compounded and made even more ghastly if he happens to be an American Negro in America.

EF: Perhaps you could just give us a brief synopsis of the storyline of the play because when you talk of this incident you didn't mention what it was.

LH: Well, I'll try. Of course, I don't do as good a job as theater critics who can sum it up in a paragraph but what it has to do with is a family that has an insurance check left by a deceased father, the sum of $10,000, and every member of the family has some sense of what they want to do with this money to change their lives or to embellish their lives in some way. The women of the family tend to want to put it into a home, the young daughter wants to use a portion of it to get herself through medical school, the son wants very much to go into business because that's a big American thing right now is to be a businessman and an affluent one, and he has simply been caught up in this. And ultimately the mother takes the money in a moment of family crisis and buys a home in a white community and the son is shattered by this because he had his own designs on the money and there is another family crisis. The play is full of crises. And the white community represents itself by sending a little man who says, "We don't want you. Please don't come out into our neighborhood." And at this moment I use this as a device to resolve problems of character in the son who decides since they have been offered a great deal of money not to come, that even in spite of that it is the moral obligation and the historical necessity of this particular family to move where they feel they have to right to be as human beings even though they don't get the money.

EF: When the play first came out, I recall the reviews said one of the great things about it was that it was not a play about race problems. Now did you really intend to play down the question of race relations as much as that except as a means of resolving personal characters?

LH: Well, I think that we are all what our lives are. It really doesn't matter who you are talking about; whether you are talking about Willy Loman or the man in *Rhinoceros* or Julius Caesar in Shakespeare or anyone else. We are what the nature of our lives makes us so that it's impossible to divorce the racial fact from any American Negro. Part of his daily experience is that of being a unique person in American culture who is a Negro and the reason these people are in this dreadful place anyhow—which, I should say, to make it clear is not particularly squalid or horrible in itself but . . . their home, when the play opens, is an expression of the ghetto. The fact that thousands and thousands and thousands, hundreds of thousands, really, of people are jammed into areas which should only accommodate a few thousand. So it's the overcrowding. So that from the moment the first curtain goes up until they make their decision at the end, the fact of racial oppression, unspoken and unalluded to, other than the fact of how they live, is through the play. It's inescapable. The reason these people are in a ghetto in America is because they are Negroes. They are discriminated against brutally and horribly, so that in that sense it's always there and the basis of many things that they feel and which they feel are just perfectly ordinary human things between members of a family are always predicated, are always resting on the fact that they live ghettoized lives. So, in that sense, it is always distinctly there but overtly it isn't introduced until they are asked by the author to act on the problem, which is the decision to move or not to move out of this area.

EF: In this portrait that you gave of a Negro family in Chicago, is just that a portrait of a Negro family, [or] did you expect it and do you think that had, to white audiences, a more universal appeal? Do you think it made them conscious of something else that you were trying to say outside of the question of race or the question of the problems that exist between the white and Negro in the United States today?

LH: Well, to be quite honest, I don't there is anything more universal in the world than man's oppression of man. That this is what most great dramas have been about, no matter what the device of telling it is and we tend to think, because it is so immediate with us in the United States, that this is a unique human question where white people do not like Black people in the United States but the fact of the matter is wherever there are men, there are oppressed peoples. And the universality of the play, and I say this everywhere, has to do with the fact that, if I may say so, to the extent that it is a successful piece of drama, it makes the reality of this oppression true, and people feel, I think, white audiences are able, which is the reason those people seem to have burst into applause in Washington the other day— that a human being sitting in the audience feels himself involved with what has become to him, after two acts, by the time the racial thing becomes paramount—we're human beings who are not getting an even shake in the world. This is always what commands our sentiments in the theater and always will, I think.

EF: What about the idea that I believe you have expressed before, that one of the issues in *Raisin* was the issue raised by American culture in general, the attitude towards money and the approach towards gain. Would you say that this is one of the prime aspects of your play?

LH: It was one of . . . my primary intentions, yes. Because, well, we've gotten a little confused or very confused, I should say. We have confused acquisition of what I call trivia, of the paraphernalia of life, with a good life, I think in America, in the United States, and we have gotten to a place where on the one hand you have the intellectuals turning a very long nose towards what they think is materialism. They have confused trivia with the material base—the material good base of life which all human beings need in order to live and just a level before they can even discuss happiness philosophically, they at least have to have everything that it requires just to bring up your children without rickets or without tuberculosis. And this confusion results in people saying, "Well, we've got too many automobiles in America, we've got too many Cadillacs and television sets and all of this"—when the fact of the matter is that there are thousands, millions of people in the United States who don't have too much of anything. They don't have enough. And there's a fine and important distinction between that kind of material base of life which simply provides what people need to live a decent life and the middle-class preoccupation with acquisition, with affluence, with those things that they can demonstrate to their neighbors that show that they are keeping up with the fashions. And these people are between, you see. They really don't have enough yet. The fact of the family that I was writing about not having a home where a child can have his own bedroom in a country quite as wealthy as this, shouldn't be confused with the fact that some American children drive to school every day in their own private automobiles. Those are two different questions. There are people who are still trying to guarantee just the basic things of life. At the same time, if I may say so, the complication of the play is that I don't want the hero of the play to get lost, the young man who thinks that he wants yachts and pearls because this is what he sees all around him; that the people who seem to command his world, to be in charge of it, are full of yachts and pearls in their lives. I don't want him to get confused about the reality of the one thing he really does need for his family with the other. One is paraphernalia, one is fluff, and the other is a real base of good life and good living. And he is confused. He is representative of those people in our culture who are. And the play makes the statement at the end that when money intrudes on those things which we know that we have to have for any kind of moral health as a people, and I mean all Americans, by Heavens, let us choose for the other thing, not for the money. The focal moment of that[2] play very much hangs on the denunciation of money values when the mother confronts the son who is considering this betrayal of his heritage of a great people and says, "I want what the bourgeoisie has." The mother says to him from her resources as a daughter of the Negro peasantry, of the Negro slave classes, "I come from five generations of slaves and sharecroppers and ain't nobody in my family never taken no kind of money that was a way of telling us we wasn't fit to walk the earth."[3] And she is the heart and soul of this play in that respect, even though the more—as I have said elsewhere—the more articulate, the more sophisticated and refined expression of this does come from the African student, who has a way of dismissing this question and saying that—

EF: The African student, what role did he play in the drama?

LH: Well, in popular terms, he is simply one of the girl's—the daughter of the family's—suitors, who comes and likes her and wants to marry her and go off to Africa, but in the course of doing this he explains that he doesn't think that the—this is particularly more pronounced in the movie script where I took care to put it in a way that it wasn't in the play script, apparently—he doesn't think that these people should allow themselves to get lost in the mystique of accident and life. . . . That they mustn't allow themselves to think that accident—that is the death of the father, the insurance money, is the thing that can guide their futures. . . . That, after all, it is how we act and what we make of life that is going to make all of the difference in the world eventually. And I tend to think that Walter is not a hero in terms—

EF: Walter is the young man, the head of the family.

LH: Yes, the pivotal character who eventually makes this decision. I tend to think that he isn't a hero in my terms. I would like him to have a much larger view of the world . . . a much larger and deeper and more profound understanding of his own class situation in society and his position as a Negro. But that's the difference between what I hope I write and [*laughs*], I'll say, more agitational type of material. I wanted to write about him as he existed at this moment in history. What he will be in twenty years I can't say, what his son will be. But John Howard Lawson might possibly understand and sympathize. But I wouldn't say that because he has a particular moment of truth that the author thinks this is what Negroes should be at this moment in the world.

EF: The young student, the boyfriend of the daughter, he expressed as you said a point of view that you were trying to get across. Why did you make him an African student? Couldn't you have gotten the same point of view across if you had kept him in the context of the purely American society?

LH: Not the same degree as reality. I felt the need in writing this play for a very sophisticated figure who would articulate some of the things that I felt. Who would have something of a larger historical view. And at this moment, well, first I should say this, that between American Negroes and Africans we can't forget that oppression has been welded together in a way that the mystique of race has not. The kinship that American Negroes feel with Africa has nothing to do with the bloodstream. It has a great deal to do with the fact that we are only now on both sides of the ocean coming into our destiny, so to speak, as emergent peoples and self-assertive peoples. So that he really isn't an alien figure in the play. And because he is an intellectual and one who is both of age and experience to be a little more fully formulated than the daughter, who is sort of an embryonic [*laughs*] intellectual, you know, he can say things that no one else in that particular setting can, no matter what their depth of understanding. . . . Their way of saying it would have its own limitations, and I chose him quite arbitrarily in that sense.

EF: Do you really feel that, moving away just from the strictly dramatic point of view, when you commented about the relationship between the African and the American Negro in the totality of the social setup that there is this bond that has grown up between the American Negro and the African, not in terms of race but in terms of oppression, and that this is felt and realized by the American Negro, and that the American Negro, in watching this play or seeing this movie, would have the same feeling?

LH: The same feeling as . . .

EF: As to this bond that you were speaking of, the bond of oppression, the bond, as to your reasons, your motives, for using the African in the play.

LH: Well, I don't think that people understand a number of things about this, because after all American Negro culture is very much isolated from many of the mainstreams of the rest of American life. . . . That in spite of all of the things, which are true, that Negro children are taught to look down on the African through all of the cultural media and all of this and they think in terms of Tarzan and the apes and people running around with loin cloths and all of that—at the same time and almost concurrent with it we mustn't forget that oppression—the fact that the Negro has never been fully absorbed into American society—has forced him to have certain profound emotional relationships with oppressed peoples everywhere in the first place and with Africans in particular. We forget, for instance, that in the twenties the largest and most potent organization of Negro life, in my mind, happened to be under Marcus Garvey who organized Negroes on the basis of an African orientation of African nationalism. Millions. Not hundreds of thousands. No one has equaled this in Negro politics or Negro society since. And this was back in the twenties. This was before what we now call the ascendancy of Africa. And it is not an alien thing in American Negro life. It died out and became latent and then now—with the emergence of Ghana and Nigeria and the other independent African states—is very new, but it has never been alien. Growing up in the heart of the South Side of Chicago all my life hearing people on the street corners speaking of Africa, Africa. We didn't know which part was the east and which part was the west, that's true, you know, but we knew that there was an emotional relationship.

EF: Well, I know that some students from Kenya were telling me not too long ago that they had been down South and they discovered that many of the southern Negroes looked upon them with a great deal more suspicion than the white people did, and that they had several Negroes come up to them and say, "Do you wear shoes in Africa?" and they were quite shocked by what they felt was the lack of understanding and the lack of identity of the American Negro with the African.

LH: Well, yes, that's part of their lack of development with regard to understanding of the American scene, because there is no particular reason why—in fact, a remarkable thing is that American Negroes have any sense of identity at all with Africa because quite a job has been done on us. We have been taught from cradle to grave that there is one thing that you must try and negate and that is your sense of African heritage. This has been drilled into us by every aspect of American culture. The one feature, the one aspect that you were supposed to know is that this is a savage past, and what you want and what you want alone is to try to prove that you are worthy of this Western, American identity. And I think part of what you are trying to ask is: is there some distinction between what the Negro intellectual feels about Africa and the Negro masses?

EF: The average person, yes.

LH: Well, there's a little bit of both, I think, and I try to deal with this in the play. There's a scene when the mother—

EF: Yes, there is.

LH: —shows her alien sense with regard to Africa, and I tried to treat it in such a way that the daughter presumed her question and said, "Mama, please don't ask him a lot of questions about 'Do they wear clothes?'" However I must say, to the extent that the play is dated at all—having been written in 1957 or '8, and [now it's] 1961, and this is the rapidity of world events today—that to that extent the play is dated, whereas it would be more likely perhaps at this moment that the mother—I can't speak for the person in the South, that's a different question—but the mother in Harlem or the South Side of Chicago would be saying to her daughter, "Get yourself fixed honey, if you're having a young fellow come. . . . Oooh is he . . ." You know. She might have it all wrong. She might want to know is he a prince, or something like that. Or is he in the government, or something. You know, she would have her own class attitudes about it to look up to. But to be a young African today, you know, I think it would be a slightly different quality.

EF: Well, where do you go from here in terms of writing a drama, let's say about Negroes. You are a Negro playwright. You're a woman, They're two very unusual things for Broadway. You're the first, um . . . [*laughs*][4]

LH: [*laughter*] Thank you, that's very true. . . . I'd like to talk about the second a little bit too. [*laughter*]

EF: My train of thought has just been interrupted. [*laughs*] Yes, you are the first Negro playwright to have been represented on Broadway—Negro woman playwright—and I doubt now how many woman playwrights have been represented on Broadway either, for that matter, I think very, very few. But you have involved yourself in a particular way of looking at the material for drama. You've involved yourself with writing, so far anyway, about Negro family, about human beings, basically, but about a human, a Negro family, actually. Where would you go from here? What will be the issue? What will be the things that you would consider using as material for a play in the future?

LH: Let me say this as a preface to that. I've said some of the things and I've gotten into the habit of talking about why I wrote *Raisin* in a certain way, but I should say this, which I very seldom say because I think it is so apparent in the play and I probably shouldn't assume it. One of the reasons I wanted to write about Negroes as I knew them is because I am very concerned about my country. I think that we have—all the things I've said before—we have become, in large measure, a country which insists on acting as if the American middle class is the base and almost the totality of the world—which, in fact, of course it is not. Most people in the world cannot read a book and most people in the world do not even eat properly, so that this vantage point of looking at the world is a distorted one, is one that gives us a false view of the world. And at the same time that that is true, well, there are many, many, many wonderful things about the nature of middle-class life—that is, comfort, the capacity to give one's children the proper education and all of that. Given a certain context, given a world where most people don't have these things, it tends to bring with it, it seems to me, a certain amount of sterility, a certain amount of deadliness, of inverted values, of confused thinking, of a profoundly awkward way of treating of human questions and spirit and soul and all of this. And it seems to me that Negroes in the United States, all twenty million of us, do have vitality, do have a preoccupation with life and a rapport with those things which excite and move people. And I think that one of the things that I wanted to contribute to American drama was a little bit of this life, that these people were genuinely more interesting than most people who are being written about in American drama today. And people sit there you know, they're sort of like this, because there's so much "life" going on on the stage. Well, that life came out of these streets in Harlem, and the South Side, and it's there and I wanted very much to share this because it is theatrical, because it's so human; not because it's exotic, but because it is human. That was the thing. So that my point of departure from that, to try and get back to your question is: as great as I think Negro[5] culture is, as great as I think they are as a people, I don't consider myself in any way restricted to any part of the world. I plan to write about everybody that I know anything about. I plan to write about my own generation be they white, Black, or Puerto Rican. I am doing so at this moment as a matter of fact.

EF: What are you doing at the moment? May I ask or is that private right now?

LH: [*laughs*] Well, I don't think I could speak about it very lucidly because it's still in the process of work—but always in the same vein, whatever the political question, whatever, what we call the social aspect of people, I want to write about them [as] human beings and let the political essence of it be implicit. And I hope that this will always be some hallmark of my work, that you have to look to find what other people will call the message. That you will become so involved with people, no matter what the question, be it war and peace, or the working classes or what have you, that first you will feel involved with people.

Notes

1. Editor's note: Self-prepared transcript. The audio of the original, full interview is available in two parts in 1) the Lorraine Hansberry papers located in the Moving Image & Recorded Sound Division of the Schomburg Center for Research in Black Culture at the New York Public Library, and 2) online via the WNYC Archive Collections: https://www.wnyc.org/story/lorraine-hansberry/. The opening portion and final moments of the interview are preserved in an edited version of the audio interview, held at the Schomburg, but Fischer and Hansberry's discussion of the African student was cut from that recording. However, this discussion was preserved on Fischer's private field recordings and donated to the WNYC Archive Collections after Fischer's death. It has been reinserted into the transcript printed here. It is not clear whether the interview was ever broadcast by CBC, as they have no record of it.

2. Editor's note: The WNYC recording picks up here.

3. Editor's note: The Schomburg recording cuts out here.

4. Editor's note: The Schomburg recording picks up again at this question.

5. Editor's Note: The WNYC recording cuts out here.

Miss Hansberry and Bobby K: Birthweight Low, Jobs Few, Death Comes Early

Diane Fisher / 1963

From *Village Voice*, June 6, 1963, pp. 3, 9. Reprinted by permission of *Village Voice*.

"When we left the Kennedys' apartment, I had a feeling of complete futility, and as we got on the elevator I wondered if there is any way to make the white people in this country understand . . ."

Playwright Lorraine Hansberry discussed the meeting she, James Baldwin, Lena Horne, Freedom Rider Jerome Smith, psychologist Kenneth Clarke, and a number of other Negro entertainers and leaders had with Attorney General Robert Kennedy in late May at the Kennedy family's Central Park South apartment. It was her first interview since then.

"Mr. Kennedy seemed to have the least rapport with Jerome Smith," Miss Hansberry said, "and would have dismissed him entirely, I think, if the rest of us hadn't made it clear that we considered him the most important person in the room. Mr. Smith told Mr. Kennedy that a time may come when he will, no matter how reluctantly, hand arms to a militant integrationist—even a Black Muslim."

Smith, married and the father of two children, dropped out of college to become a Freedom Rider for the Congress of Racial Equality. He has been beaten and arrested in the South and served a jail term in Jackson, Mississippi, as a result.

Discussing the increasing attraction of the activist approach to integration over the moderate, she said, "Negroes aren't violent by nature, and I don't think the Black Muslims can become too powerful. Yet there comes a time when a person has taken so much hurt and insult and he rebels, and so with a people. At a rally in Harlem in April, I felt a tension in the air I had never experienced before. White people have always been welcome in Harlem, and for the first time I felt apprehension for the ones who were there, and there were quite a few. The Muslims, and there weren't that many, started chanting, 'We want Malcolm, we want Malcolm,' and dominating the rally. I left soon after and heard that evening in the news that there was violence then.

"This new tension was what we tried to convey to Mr. Kennedy." That the attempt failed has seemed evident in every comment made publicly by every person who was present at the meeting.

The rumbling has become a roar. The steadying voice of the moderates is being drowned by the battle cry of the extremists. Inaction once again has bred crisis. This has become a time of the instant, on-the-scene, unconsidered decision. The followers are leading, and the leaders are hard put even to keep up with the will of the followers. We've watched the Eisenhower-like paralysis of the administration, paying lip service to civil rights, playing a game of politics. Now, from one person after another we hear, "It's too late for politics!"

I brought up one of the most widely quoted incidents of the meeting, the suggestion that President Kennedy escort two students into the University of Alabama next week. "The suggestion was symbolic, of course," Miss Hansberry said. "We were trying to make the attorney general understand that the president must make a strong, definitive personal commitment. We were saying that the president must use that creative vigor of his to obtain equal rights for twenty million Americans.

"I don't think white people are as prejudiced as they think they are," she said. "I think when they are confronted with their prejudice, it tends to melt away. But I do think they have a great naivete about what it's like to be a Negro. I have a lot of white friends, and I have taken this understanding for granted until recently. For example, I was thinking of going to Birmingham. I don't fly, and I mentioned the physical problem of getting there to a friend of mine, a white girl. She asked me why I didn't drive, and I realized she had no understanding of what it would involve for me to drive to Birmingham, a Negro woman driving alone in the South. I can't just get in a car and drive to Birmingham. I don't know where I can stop and eat. Negroes fighting to be served hot dog and Coke is true literally as well as symbolically."

The gulf, the chasm, the ocean of misunderstanding between the administration and the Negro community is daily more obvious, as is the absence of the body of common interest assumed by the Kennedys. The game-loving president says to Negroes, in effect, "You know we're all on the same team, now just be patient and play by the rules." But Negroes are just beginning to learn there is a game, and if they find it's a waiting game and won't play, the administration might be well-advised to forget games.

President Kennedy, a well-educated man of wealth, speaks a different language from the Negroes. He never came close to being killed by a brick thrown through the window of his family's house (Miss Hansberry did when her family moved into a white neighborhood), he never needed to worry about which hotel or motel or restaurant or lunch counter would serve him, and luckily for us all he needn't concern himself with his safety in driving to Birmingham—a very efficient Secret Service handles the concern.

But if Kennedy cannot feel each of the terrors, receive each of the insults, and endure each of the inequities—in short become a Negro woman driving to Birmingham—if he cannot drop his political self-consciousness and achieve complete empathy with her and twenty million other Negroes and react passionately, then this country is going to see a crisis that cannot be predicted now.

Departing again from the subject of the Kennedy meeting, I asked Miss Hansberry how she would set up a timetable to accomplish the reforms she considers most important.

"We need legislation to guarantee any right a person can be denied," she replied. "The first thing that must be achieved is equal job opportunities for Negroes, then equal housing. When unemployment is 6 per cent nationally, it is as high as 30 per cent among Negroes. Education isn't as important as it used to be; Negroes are the last chosen for any job, skilled or unskilled. It's a matter of life and death, literally. Negroes are starving to death.

"And the ghetto kills, literally. Statistically, Negro men die the youngest of any group in this country; white men, Negro women, and white women follow in that order. I think housing is so important I wrote a play about it.

"I don't think Negroes give a damn about social integration. I never heard a Negro say he wants white friends. Negroes just want a chance to live their lives with the same rights as white people."

Negro babies are born smaller than white babies. The half-pound disadvantage of a newborn Negro baby forecasts a childhood that will be spent in the streets and an education that will come in underequipped, overcrowded schools, from uninterested teachers who will not endow him with an intellectual curiosity. The gap widens more when he is forced out of school early to the bottom of the job market. He won't earn as much as a white man, even if his job is the same. He can't get into a union. The Human Rights Commission estimates the percentage of Negro apprentices in New York

Unions as 2 "at most." He starts his married life in a high-priced apartment in a slum, and he can expect at this point to bear children who will be smaller than white children, get a limited education, live in a ghetto, and die young. The birthweight's low, the unemployment rate's high, and death comes early.

A painful situation becomes intolerable when its solution becomes possible. American Negroes are becoming aware of pains that were always there, but they never noticed before. They are being educated to the fact that they have a right to the civil liberties they have been denied for three hundred years, and they know instinctively that freedom has never been won by asking for "equality tomorrow." And this is exactly what the administration is asking them to do.

Between the time this piece was written and this moment in which it is being read, the president was expected to send a civil rights message to Congress, and this was expected to set off bitter debate. And in this same time, there has matured by a few days a restless urgency that has united twenty million Americans who demand their constitutional birthright now, and not tomorrow.

Miss Hansberry has been a Village resident for ten years, and says she intends to spend the rest of her life here and at her commuting-distance country place. The only thing that distinguishes her apartment from hundreds like it in the West Village is a phone with six buttons. She is pretty and small; a halo of soft black hair accentuates her large eyes. She dresses smartly, is sophisticated and poised. She speaks quietly and with intense conviction, but not with the fervor of a professional crusader; she is a writer, and her current project is a play, *The Sign in Sidney Brustein's Window*, which will be staged this fall—set in "the bohemian quarter of any large American city." *A Raisin in the Sun* was produced about four years ago, and it took about a year for the din to die down (Miss Hansberry doesn't like the concomitants of being a celebrity). Since then she has lived quietly, she says—that is, "B.B."—Before Bobby. She has been besieged by newspapers and national media since.

As our talks became more general, we discussed Jim Crowism in the Village, which she says is strong among real estate agents. "They'll make one excuse or another, but a Negro just can't get an apartment," she said. "Restaurant owners have pretty much had to give in."

About James Baldwin: "He is a great writer, a great essayist, and his greatest gift is that he truly understands not just Negroes, but the American people."

On differences between Negro [sic] and white people: "You know, Negroes I went to school with in the Midwest, who had been raised in predominantly white communities, had midwestern rather than 'Negro' accents and personalities. I think differences in attitudes and personalities are more cultural, environmental, than racial.

"I don't know why it should matter, but it bothered me that he wouldn't meet my eyes," she said of Bobby Kennedy the man.

"I've been encouraged by the press coverage," she added. "Lippmann, editorials in the *Post* . . . there's been an honest feeling of the course of the meeting. I did not, however, as was reported in some quarters, walk out. When I got up to leave, the meeting had gone on for about three hours, and everyone got up, said goodbye, and left.

"The most shocking aspect of the whole thing," Miss Hansberry concluded, "is the waste of our youth—when they should be in school, or working, or just having fun, instead having to ride freedom buses, be subject to police brutality, go to jail, to get rights that should be unquestioned."

The Black Revolution and the White Backlash: A Town Hall Forum

Association of Artists for Freedom / 1964

From the Association of Artists for Freedom's Town Hall forum held in New York City on June 15, 1964. Audio broadcast on WBAI, August 10, 1964, with an introduction by William Tatum. Partial transcript (below) printed in *National Guardian*, July 4, 1964, pp. 5–9.[1]

The June 15 Forum in Town Hall, New York, on "The Black Revolution and the White Backlash" marked a significant step in the developing dialogue between Negro militants and white liberals. The panelists examined closely the resentments and disagreements that have resulted from racial separation and the approaches and methods needed for success in the civil rights movement. The *Guardian* here presents a verbatim transcript of the meeting, with some minor elisions. The program was presented by the Association of Artists for Freedom. The moderator was David Susskind, president of Talent Associates and moderator of *Open End*. The panelists were Ossie Davis, actor and playwright, author of *Purlie Victorious*; Ruby Dee, actress; Lorraine Hansberry, playwright, author of *A Raisin in the Sun*; LeRoi Jones, poet and playwright, author of *Dutchman*; John Killens, author of *And Then We Heard the Thunder* and *Youngblood*; Paule Marshall, author of *Brown Girl, Brownstones*; Charles E. Silberman, author of *Crisis in Black and White*, member of the editorial board of *Fortune* magazine; and James Wechsler, editorial page editor and columnist, *New York Post*.

Opening Statements

LeRoi Jones [Amiri Baraka]: I see that question is: "Is there a necessity for new honest dialogue between white and Black Americans." The "new" part doesn't seem right, but for an honest dialogue, I think if there's going to be one, it would have to be new because I don't think there's ever really been an honest dialogue between white Americans and Black Americans.

Ruby Dee: I thought I'd deal with the word "backlash," as I think when I first heard the word it was in connection with some countries in Africa. . . . Backlash I think is much more a class action or attitude than a race one, manifest maybe in its earliest stages as conflict between races.

In Sharpsville in South Africa when the police opened fire on unarmed men, women, and children who had gathered nonviolently to protect the passbook laws, more than seventy Africans were killed, and the South African government reached the point of no return in their dealing with African people.

But with Sharpsville, the policy of nonviolence was felt to have proved itself inadequate and a policy of resistance to apartheid by whatever means including violent means was embraced by the leaders of African National Congress, most notable of whom is Nelson Mandela, recently sentenced to life imprisonment. . . . Coincidental with these developments and the Africans' drive for freedom and equality at Sharpsville has been a falling away of the former support the Africans used to get from the white liberals. . . . With the example before us of what happened to the majority of white liberals in South Africa when the chips were down, we cannot help but wonder if the present white backlash does not indicate which way the white liberal will go when and if violence erupts. Nobody wants violence, but . . . consider the following statement from a reporter by the Ad Hoc Committee on the Triple Revolution which says:

"The Negro claims as a matter of simple justice his full share in American economic and social life. He sees adequate employment opportunities as a chief means of attaining this goal. Negroes are the hardest hit of the many groups being exiled from the economy by cybernetics and automation. Negro unemployment rates cannot be expected to drop substantially. . . ."

When the time comes as indeed it must if things do not change and change overnight, that the Black worker winds up in the street fighting the white worker over the fewer and fewer jobs left by automation, will the white liberal in America throw up his hands like the white liberal in South Africa, or will he, like the two white men just sentenced along with Nelson Mandela to life imprisonment, remain committed to this struggle even to the point of revolution and beyond?

Charles Silberman: What I'd like to address myself is what is necessary on both sides of the dialogue for a dialogue to be established. . . . It's essential, it seems to me, that white liberals understand why the present strain exists, why to their apparent surprise in the past year or two they've found themselves under attack, frequently very bitter attack, from Negro activists. The reason was expressed succinctly in 1827 in the first editorial in the first Negro newspaper to be published in the United States. The editorial began: "We wish to plead our own cause. Too long have others spoken for us."

This, I think, lies at the root of the strain. Until very recently, Negroes have been the junior and usually the silent partner in the great liberal coalition, deferring to white judgement on strategy and tactics. However unavoidable, this relationship had unfortunate consequences for both the Black and the white partners. The white allies acquired the habit of speaking for and doing for the Negro. The Negroes consequently were never able to break the habit of having things done for them. White liberalism, white sympathy and support no less than white bigotry and discrimination, have had the effect of preventing Negroes from standing on their own feet and from exercising their full manhood rights, to use the phrase of W. E. B. Du Bois.

The Negroes always have resented the relationship. Their dependence on their white allies created an underlying animus that was no less real being carefully suppressed. Besides resenting their dependency, Negroes have not really trusted their white allies. They have always had a nagging suspicion that the whites were holding them back. . . . At the meeting at which the NAACP was founded, one of the Negro participants shouted, "They are betraying us again, these white friends of ours." And other Negroes with all too much cause have echoed this cry ever since.

What is new in short is not the strain between Negroes and white liberals, but the fact that the white liberals are just beginning to discover how Negroes feel, how they have always felt. They are making this discovery, of course, because Negroes are now expressing the anger and resentment they had felt but had carefully hidden.

If the dialogue is to be restored, therefore, whites will have to abandon their tradition of command and their habit of speaking for and acting for Negroes. . . . For if Negroes are to gain a sense of potency and dignity, it's essential that they take the initiative in acting on their own behalf.

There is another source of strain between Negroes and white liberals, one that is unlikely to take on more importance as the years go by—the fact that when the struggle takes to the streets, the majority of liberals are reluctant to move along with it. The problem is a real one. It is the fundamental difference in the situation of Negroes and of whites that leads almost inevitably to conflict over tactics and strategy. Negroes are outside the mainstream of middle-class American life, whereas their white liberal allies are on the inside. Hence, the liberals have a deep interest in maintaining peace and harmony. . . .

The changes of the sort Negroes now demand at the speed which they now insist upon cannot be provided without considerable conflict. Too many Americans will have to give up some privileges or advantage they now enjoy or surrender the comforting sense of their own superiority. Hence, white liberals must develop a new ideology or a new theory of politics, one geared to rapid change rather than one designed to eliminate conflict.

I would like to address myself to the Black liberals for a minute. The question, how to establish a dialogue? This is a real question for a great many whites with deep convictions about equality and justice. At times, there seems to be no way. What everyone says or does is received with hostility. James Baldwin has gone so far as to say flatly, "There is no role for the white liberal. He is our affliction." [*laughter*] . . . In Baldwin's cosmology, there seems sometimes to be no way a white can prove his decency. If you're hostile, you're obviously a racist. If you express friendship or sympathy, you are a fuzzy liberal.

At times, in short, Baldwin seems guilty of the same sin with which he charges whites, of seeing men of different color, not as individuals, but as stereotypes, as nameless, faceless men. He does this for artistic purposes, to try to arouse the white conscience. But for a dialogue to take place, there must be two people at the very least.

If whites bear the main responsibility for establishing, for creating the dialogue—and there's no question that they do—the fact remains the Negroes have responsibilities too. . . .

Paule Marshall: I would like to begin by saying something about the two words which form the poles of our discussion this evening, the words "Black" and "white," and how, in my mind, they have become less important as a description of a man's color and more important as the description of an essential attitude of mind and heart.

White has come to suggest more and more to me a moral callousness and timidity, a kind of rigidity and blindness, the childish belief that if you close your eyes tightly enough, the bad man will disappear. White is wealth without wisdom and an incredible innocence which is matched only by arrogance. In a word, it is the force in the world today which is opposed to change, even when the change is necessary to survival. Under the terms of my definition, there are many Americans who are hopelessly white, so that what we are referring to here tonight as white backlash is inevitable and it can be expected to grow increasingly ugly as this white, truly white, American realizes the hard fact that in order for the Negro to participate fully in the American life, he, the white man, will have to relinquish some part of his comfort, and that the system which has permitted him a privileged place at the expense of the Negro will have to undergo fundamental changes.

At the same time, the word Black is also expanded in meaning. It has come to stand for that force which recognizes that change, social and political change and movement and struggle are essential realities of human existence. It is the willingness to question and reject the old established institutions once they are proven obsolete and unjust. Black is to see a new way.

The Negro is symbolic of the force for change in America today and his demand for complete equality is part of the larger demand for human dignity and fundamental freedom being sounded all over the world. So often we think of ourselves as a hopelessly outnumbered embattled minority and thus tend to settle for much less than our demands, such as this present civil rights bill which has been practically amended to death, when in truth and in fact, we are part of a huge world community and our struggle here part of the world-wide struggle for human rights. This larger aspect of our revolution has to be stressed . . . if we are to recognize and accept also that the civil rights movement in our country has to widen in scope and take on a more militant tone.

This is not to say that I personally reject nonviolence as a method of struggle, but I am coming more and more to the conclusion that there is a need now for the establishment of a nationwide organization that is far more militant than any today. An organization with its base in the South where the potential political power of the Negro lies, with its roots reaching down into the mass of the Negro community, an organization with a well-planned and sustained program of action. . . . An organization, finally, which is totally committed to the liberation of the Black man in America by whatever means prove the most effective.

Most important, this organization must be truly independent. By this, I mean that it should not have to look for its financial support from the very sources it is working to overcome. Rather, it must be both financed and led by the Black man himself. . . . Politically, it must work to secure the vote for every Negro in this country. . . . Economically, there is a need to start exposing the many faces of the man downtown. For some reason, there has been a failure even on the part of the most radical groups in this country to spell out in clear terms, in clear language just how this system conspires to deprive the Negro of his basic rights.

In addition, strong economic pressures must be applied in the forms of carefully planned boycotts and other means of economic protest.

There is yet another task and it is one which involves the people sitting at this table here tonight and those in the audience. It is the task to establish not only a dialogue with the white man in this country, but even more so, a dynamic dialogue with the Black man at the bottom of the heap, because one of the most insidious features of this society is that it has made for economic and social separation between the Negro community—the old colonial tactic of divide and rule still obtains—and it is this separation which is in part responsible for the limited effectiveness of the civil rights movement today.

John Killens: I think the first think I'd like to say is that there is a misnomer here. There is no Black revolution yet. And I think Miss Marshall has indicated some of the reasons why there is no Black revolution. There is a Black revolt. White liberals have become disturbed. I understand there was a white newspaper writer who first dubbed the Negro revolt as a revolution. White liberals have called this revolt a revolution because of an inconvenience when we stalled their motor car on the bridge. In revolutions, people blow up bridges. [*laughter*]

One white patriot a long time ago, almost two centuries ago, said that these are the times that try men's souls. It was Tom Paine who said this almost two hundred years ago. Well, certainly he could have been talking about today. These are the times that try men's souls, these are the times that divide, indeed, the men from the boys. There are the times when the Cold War liberal must somehow, somewhere down the line, make up his mind, make a choice between the Cold War and the freedom movement. Because the struggle is to free America and not to help the downtrod Negro, which is the way many of the white liberals and white Americans like to look at it. . . .

How many are the winter soldiers of white America? How many are the sunshine patriots? How many Cold War liberals will desert our ranks when we assert the right of self-defense? Because we must assert this right. . . . Will the liberals of white America desert our ranks when we say that we will not love our enemies? That's a pretty sick but, anyhow, unrequited love. For example, what if Harlem organized a vigilante group? Would the newspapers and the police be so tolerant?

And another big test is, where will the Cold War liberals be when we place our case before the United Nations, which we must do in due time since it is a case of denial of human rights? . . .

America is sick, America is sick and is in need of basic surgery while the Madison Avenue fellows with more sense than anybody sitting here try to cure the world with plastic surgery, with a face-uplifting job.

There are a few myths we must be willing to relinquish. The one that I mentioned before that there is no revolution yet; another one, that we have let the establishment get by a long time on is telling us that we are second-class citizens. Who in the hell ever heard of a second-class citizen until they were invented in the United States? . . .

The backlash is a counterrevolution before the revolution has gotten underway.

So many liberals in the freedom movement are long on advice and short on action. Too many are willing to lead us down the freedom road but not to follow Black leadership. But in the final analysis, that is how it must be, that is how it will be. American Black folk will—with white assistance great or small—change America if it can be changed and that's what it's all about, to change the country fundamentally and lead her out of the muck and mire of obsolescence of nineteenth-century racialism into the new world of the freedom century which is already magnificently here all over the world. You know, I really marvel at the patience and fortitude displayed by many liberal Americans in the face of other people's degradation. They remind me of that great liberal, William Faulkner, the great Nobel Prize winner, exponent of noblesse oblige and plantation owner. His advice to the American Negro is still typical of the complacency of the Cold War liberal. You remember those three great revolutionary slogans he gave us: Patience, courtesy, and cleanliness, or words to that effect.

James Wechsler: Perhaps I should first begin by disagreeing with Mr. Silberman's suggestion that the white has the role of waterboy in the freedom movement and that he'd better damned well accept it. I find myself increasingly, as I grow older, feeling that old-fashioned American liberalism had some great, deep strengths. One of them was the sense that separatism was disastrous to any human cause. I am deeply disturbed this evening to learn the civil rights bill, which has just been passed, is really no bill at all. It is a matter of fact that the bill is stronger than the one proposed by the late John F. Kennedy to the Congress of the United States and no one performs any service by an attempt to deny the fact.

Similarly, let me say that I never believed that the civil rights bill was the answer to all our problems. It will not be. Nobody seriously alleged that it would be, but now suddenly to derogate it and to suggest that this whole effort was all in vain and meaningless seems to me a form of political irresponsibility. . . .

We talked, in some of the discussions of what this meeting was about, of who spoke for whom. I should like to venture the opinion that all of us on this platform don't speak for a hell of a lot of people. I should like to venture to remind those who have spoken here tonight with great militancy on certain aspects of this situation that the latest opinion polls show that among Negroes as well as among whites, Lyndon Johnson is the most popular American. . . .

There were many moments this evening when I felt that the discussion here did not involve white liberals. It involved the question of whether Jim Farmer was Jim Crow. Now, I submit that this suggestion that the Negro leadership has somehow betrayed the cause of civil rights, that we need some great new organization under some undesignated auspices is to me again no contribution to the very difficult and dangerous and dramatic times in which we live. And I do not believe that those who say these things do speak for any substantial portion of the American community. . . .

It is easy to say that in revolutions we blow up the bridge. The truth of the matter is, however, that one of the greatest revolutions in our time was conducted by a man named Gandhi. The truth of the matter is that he didn't blow up any bridges.

I don't know what the phrase "Cold War liberal" means. It does not seem to me that I must not care about the fate of Djilas in a Yugoslav prison in order to care about the freedom struggle in America. It does not seem to me that I must be tolerant of oppression and tyranny and enslavement in fascist and Communist countries in order to be a participant in the freedom movement in America. . . . It seems to me that if there is any meaning to our struggle in this country it is the obvious point that freedom and liberation are indivisible and that goes from Africa to Hungary to Mississippi to Manhattan.

Lorraine Hansberry: Was it ever so apparent we need this dialogue? How do you talk about three hundred years in four minutes? I wrote a letter to the *New York Times* recently which didn't get printed—which is getting to be my rapport with the *New York Times*. They said that it was too personal. What it concerned itself with was, I was in a bit of a stew over the stall-in, because when the stall-in was first announced, I said, "Oh my God, everybody's gone crazy, you know, tying up traffic. What's the matter with them? You know, who needs it?" And when I noticed the reaction, starting in Washington and coming on up to New York among what we are all here calling the white liberal circles, which was something like, you know, you Negroes act right or you're going to ruin everything we're trying to do—that got me to thinking more seriously about the strategy and the tactic that the stall-in intended to accomplish.

And so I sat down and wrote a letter to the *New York Times* about the fact that I am of a generation of Negroes that comes after a whole lot of other generations, and my father, for instance, who was, you know, real American-type American, successful businessman, very civic-minded and so forth, was the sort of American who put a great deal of money, a great deal of his really extraordinary talents and a great deal of passion into everything that we say is the American way of going after goals. That is to say that he moved his family into a restricted area where no Negroes were supposed to live and then proceeded to fight the case in the courts all the way to the Supreme Court. And this cost a great deal of money. It involved the assistance of the NAACP attorneys and so on, and this is the way of struggling that everyone says is the proper way to do and it eventually resulted in a decision against restrictive covenants which is very famous. *Hansberry v. Lee.* And that was very much applauded.

But the problem is that Negroes are just as segregated in the city of Chicago now as they were then, and my father died a disillusioned exile in another country. That is the reality that I'm faced with when I read that some Negroes my own age and younger say that we must now lie down in the streets. Tie up traffic, stop ambulances, do whatever we can, take to the hills if necessary with some guns and fight back, you see. This is the difference.

And I wrote to the *Times* and said, "You know, can't you understand that this is the perspective from which we are now speaking. It isn't as if we got up today and said, 'What can we do to irritate America?' It's because that since 1619, Negroes have tried every method of communication, of transformation of their situation from petition to the vote, everything. We've tried it all. There isn't anything that hasn't been exhausted . . . and now the charge of impatience is simply unbearable. I would like to submit that, yes, there is a problem about white liberals. . . . We have to find some way with these dialogues to show and to encourage the white liberal to stop being a liberal and become an American radical. . . . [*long applause*] The basic fabric of our society, after all, is the thing which must be changed to really solve the problem. . . .

When someone uses the term Cold War liberal . . . I can't believe that anyone who is given what an American Negro is given can believe that a government which has at its disposal a Federal Bureau of Investigation which cannot ever find the murderers of Negroes—and by that shows that it cares really very little about American citizens who are Black—really are over somewhere fighting a war for a bunch of other colored people, you know, several thousand miles. . . .

Ossie Davis: We can understand the concern expressed by some of us about the sharp attack that we've launched against the white liberal and I don't think it's a vicious attack. It's based on a desire to establish a communication because we have found that when they listen, they are not listening to what we're saying enough. The white liberal showed his color and his response to Senator McCarthy and we never learned to respect him since that time. And the great coalition put together by President Roosevelt which included white liberals, labor, and Negroes, etc., began to go apart at that time. I don't think that anything has happened, even with the appearance on the scene of President Kennedy, to mend that kind of separation.

We know from the fight waged or not waged against McCarthy that when McCarthyism is translated into anti-Negroism, we suspect that the white liberal will behave as he behaved in the past, and that leaves us somewhat frightened and naked.

Another question which bothers us very deeply is that a lot of the crimes of which we are accused as a people and of which we are guilty can only be explained in terms of the environment in which we grow up and live and breathe and fight and draw our switchblades and die. Now, there are many studies made every year of Harlem and who lives there and what's wrong with the people of Harlem. And yet, if you were to study the one question which is relevant—Who owns Harlem? Who profits from Harlem?—you would come up with a great number of liberals who see no discrepancy between profiting on the degradation of a people and taking 10 percent and giving it to the NAACP. . . .

Ten years ago we were held out the promise of integration and ten years has passed and not much has happened. There has been some integration believe me, and I appreciate that. There's been integration on the higher levels, in the middle-class Negro, the Black liberals, etc., but in the other areas where the mass of us lives, we have not been not only not integrated into society, but by automation, we have been out-egrated—we have been computed out of the society so that even the security we had in slavery and in segregation when we had the inherent right to shine the shoes—we were at the bottom of the totem pole, but that belonged to us, and we could build our churches, build our schools and send our children to college and support our newspapers and our organizations and our freedom movement from these jobs, but automation has taken those jobs from us. We are the first people who no longer have any stake in the economy of this country and that is what puts us in the street and that is what we are screaming about.

I am as careful as anyone to nurture the kind of unity in Negro-white relationships as was manifested by the March on Washington, August 28, 1963. I was very proud to be a part of that. . . . And yet at the same time when the question of responsibility arises, we must decide how to phrase the question before we can answer it properly. If the Negro leadership is responsible or irresponsible, we must ask the question: Responsible to whom? And this is a key question, because if they are our leaders, then they should be responsible to us. . . .

This leads me to the consideration of the question, who speaks for the Negro, and I'd like to read a few things which I think are relevant to our discussion. I take this from an article called "The Establishment" written by Mr. Lerone Bennett in the *Negro Digest* of April 1964. This is not necessarily a direct quotation, but I do not think I have done him injustices by making a few changes:

"The struggle for civil rights in America has been waged principally by several organizations dedicated specifically to that purpose, NAACP, Urban League, CORE, Southern Christian Leadership Conference, Negro American Labor Council, and SNCC, the major ones.

"And it might pay us to examine who has power in these organizations and how that power operates. . . .

"Racial policy is subtly shaped and diluted by the expectation, priority, and fears of liberal, labor, religious, and minority groups. From this white liberal nexus, these civil rights organizations seek allies and donations. And these allies have definite ideas about the goals and directions of Negro policy. And it is not always possible to accept the donations without accepting the donor's ideas about how Negroes should go about trying to get their freedom.

"Among the leading organizations having influence in civil rights groups are the UAW-CIO-United Auto Workers and other liberal unions, the American Civil Liberties Union, the American Jewish Committee, the American Jewish Congress, the Race Relations Departments of the YWCA-YMCA, the National Council of Churches, the Roman Catholic Church, the American Friends Service Committee.

"Another layer of power operating on the fringes of the civil rights organizations centers in the philanthropies. The Rosenwald Foundation, the American Missionary Association of the Congressionalist Church, the Rockefeller Foundation, and the Harmon Fund have played a huge role in shaping and breaking Negro policy. Of crucial importance in the context of current power realities are the Taconic Foundation, and the Phelps Stroke Fund. These organizations and their representatives are part of the formal and informal network of power surrounding the core organizations of the civil rights movement.

"Some of these groups send white delegates to the civil rights organizations. Some groom specifically selected Negroes who represent them in the inner councils of power. Certain positions are apparently reserved in these organizations for white men. The NAACP Legal and Defense Fund have never had a Negro president or a Negro treasurer. Nor, for that matter, have many other Negro institutions of power. Final control . . . is generally vested in white hands.

"Not only has Black nationalist, Black minister Malcolm X deplored the presence of so many whites in positions of power and authority in our own Negro organizations, not only men like Paul Robeson, W. E. B. Du Bois, have raised their voices against it, but even Ralph J. Bunche has sharply criticized the situation. . . . [*laughter*]

"Now, this is not to imply that these (Negro) organizations are centers of treason or that they set out to betray the Negroes or that the Negro leadership in them does not command a great deal of respect and even admiration from all of us, but it would seem to us that it is now a time of change. In our struggle for freedom and equality, we welcome the white man as an ally, as a friend, as a brother, but not as a boss.

"The basic difference, which is simple yet profound, is that the whites naturally, inevitably believe in the maintenance of order, because they benefit socially, economically, spiritually, in all other ways by the maintenance of order, orderly process, due process of law, order at all costs. Countered to them are the Negro people who do not believe that order is more important than either freedom or equality. And however, we have seen ten years of nonviolent orderly struggle to secure the freedoms and rights which are ours come not nearly to fruition, and if it were possible to believe that it could be done, I would say, let us have another ten years of quiet disciplined orderly protest, but I submit that another hundred years of protest cannot secure integration into a society which is automating even its white workers out of existence. It is an impossibility, and we must address ourselves not to a revolution of anger and vengeance against our white brother, but a constructive way to use the revolution which is already upon us created by the technology of our times."

David Susskind: I must say that until tonight I did not realize that the mortal, two-faced, ugly, double-dealing enemy of the Negro people were the white liberals. Ossie Davis said, "Where were the white liberals in the case of Senator McCarthy?" I know where they were. They were Herbert Lehman, Paul Douglas, President Pusey of Harvard, Jimmy Wechsler of the *Post*, Ed Murrow. In a terrible little area that doesn't matter much like show business, I was double-dealing the blacklist every day of the week. I know where the white liberals were. They were fighting with whatever tools they had.

I think that white liberals are the American radicals, Lorraine. [*laughter and murmuring*] I think—enjoy yourselves. Get it out of your systems—I think the white liberals are really right alongside you in the fight that they feel is not your fight, but is a deep and absolutely inescapable fight for freedom, for equality, for themselves as well as for you. . . .

I'm appalled. Several speakers complimented previous speakers on their eloquence. I can't quite agree. I never heard such carefully couched calls for violence and bloodshed in a long time and I think it's dangerous, irresponsible, and ineffective talk. [*booing*] Get it out. You'll feel better.

Ruby Dee, whom I happen to admire enormously, says "when violence erupts." Paule Marshall says we must be totally committed by whatever means. Paule Marshall again said we must become far more militant. You might be interested in researching William Buckley, who doesn't happen to be one of your white liberal enemies. He equally calls for the hanging of Supreme Court Justice Earl Warren and he speculated in print why President Kennedy was not torn limb from limb in Florida while addressing the Cuban patriots.

John Killens said we got to heat up the Cold War. That sounds like violence to me. I'm used to understanding words in their normal context. He also says we haven't had a Black revolution, we need a revolution. You don't stall bridges, you blow them up.

Of course, Ossie Davis says who owns Harlem? I think I can help him a little. Banks own Harlem, insurance companies own Harlem, and powerfully politically connected law firm rich guys own Harlem. They are not particularly liberal, Ossie, and they don't make contributions, those guys, to CORE or NAACP.

When you negate the civil rights bill, when you suggest that it's nothing except white man tokenism to a cause that needs far more, you are making a criminally irresponsible mistake. As a symbol—as a piece of legislation, as a focus point for millions of people's aspirations, it is deeply significant, far-reachingly important, and will have an enormous impact whether you believe or like it or not.

The white liberal is not your enemy. The real white liberal is not a double-talking hypocrite. The real white liberal is on the firing line of your cause and the cause of free speech and the cause of human rights.

Now, some questions for the panel. I would suggest from what you said, Ruby, Paule, and John Killens, that you would repudiate the leadership and the philosophy and the tactics of Martin Luther King, Roy Wilkins, and A. Phillip Randolph. Is that true? Paule.

Arguments Expanded

Marshall: Well, I think somewhere in my statement I made the point that this is not to say that I personally reject nonviolence as a method of struggle, but I think that we have all fully recognized that our struggle in order for it to move to another stage has to adopt other tactics. What has been going on here says very eloquently how impossible right now it is to carry on a dialogue with a white man. And that he is not ready. At this point, our full energies in this struggle have to be directed toward bringing together the mass of the Negro people, because there is no point in looking for support and help from the white liberal or from the white man. Period.

Wechsler: I'd like to just clarify once and for all that this is not a conflict here between the white liberal and the representative of the Negro people. . . . What has been stated tonight is a rebellion of some Negro intellectuals against the leadership of the freedom movement, which happens to be overwhelmingly Negro. . . . If anyone here really professes to be a spokesman of some great mass movement, I would like to see their credentials.

Susskind: I want to know whether blowing up bridges and becoming far more militant coincide with the philosophy of the leadership of Martin Luther King and A. Phillip Randolph and Roy Wilkins, or do you repudiate that leadership?

Killens: You and Mr. Wechsler did the same thing. Instead of answering our reasonable and not irresponsible statements, you are trying to divide us from the Negro leadership. This to me is something that was not suggested in anything that was said. . . . Somebody asked my credentials for speaking for the Black masses. My credentials are my frame of reference as a Black man in this county.

Davis: My relationship, and the relationship I think of most of us to the Negro leadership, can be expressed very succinctly. I feel that the Negro leadership has through an unparalleled example of discipline and pleading and skilled handling of affairs given the country ten years of peace and ten years of chances to solve the problem. . . . But the philosophy, the tactics that the Negro leadership had to work in, had to be complemented by the white people of good will in this country coming to their rescue, giving them victories enough to go back to their people and say, "Look what nonviolence has gotten you, look what peaceful demonstration have gotten you, look what all of the ways that we have developed have gotten."

Now, nobody needs to quote what the figure for integration in the schools in the South is. It's awful. We're all ashamed of it. Nobody needs to quote what the conditions are in Harlem. I was up to see the world's worst fair. Believe me, the fact there is no violence now still shocks me.

Susskind: Ossie, is the leadership now ineffective and passé by your lights?

Davis: No, no, no. Let me finish, please. That leadership will shortly be made ineffective because the white friends who should have come to the rescue in those ten years were too weak, could not fight the power sources and bring the changes that were necessary to make that leadership effective. Now, I prophesy that unless that leadership can come up very quickly with some answers . . . they will be superseded by younger more daring, more reckless men. . . .

Susskind: A short answer, Ossie. As of tonight, the best and most effective hope for the Negro movement is for rights, for equality of opportunity, housing, jobs, schools. Does it, in your opinion, rest more in the leadership of Bayard Rustin and Rev. Galamison and Jesse Gray than in A. Philip Randolph and Martin Luther King and Roy Wilkins? Answer that directly.

Davis: At this moment, I would say that it does not. But I couldn't answer for tomorrow.

Susskind: Where does the best hope lie, with which group?

Silberman: I thought we were supposed to have a dialogue and not hurl speeches at each other. Part of the problem, it seems to me, is that there's an awful lot of stereotyping going on. Mr. Susskind has talked about the white liberal. Mr. Killens has talked about the white liberal. And there are two white liberals on the platform here and I don't think we're in complete agreement, so I think the starting point is that there are white liberals of many sorts. . . .

The crucial point, it seems to me, is the one Mr. Davis was just talking about which took up from Miss Marshall's talk, from Mr. Killens's talk. Mr. Killens said that the white liberal was long on talk and short on action and I think the criticism is essentially true of a great many white liberals. But

I think the same thing unfortunately is true of the Black radicals. It's true, Mr. Davis, the relevant question to ask when responsibility comes up is, "Responsible to whom?" But responsibility to the Black masses of whom you spoke, it seems to me, involves doing something substantially more than merely ventilating the anger that has been repressed for three and a half centuries.

It is essential to ventilate the anger. It has to come out, but the answer has to be channeled into some kind of action and I have not heard from Miss Marshall, from Mr. Killens, from Miss Hansberry, from Mr. Davis any concrete definition of what this action is supposed to be, what these new techniques are supposed to be. . . . The point is that no one, no one in the Negro community has yet done the hard, mean, dirty job of building that mass-based organization that you are talking about and it is a hard, mean, dirty job that has to be done seven days a week, fifty-two weeks a year. . . .

Q. and A. Period

(At this point a recess was taken. Then a question-and answer period began.)

Susskind: Let's go, Mr. Wechsler, these are questions from the audience. If they are militant or angry, that's the mood of the audience. "Mr. Wechsler, I charge that the *New York Post* has become an evening *Daily News*, capitalizing on race stories to sell newspapers; also, as a result, helping to create a climate in New York City that might be a cause of a race riot. How do you plead?"

Wechsler: Well, I just stopped beating my wife. . . . I do not happen to be in charge of the news columns of the *New York Post*. I run the editorial page and write my column.

With respect to the general question of coverage of the racial crisis in New York City, I think it is so damned complicated that if one were to read the *Amsterdam News*, let's say, and the *Daily News*, I suppose one could charge that both, and perhaps the *New York Post* and even the *New York Times*, that all were in some degree promoting a crisis by the coverage of it. . . . It is my own view that there is a therapeutic value in getting these matters into the open. They exist, the tensions exist, we would not be here tonight if they did not exist. . . . You know, in the late 1930s there was a theory that if you didn't talk about anti-Semitism and Nazism and Hitlerism, somehow this thing would go away. Well, I didn't believe that then and neither do I believe that by pretending that we aren't living in a very explosive city in a very explosive time, that we're going to kid anybody. . . .

Susskind: Next question to Miss Hansberry: "I am a white liberal with a desire to be a white radical. I don't want to be read out of this battle. What can I do to earn a chance to work with the Black revolution?"

Hansberry: Radicalism is not alien to this country, neither Black nor white, and we have a very great tradition of white radicalism in the United States, and I've never heard Negroes boo the name of John Brown. So there's no problem that anybody at this table wants to read any patriot out of the Negro movement. That's not the point. Some of the first people who have died so far in this struggle have been white men and I for one would be prepared to accept the leadership of the person who gives that much devotion as against someone who would exhibit the traitorous character of, say, a Moise Tshombe. I don't think that we can decide ultimately on the basis of color that kind of thing.

The passion that we express should be understood in that context. I think it's unfortunate, for instance, at this very evening that Mr. Susskind, whom I know, and Mr. Wechsler—not Mr. Silberman—have presumed, for instance to almost adopt a tone of scolding to those people who have exhibited passion here.

The thing that is trying to be said is we want total identification. It's not a question of reading anybody out. It's a merger, but it has to be a merger on the basis of true and genuine equality and if we think that it isn't going to be painful, we're mistaken. That's what Jimmy Baldwin is trying to say. . . .[2]

Susskind: The lady asked you how as a white liberal she can become a white radical. You haven't answered that.

Hansberry: I don't know how to answer that. . . . I think as the movement goes on, we each see our place and we get into it.

Davis: I would like to express some thoughts on this that tie up directly with something that was mentioned before we came down, which was: What do we suggest as means of tackling problems, ways and means of getting together? People unite themselves not on the basis of color or heritage or whatnot. They unite themselves when there is a program that they need to accomplish and they can't do it without the other guy they need to unite with. This is always the basis of unity and it always will be.

Now, the problems we face are not insoluble. The problems of the rats in Harlem can be solved. The problem of everything that's wrong with this country can be solved. . . . However, the solutions which are the most logical ones are the ones which nobody wants to face and that is why we talk at cross-purposes. . . . Suppose we could have full employment in this country. I would be for nonviolence and everything that leadership could offer if we could get full employment, but I know as you do, full employment is not only not possible, it becomes less and less possible. And because our leaders white and Black have no program to deal with this problem, we will wind up shooting each other. It will not be because of race, but because we haven't faced the problem in front of us. . . .

Susskind: Ossie, you're an eloquent and passionate man and I would ask your help on something. A person of genuine candor says, "I don't want to be read out." The biggest hand of the evening or one of the biggest was gotten by Lorraine when she came up with the phrase, "It's time for the white liberal to cease being a liberal and become an American radical." Now when asked how do you do that, she said I don't know. Do you know how? I think the woman who asked the question is still wondering what the answer is.

Davis: Well . . .

Susskind: All right, let me—here's a question. Next question: "Whom the gods destroy, they first make mad. I as a Negro am interested in a sane leadership, a leadership able to think, reason, and view issues with a long perspective. It is poor strategy to adopt a tactic which poses more problems than it solves, which has every chance of making things more difficult for many who have given so much to the Negro struggle. Now, the question is, how can we get less heat in this discussion and more rational thought?" And the question is addressed to Paule Marshall.

Marshall: I think that the person who asked the question has bought lock, stock, and barrel the white man's definition of violence. And that is a picture of Negroes running through the streets armed to the teeth. No one at this table tonight has projected that kind of picture. What I said is, there is the need for an organization which will take on a more militant tone . . . an organization which is so well organized, which is so tightly knit that they can act in response to the abuse that we as Black people in this country are subjected to every day of our lives.

Now, the form that this kind of response will take will be in terms of the kinds of abuse to which we are subjected, because, you see, the whole principle of nonviolence—which I accept as a method of struggle—is only feasible when you are dealing with a reasonable people. It has no meaning when in response to that nonviolence we are beaten, cigarettes are ground out on our backs as we sit at counters, where the police dogs are put upon us, where the fire hoses bash us cross the street.

Susskind: Not in America.

Hansberry: Only in America.

Marshall: Only in America. And so there is the need to find some response to this kind of abuse and I say it is the job of the organization of which I am speaking to find that response—a more militant response to the kind of abuse we are subjected to.

Hansberry: [*to Susskind*] I'm a little surprised that you got quite as exercised as you did about some of the things that were said here. I know that you, for instance, are an admirer of our late president and he presumed— with all respect to the dead, but he happens to have been our president, so I have to talk about him that way—to have suggested to the world that if our foreign policy were not honored in regard to Cuba that we would blow up the world, you see. And we live in a nation where everything is talked about in terms of the fact that we are going to be the mightiest, the toughest cats going, you know, in the whole world. And when a Negro says something about I'm tired, I can't stand it no more, I want to hit somebody, you say that we're sitting here panting and ranting for violence, you know. It's not right.

I think it's very simple. I think it's very simple that the question of the whole idea of debating whether or not most Negroes should defend themselves is an insult. If anybody comes and does ill in your home and your community, obviously you try your best to kill them.

Susskind: Your playwriting is superb, but your dialectics is somewhat wanting. I fail to see what President Kennedy's decision at the Cuba showdown had to do with the Black-white dialogue. Mr. Killens, there's a question for you: "Mr. Killens, as a decent human being, what do you want an individual to do?"

Killens: I want to say, as a decent human being, that I think the white liberal should be more ready to listen and not so quick to scold—you know, to act like a spoiled boy or something. . . .

Susskind: This question is not addressed to any particular person. "If the liberal is your somewhat impotent ally, who is your enemy? Who is holding back your progress?"

Jones: I've been sitting here trying to figure out what was happening, and it's very strange, because I look up and see people sitting at the table with me that abstractly I despise. For instance, someone from *Fortune* magazine— and it seems to me the can of all the filth in America must rest somewhere close to where they live. The *New York Post* to me represents the same kind of unrealistic understanding of the world that only leads to debasing human beings, lying to people, telling them they're one thing when they're another thing. I said before about a dialogue that there never had been one, and the reason for it is: here are some artists sitting at this table and who are we offered to talk to? The editor of the *New York Post*. What is that? Or somebody from *Fortune* magazine. If I wanted to talk to somebody about

America, I would want to talk to somebody who knew something about it, including the moderator. . . . It's all the same person, and David Susskind represents the same people, to my mind, that are sitting on everybody, Black and white, that's being sat on. . . . There's so much, like, static and lies and the mass media in the hands of thieves and fools. People put so much stuff in your way that you can't really see what's happening. Here are some artists, Black artists, sitting here not doing anything but talking to some possibly, possibly liberally educated white men, you see. That's what's happening.

Susskind: Mr. Jones indicted the *Post* and me and Wechsler and everyone else. . . . Who of white complexion, whether running a magazine or newspaper, in politics, who is in your view honest, sincere, and dedicated in his conscience and his effort to helping?

Hansberry: The white kids on the firing line in Mississippi as we're sitting here.

Susskind: Anybody else? LeRoi, anybody else?

Jones: No, she's right, you know. There are people getting knocked in the head like that, but again, essentially I think in the wrong direction, you know. The method is wrong. You know, finally, it's not Black—it could never be about Black and white. But it has to do with a message. What are you trying to do, what is your intent, what do you want to happen, you see. Now this man from *Fortune* magazine cannot afford to see this thing fall, you see. But I can afford to see it fall because I don't have anything to lose.

Silberman: I thought I was sitting on a chair, not somebody's back. But I have been waiting through the discussion and now through the question period for some concrete definition of what it is that Mr. Jones wants to do, of what it is that Miss Hansberry wants to do. I've been waiting for a definition of what a Black radical is and I'm afraid I have to repeat the statement that I made before: it would seem to me that it's not just the white liberal who is long on talk. The Black radical seems to be long on talk and short on specifics. What is the program? What is it that is supposed to be done?

Susskind: Here's a question addressed to Mr. Killens, Paule Marshall, and I guess Ossie Davis. "I am white, have been jailed in the freedom fight, am an artist and a member of a minority. Six million of my people were destroyed in our time. I am willing to follow Negro leadership. Who is the leadership I should follow?"

Marshall: Perhaps a person of your dedication and obvious sincerity might best direct his or her energies to something which I heard suggested last Sunday, that is, to those like-minded whites, those whites who by my definition think in terms of Blackness. It might be best if you formed an organization and went into the white community and there try to change them, to bring them around.

Davis: I think I can answer two questions at once. You asked a question: "If the liberal is an important ally, who is your enemy?" The enemy that we face . . . is more viscous than the bigots, and the enemy is the apathy of the American people and that apathy inflicts Black and white, the thirty-eight people who refused to pick up the telephone when a woman screamed help to call the police, that kind of impotence, that kind of not-caringness in the face of what happened to us or to the children in Harlem or to the people down South.

How can we scream loud enough in an affluent society when our biggest commercial enterprises are making profits hand over fist and are so busy counting their money that we can't get in their ear. How can we tell them that the little man is being booted out of the society, more little whites than Negroes. The forty million starving Americans, forty million, who have to depend only on the President's program for poverty, which will certainly not give them what they need, these are the people, there are the people around whom any program for the future must be built.

We live in a society that can produce what it cannot consume and because this is so, all of our institutions are being gouged and dislocated out of existence. Let those of us who are liberals or radicals or whatnot or who care put person above property, even if property is owned by the banks, by Rockefeller, by anybody—let us call his name and hold him to account. . . .

Hansberry: I think the enemy is also the political structure of the county, every senator and congressman from the captive states below the Mason-Dixon line who does not represent the people of the South equally and proportionate to the population; these people who not only presume to sit in Congress and tie up the affairs of the United States sixty days, for an unlimited amount of time, but are the same illegally represented figures who pass on our foreign policy and decide that the money that you and I pay in taxes will go to things that don't have anything to do with improving the way of life for the American people. That's the enemy, too.

Susskind: Here is a question that's pretty specific. Ruby Dee. "P.S. 139 in Harlem is a public junior high school, all male. The teaching is inferior, the curriculum is inferior, the students are rebellious and not anxious to learn. What is the specific answer in this specific school to make these specific students, teachers, and curricula perform up to standard?"

Dee: How can one community long deprived, long degraded, expect to conquer in that particular area?

I have to say here now, I don't believe in violence. I deplore it with my whole being. Six million Jews, six children in Birmingham, the violence of the lynchers in the South—violence is no answer. The Negro has perpetrated very little of this violence. It has been perpetrated against him in this country. . . .

I'm hoping that as Mr. Silberman said we will come to the point where we have programs for schools, programs for people, programs for the nation. I think one of the things that we have to do is address our congressmen, address our government, let them know that the economic system under which we live is passé.

Susskind: What economic system would you substitute?

Dee: I think that we are afraid to talk about socialism. I don't know much about socialism in all its details, but I think America has started something that is a little bit beyond socialism. I think in terms of socialism, a lot of people working, there are jobs for everybody under socialism and we share the wealth that we make from our labor; but in this country, our wealth is no longer dependent upon our labor, so therefore socialism itself does not seem to be the answer. We live in a time now where man is entitled to life, liberty, and the pursuit of happiness without a job. . . .

All of us here tonight, I think, are scratching through to what shall we do for the real issue. We aren't even talking about it. It's distressing to think that Negroes and whites may fight in the street, because they aren't fighting each other. It's like people in a family distressed over something and the wife screams at the husband, but that's not the enemy. It's the poverty that's the enemy and it's the dripping water that's the enemy and it's the rats that are the enemy, but this is only symptomatic. The enemy are the people who have taken what we have invented in the factory and claimed that it is theirs when in fact it belongs to all of us because through government subsidies, through tax write-offs, and through the tax money that we pay to the American government, the factories belong to the American people. I don't know what you call this, socialism or . . .

Susskind: Time for one more question. Mr. James Wechsler: "How do you expect the government to enforce the civil rights bill when it has never in 343 years enforced the Bill of Rights so far as the Black man is concerned? Do you believe that nonviolence will change the racist mind?"

Wechsler: On the first, let me say that I think there is a slight overstatement in the rhetoric. I do not believe that we would be assembled here this evening and that some of us would have been saying some of the things we've said if we didn't have some approximation of a Bill of Rights that rather transcends the conditions existing in Communist and fascist societies and I trust that it is not an offense to get any Americans in the audience to suggest that. . . .

With respect to enforcement of the civil rights law, this will be the battle of this year and perhaps the battle of our century. The battleground perhaps most immediately will be Mississippi and when some people have asked whether anything can be done, it seems to me that those who are not at the front in Mississippi can do very many things. There will be battles at both national conventions about the seating of delegations. There will be the issue of what the Justice Department does in Mississippi. Now I don't want to suggest any naive optimism about the outcome. The plain truth of the matter is that marshals have been used in the South and that if there is a sufficiently purposeful disciplined resolute mobilization of the freedom movement in America, this government will move. And I should like to say to the question that has been asked as to whether there are any specific and tangible dramatic goals, I would suggest that the answer very concretely is in Mississippi this summer. . . .

Susskind: Mr. Jones: "In the predictable future, in your view, can the northern Negro attain his rights and his ambitions without violence and bloodshed?"

Jones: Well, I don't know. When people talk about violence, they usually mean violence to the white man, not just violence, because that's sort of an everyday fact of a lot of Negroes' lives—violence. When you say violence and bloodshed, you mean violence to white men and maybe violence to social, economic, political structure. I think that that kind of violence is going to happen, because I don't really see anyone doing anything about it. This gentleman here is talking about local organizations, when he must know as well as I do that it's about money, finally, and that you make $85 billion a year and that we want 10 percent of it. Think of it as a stickup, you know. [*laughter*] So that obviously, and with enough pressure from outside, it's either you're going to give it over or something else will happen. And we're trying to find out what that's going to be now, you see. But as far as violence, you can walk down 125th Street and see a hundred policemen from Amsterdam to Lenox and I don't know if that's promoting an intelligent discourse.

I don't think that any Negro can represent any mass of Negroes because that's what we've been fighting, the right to be singular, the right to be individual, not to be abstracted, you see, but also the right to choose, so that one thing you can say we want along with the money is also the right to say who we have to fight, for instance, you know, in war, and also, who is collecting the taxes and where that goes and who is to select a man to sit in the post of judge, whether another man is fit to be rich or not. We want all those rights. What you have—that luxury—that's what the great majority of the people pushing up toward middle class want. . . . If you're not prepared to go for that, then you'll have to go for something else. It'll probably be worse.

Silberman: I think Mr. Jones used the wrong metaphor. From the way he spoke, it sounded more like a mugging than a stickup. [*murmuring*] It seems to me the question that I'm left with by this discussion is whether Mr. Jones and a good many people in the audience really want the merger which I think Miss Hansberry spoke about or whether they want to bring down the whole structure.

Hansberry: The latter may be necessary to make the first possible.[3]

Notes

1. Editor's note: The original audio is available in the Lorraine Hansberry Papers in the Moving Image & Recorded Sound Division of the Schomburg Center for Research in Black Culture, New York Public Library, and also in the Pacifica Radio Archives. Hansberry's full opening statement is available in Catherine Ellis and Stephen Drury Smith, eds., *Say It Loud: Great Speeches on Civil Rights and African American Identity* (New York: New Press, 2010), 19–24 and online at http://americanradioworks.publicradio.org/features/blackspeech/lhansberry.html.

2. Editor's note: In the original audio, Hansberry continues to praise Baldwin for having "made us want to talk to each other," and goes on to argue that "to do that he has had to say things that—yes—shock. He has had to say things that even I must criticize, myself, I have hesitated to say, before he led the way. This is what he has accomplished, and we should thank God for him."

3. Editor's note: In the original audio, Susskind tries to close the panel and Hansberry asks, "May we please have the last word once though." Susskind responds, "Last word once . . . I thought you had the last word all night."

A Lorraine Hansberry Rap

Lerone Bennett Jr. and Margaret G. Burroughs / 1979

From *Freedomways* 19, no.4 (1979): 226–33. Reprinted by permission of *Freedomways*.

For this special issue [of *Freedomways*], Lerone Bennett Jr. and Margaret G. Burroughs came together to discuss the life and work of Lorraine Hansberry. Dr. Bennett is a leading historian and senior editor of *Ebony*, whose numerous books include *Before the Mayflower* and *Wade in the Water: Great Moments in Black History*. Dr. Burroughs is a prominent artist and teacher, a contributing editor of *Freedomways*, and director of the DuSable Museum in Chicago. Following is the transcript of their discussion.

Margaret G. Burroughs: In our effort, Lerone, to estimate the career of Lorraine Hansberry—the contribution she made and the relevance of her work—the first thing that comes to mind is that here we are in 1979, fourteen years since she passed away, and the person seems to be still very much alive. Did you know Lorraine Hansberry?

Lerone Bennett Jr.: I didn't know her well. As a matter of fact, I should say that I didn't know her at all. I saw her two or three times I think in my life. The first time was when *Raisin* opened in Chicago. I was doing a story at the time on Sidney Poitier, and I was backstage running around. I saw her then from a distance, and I was interested in her. I knew the Hansberry name—the Hansberry family is well known in Chicago. I knew her sister Mamie who was married to a very good friend of mine. I knew Mrs. Hansberry; I knew Perry, her brother. He was well known here in the fifties as a very militant type and I had been at several parties with him. In addition to being interested in her from this general background, I was also interested because of what seemed to be an emerging bombshell success— that is, *Raisin*—which naturally attracted the attention of young writers. Through Mamie or Mrs. Hansberry, I was invited to the house for a reception a few nights after the opening. I went and it was that kind of party, you know . . . an emerging celebrity, Chicago girl, old Chicago people who hadn't seen her in a long time. It was no time really for a very serious discussion. But near the end of the party six or eight people, writers mostly, got together and discussed art and struggle. I remember Oscar Brown Jr. was there, pregnant, at the time, with *Kicks and Company* and various other things he was planning to write. He talked about that, and Lorraine talked about some things she wanted to do. But she was in the middle of a media volcano right then; she was being transformed from an anonymous person into a celebrity, and so there wasn't much time to talk. I was very much impressed with her. She seemed to me to be very intense, very dedicated, very determined; and I don't know from this distance, but she seemed to be something that I admire in Black women as you know—she seemed to be tough.

MB: You mentioned some other members of her family. What do you know about the family environment this young woman came out of and about some of the struggles the family was engaged in?

LB: Well, the Hansberrys, as I said, were well known in Chicago and well-to-do—the father was a major real estate broker and developer. The family had been involved, significantly I think, in the early struggles of Black people in Chicago to break down various restrictive barriers, particularly restrictive housing covenants. He had bought a house in an area that excluded Blacks and had exposed himself to some danger. In other words, he'd shown some personal courage by standing up for something. Lorraine came out of this environment, went to Englewood High School on the South Side and then left, I understand, to attend the University of Wisconsin. Now I came to Chicago in '53, and by that time Lorraine Hansberry had moved to New York.

MB: Of course, being a historian yourself you were familiar with Leo Hansberry, her uncle.

LB: That's another dimension, you're right, Margaret. Leo Hansberry was, in my opinion, the greatest pioneer in African history in this country— Harvard, University of Chicago, I'm including the whole bag. And from various things I've read that Lorraine Hansberry said about her life, he was a great influence, a great beacon in her life.

MB: How do you account for the fact that a young woman comes out of what's called a Black bourgeois background and yet develops a deep understanding of the problems of working people? Is that something that's peculiar to Chicago, or what? A number of people have come out of Chicago: Richard Wright, Margaret Walker, Charlie White, Gwendolyn Brooks, many others. What is it about this town?

LB: Well, first of all, Chicago is a very brutal city. It's a very raw city. Chicago will destroy anybody, particularly a Black person, if that person hasn't steeled him- or herself to resist. And the fact that all the people you mentioned—and you should've included yourself—the fact that these people worked and work here, indicates that a sort of strength was built into them by an environment which required them to think and resist with all their might in order to survive. That's one element. Another element—and you know more about it than I do, Margaret—is that despite, or perhaps because of the raw, brutal oppression of Black people in this city, there has been and still is a sort of community here. In Harlem and some other communities, many so-called Black middle-class people, Black professionals, move away to put some distance between themselves and the great mass of Black people. But for geographical and a lot of other reasons, here you find Black middle-class people living on the South Side and the West Side. Now they might have a few more amenities, but they're not more than three or four blocks away from the people. And that has produced a sort of community feeling which makes it impossible for the Black middle class, in general, to ignore those Black people en masse a few blocks away who are living in poverty and misery. There are perhaps other reasons, and somebody needs to think about this: Since the great migration of Blacks in the early part of the century, Black Chicago has developed a number of extraordinary business institutions. And the question to investigate (I'm not really competent to talk about it) is the relationship between the development of this huge, vital Black economic foundation and the development of artists like Richard Wright and Lorraine Hansberry.

MB: There's much more research yet to be done on Lorraine Hansberry and her contacts while she was here. But I do know that during her formative years, in Chicago, some of her mentors were people who were socialist, Marxist in their philosophy. For example, she spent many evenings at the knee of, say, Raymond Hansborough (deceased) and his wife Romania Ferguson Hansborough, who were certainly Marxists. Then later, she went to New York and worked on Paul Robeson's paper *Freedom*, where she certainly met other people of this persuasion. Now those influences might have been what led her to identify with the working class even though she came from a bourgeois family.

LB: There's just one additional point that needs more thinking, certainly on my part. That is, I'm not at all sure I understand what a Black middle-class background produces on an individual level. I'm not sure even Marx understood that, and he was a petit-bourgeois intellectual himself. It may be, and we can see this in the history of many social revolutions, that children need—"need" is not the word, I can't think of the word—children seem to need to have something to rebel against. I'm not at all sure I understand, or that anyone understands, how certain environments produce certain kinds of people. A number of very talented, very brilliant, very helpful people to the social revolution in the world have come from bourgeois backgrounds— Castro and Marx, of course, among others.

MB: Yes. But I think with Black people, it's a little different because even though they may be well-to-do, they're Black. An example is what happened to Lorraine Hansberry's father when he moved out of that area around 60th Street. Regardless of how much money he had, he was Black and that was it. And I'm pretty certain that many places Lorraine went, even though she had her own car and things like that, she was Black and felt it at an early age. So that gives you a strong sense of reality, and you see that your future is tied up with the masses of people.

LB: That brings us back to my main point, which is that, by and large and certainly up to now, it has been difficult for Black middleclass people in Chicago to ignore the fact that their ultimate fate is linked to the fate of the Black masses.

MB: Well, *A Raisin in the Sun* took Chicago by storm. Prior to its phenomenal success, if I remember correctly, we had been told that anything with Black subject matter would be rejected or certainly couldn't make it on Broadway. How would you explain the acceptance of *Raisin*?

LB: First, the timing was right—in saying that I don't mean to take anything away from Lorraine Hansberry. But the timing was perfect. Remember, this was 1959, five years after the Supreme Court decision on school desegregation, four years after Montgomery, the eve of the sit-ins. The time was ripe for Lorraine Hansberry. She was a kind of herald, a person announcing the coming of something. It was in the air, I think, and whites felt it as well as Blacks. Secondly, whatever the critical appraisals, the play was extraordinarily well done from my standpoint. I remember the Tuesday night it opened in Chicago. That was one of the most delightful evenings I've ever spent in the theater. The play—we'll come to that—the *people*: Sidney Poitier, Claudia McNeil, Ivan Dixon, Ruby Dee, Diana Sands. All that richness, all that great talent on one stage. It just blew my mind.

MB: Of course, it was at a time when if we saw one Black person in something we'd say, "Hey look! There's one."

LB: So that hit me. And—I'm not going to go into the structure of the play, into an analysis of the structure and acts and that sort of thing—the totality packed a wallop, and I think, to large numbers of Black people, the emotional message was there. Although there were some depressing things in the play, it celebrated Black life, and I think that told. Word got back to the Black community, and Black people flocked to see it. There was, also, as your question implied, a curious identification on the part of whites with the play. So they came to see it. I remain convinced after all this time—and I've seen the play over and over again with all kinds of casts everywhere—that it is a classic. The totality of it still hits me as it hit Black people back in 1959. Twenty years later, it's a classic and will endure.

MB: Do you think the phenomenon had something to do with the state of the commercial theater at that time? It was bankrupt. There was nothing on Broadway. So here comes *A Raisin in the Sun* like a fresh breeze—it was humane, its characters were real and not degraded in any way, making a lie of what had been told to us about Blacks not being able to do this or do that. It came like a fresh breeze, as Black culture so often has come, to revive, to sort of save white establishment culture. From that point on, the floodgates began to open up, and if you look today at what's happening on television or in the movies, whatever, the only thing that is giving it life is the Black presence in the same way that Western art was revitalized through the African influence a century ago. I have my students at the college read *Raisin*, and every single time we read it I find myself getting lumps in my throat even though I've gone over it many, many times. I was really very critical of some aspects of it at one time, but I've been able to look at it from a larger point of view. I think sometimes the establishment critics affect our thinking with their nit-picking, so to speak. In reading her writings, I've concluded that she had great intellectual depth—a fact which still hasn't been fully brought out. Could we discuss the play for just a minute?

LB: Sure.

MB: There's this matter of the "matriarch" character. How do you feel about that—is Lena Younger a prototype of the matriarch who robs young Black men of their strength and keeps them from developing fully as they should? That was one of the criticisms levelled at the play. Is the male role a strong one in the beginning? Does it end up as a strong role? Does Walter Lee Younger grow and develop? Does he change?

LB: That's a difficult question. I spoke earlier about the curious identification some elements of the non-Black community felt toward the play. I think, in a sense, that audiences' responses to the mother were so overwhelmingly positive that the audiences might have distorted the play. That's one point. Secondly, I think Claudia McNeil's portrayal was so overwhelming that it was very hard not to distort. On the other hand, you must say that Poitier's portrayal of the son was also masterful. Let's go back to something Lorraine Hansberry once said. She said that she created a structure in which there are two major characters, neither of which dominates.[1] On another level, I have to say that her construction dramatizes on the stage a real historical moment in the experience of Black people in this country. Whatever one thinks about strong Black women, we have had some strong Black women, so she wasn't false to our history. I think she posed that statement in the form of a dilemma which Mama Younger grapples with and Walter Lee grapples with—whether she was destroying her son trying to be too strong. I think the son grows in the play; I think the mother grows. The mother grows to the extent of recognizing that she could smother and destroy her son by protecting him from making his own mistakes. And Walter Lee Younger changes and comes into his manhood, as Mama Younger says. In sum, I'm saying that Lorraine Hansberry accurately depicted a moment in Black history. She depicted it as a dilemma, not as an irrevocable fact, not as something that should continue, but as a dilemma. To what extent should a woman who has been very strong for historical reasons appraise a situation and ask, am I destroying my son? And Walter, after a disastrous decision, recoups. One of the marvelous moments for me in the play is that he changes (and so many white critics seemed to miss this) because Mama Younger creates a situation and says, "Well okay, here's your boy. And you tell him what you're doing." And in the emotional interchanges between that boy and his father, the father grows beyond himself. I think it's very well done. But your question remains. Perhaps it will remain as long as the play is performed.

MB: But what's wrong with a matriarch? I say there's nothing wrong with a matriarch. Our strong women are accused of stunting the growth of their menfolk and after due consideration, I've decided I don't believe that. I believe it's a myth the sociologists have stock in. I think our women are solidly behind our men, and whatever they do is because they want our men to be strong and to lead.

LB: I think you're right, Margaret, and the whole thing needs to be examined. My feeling is that Black women need to be as strong as they can be. My second feeling is that Black women and men need to be as strong together as they can be. And one of the things, as I just said, about this play is that the characters grapple with that. The other point about the play, a point not often mentioned, is that Father Younger was a very strong man. I mean, the play clearly indicates that it was impossible for Mama Younger to dominate Father Younger. When he was alive, he ran that family.

MB: He spoke quite eloquently.

LB: And Mama remembers him as a strong type. Another fine moment in the work is when she recalls her late husband—his love and his strength and his sense of family. Part of the richness of this play is that all these elements are there and ought to provoke thought and discussion even today.

MB: And they are still provoking thought. That's the role her work is playing, a very significant role. In a sense, Lorraine Hansberry was a pioneer of the present women's movement, would you agree?

LB: l think she was, yes. But I don't know how far to go on this in light of something she wrote. She said that, of course, she was for what is now called the liberation of women, but she felt—if I'm quoting her correctly and I think I am—that the primary struggle was for Black liberation.

MB: Would you repeat that one please? [*laughter*]

LB: She said that she had found, in discussions with friends that she met a lot of opposition when she tried to equate or draw analogies between the situation, say, of Black people in the United States and women. And she said, here I quote: "Immediately, there is the really admirable roar of protest that 'these are entirely different questions' or the more preferred 'You must not equate!!'" She added: "Am I being facetious in calling these protests admirable because like fifteen million other Negro citizens, male and female, I naturally consider the oppression of the Negro people the more imminent and, at the moment, decisive issue."

MB: In reading things by and about Lorraine Hansberry, I've gotten the impression that her work has possibly been ignored or rejected by some of our Black critics and writers. Any comment on that?

LB: I think that would be a disservice to Black people, to Black art, to man and woman, if it happened or if it happens.

MB: Some people feel she's been placed into a niche as a Black playwright rather than as a playwright, a universal playwright. But I think you've already indicated that you feel, and certainly I agree with you, that *Raisin* is a classic, so we'll put her in a proper niche as a great American playwright.

LB: One problem there, though. From my reading of Lorraine Hansberry, I get the feeling that she struggled all her life with the whole question of "universality." And I interpret her as having struggled against false definitions of "universality." I consider her a Black playwright who wrote a classic play. To my way of thinking, an artist is most universal when he's discussing the concrete issues of his own culture. It's the task of the artist to take the concrete and make it universal. What I'm saying here is that people try to say, well, you know if X wrote a play about Black people, she's not universal.

But if an Irish playwright writes a play about Irish people, he's universal. So the play is about Black people—Black people are human. She wrote a play which is a classic, and which speaks to the human condition, not only the condition of Black people. But I consider her a Black playwright as I consider O'Casey an Irish playwright. She was universal in her particularity.

MB: Is there anything else, any other statement you would like to make about Lorraine Hansberry and her work as a conclusion to our discussion?

LB: Just two things. First, she still has something to say to young Black writers. She once warned a group of young writers against being satisfied with the undisciplined, the unstructured, the pointless. She has something to say about the need for commitment to craft and commitment to people. She stated, with her life, that all of us—young and old—are obliged to do the very best we can to illuminate the Black condition which is also the human condition. Secondly, she has something to say to the Black artist about avoiding what she talked about over and over again, and it's still a live issue, people who try to alienate them from their culture by telling them not to write about social things and not to get involved in social things. Her life was exemplary in that respect. She also says something to us about trying to open ourselves to all the intellectual currents of the world. We need to know all we can about what people are thinking in Asia and Europe and Africa, what intellectuals are thinking; we need to know what other people are doing, and then we need to work from the foundations of our own culture. I think she tells us that. Another thing we haven't had a chance to talk about has to do with Lorraine Hansberry as a witness. In *Raisin*, she announced the interconnection between Africans and Afro-Americans—Asagai symbolized the whole link. I think we need to remember that. One final point: I said at the beginning that I only saw her two or three times in my life I think. I said I think because sometime in 1964, shortly after *The Sign in Sidney Brustein's Window* opened, Gloria and I were in New York and went to see the play. I think I saw her, in the lobby or somewhere, surrounded by a number of people, some of whom might have been nurses. She seemed to be very ill, very tired; and, of course, she died shortly after that, and I never saw her again. I wish I had known her better—I would have been a better writer and a better man.

MB: Well, sometimes people make their contributions in a flash, and then they pass off the scene. Do you think, had she lived, that she would probably have given us many, many more plays?

LB: I think so, I think so. It would be very interesting to have her comments on what has happened to us, to have her insights on where we're going. And—one shouldn't say things like this—it would be interesting to speculate on what *A Raisin in the Sun*-type play of the 1970s and '80s would be. We've had so many extraordinary contributions by Black playwrights since 1959—Baraka, Douglas Turner Ward, all of them. But I think we must say, out of respect for Lorraine Hansberry and out of respect for Black people, that a great deal remains to be done.

MB: That's just as good a note to stop on as any. Thank you, Lerone Bennett.

LB: And thank you, Margaret.

Note

1. Hansberry discusses the structure of *A Raisin in the Sun* in "Willie Loman, Walter Younger, and He Who Must Live," *Village Voice*, 4, no. 42 (August 12, 1959): 7, 8. [note in original]

Key Resources

Additional Hansberry Interviews

Adams, Paul. "Theater Notes." *Michigan Chronicle*, March 25, 1961, 4–5.

Cleaves, Henderson. "Pictures, Plays, and Players: People Get Messed Up, Says Author of *Raisin*." *New York World-Telegram and Sun*, March 13, 1959.

Esterow, Milton. "New Role of Negroes in Theater Reflects Ferment of Integration." *New York Times*, June 15, 1964.

Esterow, Milton. "News of the Rialto: Hansberry's Plays." *New York Times*, July 1, 1962,61.

Fox, Penny. "Success Makes Work Easier for Prize-Winning Author." *Newsday*, February 16, 1960, 29.

"Her Dream Came True: Lorraine Hansberry." *New York Times*, April 9, 1959, 37.

Herridge, Frances. "Across the Footlights: Author of 'Raisin' Takes It in Stride." *New York Post*, March 13, 1959, 62.

"Interviews on the Arts: Interview with Lorraine Hansberry." WRVR-FM, September 18, 1962. [No recording or transcript currently available]

Kupcinet, Irv. "Interview with Lorraine Hansberry and Otto Preminger." *At Random.*, CBS-2, WBBM, Chicago, IL, May 26, 1959. [No recording or transcript currently available]

Leonard, Bill. "Interview with Lorraine Hansberry" *Eye on New York*, WCBS-TV, ca. April 1959. [No recording or transcript currently available]

Myers, Arthur. "Negro Woman Playwright Spends Weekend in County." *Berkshire Eagle* (Pittsfield, MA), August 10, 1959.

Millstein, Gilbert. "Ten Playwrights Tell How It All Starts." *New York Times Magazine*, December 6, 1959.

"People are Talking about . . . Lorraine Hansberry." photography by David Attie. *Vogue*, June 1959, 78–79.

Pitman, Jack. "Lorraine Hansberry Deplores *Porgy*: Racial Stereotype Air Debate a Feathers-Stirrer—Preminger in Rebuttal." *Variety*, May 27, 1959, 16.

Pitts, George E. "Drama Desk: Should Artists Express Political Views." *Pittsburgh Courier*, October 22, 1960.

"*Raisin* Cops Prize Despite Boycott," *Baltimore Afro-American*, April 9, 1959, 3, 15.

Robertson, Nan. "Dramatist against Odds." *New York Times*, March 8, 1959, X3

Ross, Don. "Lorraine Hansberry Interviewed: 'Whites Dreadfully Ignorant of Negro Life.'" *New York Herald Tribune*, March 13, 1960.

Syse, Glenna. "Onstage: Early Bird Hansberry Flies High." *Chicago Sun-Times*, February 26, 1961.

Willis, Ellen. "We Hitch Our Wagons." *Mademoiselle*, August 1960, 314–17.

Selected Hansberry Essays and Speeches

"About Billie Holiday." *New York Post*, July 27, 1959.

"The Black Revolution and the White Backlash." In *Say It Loud! Great Speeches on Civil Rights and African American Identity*, edited by Catherine Ellis and Stephen Drury Smith, 19–24. New York: New Press, 2010..

"A Challenge to Artists." *Freedomways: A Quarterly Review of the Negro Freedom Movement* 3, no. 1 (1963): 33–35.

"In Defense of Equality of Men," In *The Nation: Anthology of Literature by Women*, edited by Sandra M. Gilbert and Susan Gubar, 2056–68. New York: Norton, 1985.

"The Legacy of W. E. B. Dubois," *Freedomways: A Quarterly Review of the Negro Freedom Movement* 5 (Winter 1965): 19–20.

"Me Tink Me Hear Sounds in De Night." *Theater Arts*, October 1960, 9–11.

"The Nation Needs Your Gifts," *Negro Digest* 13 (August 1964): 26–29.

"The Negro Writer and His Roots: Towards a New Position," *Black Scholar* 12, no. 2 (March/April 1981): 2–12.

"Original Prospectus for the John Brown Memorial Theater of Harlem," *Black Scholar*, July/August 1979, 14–15.

"The Scars of the Ghetto." *Monthly Review* 16, no. 10 (1965): 588–91.

"The Shakespearean Experience." *Show Magazine* 4, no. 2 (1964).

"Simone de Beauvoir and *The Second Sex*: An American Commentary, an Unfinished Essay-in-Progress." In *Words of Fire: An Anthology of African-American Feminist Thought*, edited by Beverly Guy-Sheftal, 128–142. New York: New Press, 1995.

"This Complex of Womanhood." *Ebony Magazine* 18, no. 11 (August 1960): 88.

"Thoughts on Genet, Mailer, and the New Paternalism," *Village Voice*, (June 1, 1961).

"Village Intellect Revealed." *New York Times* (October 31, 1964), X1, X3.

"We Want Our Part in Full Measure, That Is All." *Everyman* 34, no. 1 (1965).

"What Could Happen Didn't." *New York Herald Tribune*, March 26, 1961, 8.

Selected Hansberry Biographies and Bibliographies

Bond, Jean Carey, ed. *Lorraine Hansberry: Art of Thunder, Vision of Light*. Special Issue of *Freedomways: A Quarterly Review of the Freedom Movement* 19, no. 4 (1979).

Carter, Steven R. *Hansberry's Drama: Commitment and Complexity*. Urbana: University of Illinois Press, 1991.

Cheney, Anne. *Lorraine Hansberry*. Boston: Twayne, 1984.

Leeson, Richard M. *Lorraine Hansberry: A Research and Production Sourcebook*. Westport, CT: Greenwood Press, 1997.

Lipari, Lisbeth. "Lorraine Hansberry (May 19, 1930–January 12, 1965)." In *Writers of the Black Chicago Renaissance*, edited by Steven C. Tracy. University of Illinois Press, 2011.

Lorraine Hansberry: The Black Experience in the Creation of Drama, directed by Ralph J. Tangney. Princeton, NJ: Films for the Humanities, 1975.

Perry, Imani. *Looking for Lorraine: The Radiant and Radical Life of Lorraine Hansberry*. Boston: Beacon Press, 2018.

Phillips, Elizabeth C. *The Works of Lorraine Hansberry: A Critical Commentary*. NY: Monarch Press, 1973.

Sighted Eyes, Feeling Heart (American Masters Pictures, PBS), directed by Tracey Heather Strain. San Francisco: California Newsreel, 2017.

Wilkerson, Margaret B. "The Dark Vision of Lorraine Hansberry: Excerpts from a Literary Biography." *Massachusetts Review* 28, no. 4 (1987): 642–50.

Wilkerson, Margaret B., "The Sighted Eyes and Feeling Heart of Lorraine Hansberry," *Black American Literature Forum* 17, no. 1 (1983): 8–13. Rpt. in *African American Review* 50, no. 4 (Winter 2017): 698–703.

Selected Hansberry Scholarship

Colbert, Soyica. "Practices of Freedom: Lorraine Hansberry, Freedom Writer." *Callaloo* 40, no. 2 (Spring 2017): 157–73.

Elam, Harry J., Jr. "Absent Presence in Lorraine Hansberry and Suzan-Lori Parks: *Les Blancs* and *Topdog/Underdog*." In *Considering Calamity: Methods for Performance Research*, edited by Linda Ben-Zvi, Tracy C. Davis, David Krasner, 39–54. Tel Aviv, Israel: Tel Aviv University, 2007.

Elam, Harry J., Jr. "The High Stakes of Identity: Lorraine Hansberry's *Follow the Drinking Gourd* and Suzan-Lori Parks's *Venus*," In *Representing the Past: Essays in Performance Historiography*, edited by Charlotte M. Canning and ThomasPostlewait, 282–302. Iowa City, IA: University of Iowa Press, 2010.

Gordon, Michelle. "'Somewhat Like War': The Aesthetics of Segregation, Black Liberation, and *A Raisin in the Sun.*" *African American Review* 42, no. 1 (Spring 2008): 121–33.

Higashida, Cheryl. "To Be(Come) Young, Gay, and Black: Lorraine Hansberry's Existentialist Routes to Anticolonialism." *American Quarterly* 60, no. 4 (Dec 2008): 899–924.

Hodin, Mark. "Lorraine Hansberry's Absurdity: *The Sign in Sidney Brustein's Window.*" *Contemporary Literature* 50, no. 4 (Winter 2009): 742–74.

Lipari, Lisbeth. "The Rhetoric of Intersectionality: Lorraine Hansberry's 1957 Letters to the *Ladder.*" In *Queering Public Address: Sexualities in American Historical Discourse*, edited by Charles E. Morris III, 220–48. Columbia, SC: University of South Carolina Press, 2007

Orem, Sarah, "Signifyin(g) When Vexed: Black Feminist Revision, Anger, and *A Raisin in the Sun.*" *Modern Drama* 60, no. 2 (Summer 2017): 189–211.

Thomas, Aaron C. "Watching *A Raisin in the Sun* and Seeing Red." *Modern Drama* 58, no. 4 (Winter 2015): 461–81.

Washington, Mary Helen. "Alice Childress, Lorraine Hansberry, and Claudia Jones: Black Women Write the Popular Front." In *Left of the Color Line: Race, Radicalism, and Twentieth-Century Literature of the United States*, edited by Bill V. Mullen and James Smethurst, 183–204. Chapel Hill: University of North Carolina Press, 2003.

Index

7; marriage to and separation from Robert Nemiroff, xviii, xxiii–xxiv, 6, 9, 18, 19, 138; move to Croton-on-Hudson, xxiv; nearly hit by brick thrown through family's window, xxiii, 22, 173; romantic view of Africa from poems of Langston Hughes, 104–5; siblings, 21, 200

interviews: Association of Artists for Freedom, "The Black Revolution and the White Backlash," 176–99; Fischer, Eleanor, "Interview with Lorraine Hansberry," xix, 162–70; Hentoff, Nat, "The Negro in American Culture," 107–34; Isaacs, Harold R., "Five Writers and Their African Ancestors, Part II: Lorraine Hansberry," 98–106; Marx, Patricia, "Interview with Lorraine Hansberry," xix, 140–48; Miller, Mitch, "Interview with Lorraine Hansberry, Leo Genn, Reginald Gardiner, and Elizabeth Seal," 135–39; Perry, Frank, "Interview with Lorraine Hansberry and Lloyd Richards," 155–61; Susskind, David, "Interview with Lorraine Hansberry, Peter Glenville, Dore Schary, José Quintero, Lloyd Richards, and Arthur Laurents," 23–58; Terkel, Studs, "Interview with Lorraine Hansberry," xvi–xviii, 73–91; Wallace, Mike, "Unaired Interview with Lorraine Hansberry," xvii, xix, 63–72. See also Hansberry, Lorraine Vivian: on art, literature, and race; Hansberry, Lorraine Vivian: on *A Raisin in the Sun*; Hansberry, Lorraine Vivian: works

on *A Raisin in the Sun*: on claims that it is not a Black play, xiv, xvii, 60, 73–74; on critical failure to recognize connection between Walter Younger and Willy Loman, xii, 92–97; on lack of a central character in, 82–83, 92; on lack of "dialect" in, xi, xxiv, 3–4; and misguided reviews and interviews, xvii, xxn7, xxin10, 65, 86; and the Nigerian character, xiii, xvii, 83–85, 99–102; on the play as protest, 60–61, 66; on portrayal of class in, 80–81; rejection of critics' white-washing of, xiv; on the response of audiences to, 31–32, 161, 204; on Walter Lee Younger as an affirmative hero, 75–77, 79, 96–97; on white view of Black characters as exotics/symbols, 119–20. See also Hansberry, Lorraine Vivian: on art, literature, and race

works: adaptation of Chesnutt's *The Marrow of Tradition*, 13; "An Author's Reflection: Willy Loman, Walter Lee, and He Who Must Live," 92–97, 208n1; *Andromeda the Thief* (unpublished play), xviii; *The Apples of Autumn* (unpublished play), xviii; diversity of material across later plays, xv–xvi; *The Drinking Gourd* (unfilmed television play), xvi, xxiv; "Flag from a Kitchenette Window," xxiii; *Flowers for the General* (unpublished play), xviii; "Images and Essences: 1961 Dialogue with an Uncolored Egghead Containing Wholesome Intentions and Some Sass" (fictional dialogue), xvi, 149–54; *Les Blancs*, xvi, xviii, xxiv–xxv; *Les Blancs: The Collected Last Plays of Lorraine Hansberry*, xxv; *The Movement: Documentary of a Struggle for Equality*, xii, xxiv; "My

About the Editor

Photo courtesy of Mollie Godfrey

Mollie Godfrey is associate professor of English at James Madison University, where she teaches African American literature. She coedited *Neo-Passing: Performing Identity after Jim Crow* and is currently working on a book project titled *Black Humanisms: Race, Gender, and the Fictions of Segregation.* Articles related to these topics have appeared in *MFS: Modern Fiction Studies, MELUS, CLA Journal, Arizona Quarterly,* and *Contemporary Literature.* Mollie has also organized several community-engaged projects dedicated to preserving and making African American archives accessible. Her work on this topic has appeared in *Pedagogy: Critical Approaches to Teaching Literature, Language, Composition, and Culture* and *Public: A Journal of Imagining America.*

CPSIA information can be obtained
at www.ICGtesting.com
Printed in the USA
BVHW082131261120
594192BV00002B/9